FAMILY, GANGSTERS &
CHAMPIONS

BOXER TONY CANZONERI'S
LIFE & WORLD

RAMON ANTONIO VARGAS

La Nouvelle Atlantide Press

Published by La Nouvelle Atlantide Press
Metairie, LA 70006

First published 2023

Manufactured in the United States

ISBN 9798397057677

Library of Congress CIP data applied for.

To Oso and Gab –
thank you two for always being in my corner.

CONTENTS

———

AUTHOR'S NOTE

It was an early evening in the late spring of 2020, and I was sitting in a sofa chair next to a wooden train set in my son's room – lost in thought – as I had done so many times when social gathering restrictions aimed at slowing the spread of Covid-19 were in full effect. At the time, I was working at New Orleans's daily newspaper, then called the Times-Picayune | Advocate, and I remember my colleagues and I were exceptionally busy covering numerous angles of the virus for which there was no protective vaccine yet and which would go on to kill more than 1 million Americans. Yet in between reporting shifts, time would slow to a crawl, and there were only so many movies or shows on Netflix or walks around my subdivision that I could take to speed it up.

I've always been a fan of boxing, an interest my Mexican parents sparked in me when we watched every Julio Cesar Chavez fight that we could together. I've also always been interested in history as well as a devoted fan of sports in New Orleans, just outside of which I've lived most of my life since I was born in 1986. It's gotten past the point of just being a hobby. My debut as an author was a book about the first of two small college national basketball championships that my alma mater, Loyola University New Orleans, won near the end of the second world war.

The only problem is there wasn't much boxing, sports or anything else going on to get one's mind off the deep part of Covid-19's lockdowns. I wasn't sure when I'd be able to again host friends and family for a boxing match-watching party like I had loved doing before the pandemic. And I don't remember exactly how or why, but it was in that chair in my son's room when it quite suddenly struck me how that might not be the worst thing.

I'd been thinking how I'd wanted to write another book like the Loyola basketball one, and maybe it could even be about boxing. Ideally it could even combine my interest in boxing with my interest in New Orleans sports' long ago glory days! Maybe now I could find some of the time I never felt that I had to do something like that.

Any of the several world champions to hail from New Orleans could merit their own biography, including the most recent one: Regis Prograis, whom I saw win a junior welterweight title about a year earlier during a fight that I covered for the newspaper about three hours away in Lafayette, Louisiana. Maybe I could do a collection of profiles of them, I thought. And so I started my research with the one whose name I remember consistently seeing in all-time rankings locally, nationally and even internationally: Tony Canzoneri.

The Italian-American pugilist had won world titles in the featherweight, lightweight and junior welterweight divisions around the Great Depression and Prohibition eras, I read. Well it's certainly impressive to have been a three-division champion, I thought. I pulled up his records on the boxing reference website BoxRec.com, saw that he made his pro debut when he was just 16, and then counted more than 170 fights before he retired 14 years later. I thought, well that's not just impressive – that's borderline insane!

A quick scan of digitized newspaper clippings available on my local library's website revealed hundreds of articles documenting his day-to-day exploits at the peak of his fame. So did the archive of the New York Times, who took a keen interest in Tony after he moved to the Big Apple as a teenager. He dominated his two towns' sports pages in his day. Writers relayed what he had to say as soon as he said it to readers who cared deeply about whether he was on the rise, on the decline and everywhere in between.

But, in my mind, whether I would dedicate an entire project to Tony Canzoneri depended on if there was enough material to do more than just recite everything he'd accomplished as well as the twists and turns of his journey. And the first hint that I may be able to do just that lay in a press release that I soon came across publicizing a book named *Saturday's Child: A Daughter's Memoir.*

A line in the press release mentioned how the book's author, Deborah Burns, was Tony Canzoneri's niece. She said she had spent some of her most formative years at a resort and hotel that her family had opened on a farm which Tony had bought with his winnings as a fighter. The hotel's guests included folks on the "sketchier" side who would only check in under aliases. "What those men actually did was anybody's guess," read a *Saturday's Child* excerpt mentioned in the press release. "No one dared ask too many questions."

Wow, okay, I thought. Maybe there's much more to Tony Canzoneri than just boxing. Tracking down Burns's phone number, calling her and managing to have a lengthy conversation with her confirmed that for me.

Members of some of New York's – and really, the United States of America's – most infamous organized crime families were all drawn to this superstar boxer and his family. It seemed Tony had little choice but to let them in his orbit while trying his best to keep them at an arm's length, she told me during the first of several hours-long conversations. I didn't see much about these underworld associations in most of the sports articles chronicling Tony's rise and fall as an athlete. But there was a mention here, and another there, and Burns herself assured me it was true, having personally met some of these figures.

Tony married an actress and then raised a daughter through the anguish of the subsequent divorce. He gave away virtually everything he had to an inner circle drawn wide enough to encompass his child, parents, siblings, friends on both sides of the law, and the many characters he met in the so-called sweet science to which he dedicated his best professional years.

Many proudly accepted being called a loved one, friend and in-ring rival of Tony Canzoneri, among other labels. And yet, when he died, it took two days for anyone to notice they hadn't seen him and to check on him, Burns and others told me in interviews as well as in long-ago writings.

It couldn't be more obvious to me at this point that there was indeed a book in all of this. Tony Canzoneri wasn't just an interesting boxing story. His was an interesting life story that happened to be about a boxer. He embodied how people can come from very little, if anything at all, to achieve things most of us can only dream of, to create a world more vivid that many of us will know, and through it all endure setbacks that many of us hope we are somehow spared from.

Burns pointed me to everything and put me in touch with everyone who I needed to get this book done much sooner than this. This includes Tony Canzoneri's daughter, who I understand has rarely spoken publicly about her father. And I did try to finish this book much sooner than I ultimately did.

But lots which sucked up my bandwidth as a journalist got in the way of doing that as the world winded its way through the pandemic. Among them: Minneapolis police murdered George Floyd, provoking worldwide protests. A mob staged a deadly attack on Congress over the outcome of a presidential election that its members didn't like. Two relatively strong hurricanes hit the New Orleans area. I went through a divorce, which was difficult emotionally and financially but has ultimately left everyone – most importantly, my son – happier.

I wasn't sure whether I'd ever finish this project until one day in the spring of 2023 my son, my partner Gabby, and I were doing his homework together at a study room in the local library near our house. We were leaving when I passed a sign informing visitors that the American Italian Research Library was on the second floor. To be honest, I'd forgotten that the research library had moved there a little more than 10 years earlier. I immediately thought of Tony Canzoneri and how a research library with a name like that must for sure have a file on him. I asked Gabby and Oscar if I could take five minutes to go upstairs and see if they did.

The two wanted to leave to get snowballs and get back home and play video games, but they let me go. Upstairs the staff helped me find a folder full of materials for Canzoneri – including words directly from him, his rivals and his associates – that I'd not come across during my first, pre-divorce push on this project. That folder helped me add tens of thousands of words to this volume, as well as some of the most vivid descriptions of key scenes in Tony Canzoneri's life that I had not seen anywhere else. And those materials have now given me the opportunity to help me thank all those who gave me a hand in turning into reality what had started out as just an idea on that chair in my son's room.

First, to Deborah Burns, her husband Bob Burns, her cousin Jay Honold, Tony's daughter Denise Freeman, and her son Christopher Freeman: Thank you for all of the time you gave me and all of the patience you showed me as I drifted in and out of your lives getting my act together to finish this project. I hope, as much as possible, that it honors your truth.

La Nouvelle Atlantide Press, thank you for supporting this project immediately after I approached you with it and for keeping your word that you would publish it whenever it was delivered. I know a lot has happened since 2020 to test that commitment, and it means so much that you never wavered. To press co-proprietor Michael Giusti, my friend and former professor, thank you for your friendship in particular.

Catherine Dorrough, my former college classmate and the most talented graphic artist I know, designed this book, helped create the cover and has always been a friend no matter how different my life has looked since the last we saw or spoke with each other. Thank you so much.

To my former Times-Picayune colleague Faimon Roberts, thank you for the edits and feedback before I handed the manuscript over to my publisher. I have been fortunate to work with a lot of amazing journalists, and you are one of the smartest and best.

Showtime boxing analyst Steve Farhood, I've seen you on so many broadcasts during my life as a fight fan, and thank you for finding time to help me explain to readers that Tony Canzoneri never avoided facing anyone, and that virtually everyone who truly wanted a piece of him got the chance to try to take one.

To my favorite author, Jeff Pearlman, thank you for your advice on how to start the book and for even just considering writing a marketing blurb for the cover. And to those who covered Tony in the days when his star shined brightest, thank you for leaving behind a record for those who want to study up on one of the most interesting – and important – athletes to ever come out of New Orleans.

To my partner Gabby Killett, thank you for helping me make some of the photos in this book, for your idea for the cover, for encouraging me to just finish the project, for loving Oscar and me, and of course so much more.

To Tony Canzoneri, thank you for making our community proud.

New Orleans is flawed and beyond maddening sometimes, but I've never been able to leave it. I know you were never able to forget the city after you and your family moved to New York, and you were always proud to represent it. Even if I wasn't here to see it personally, you are one of the most interesting subjects I've ever explored, without a doubt, so thank you for that.

And lastly but just as importantly, to you, the reader: I hope you find this biography as inspiring, intriguing, amusing and, at times, heartbreaking as I found researching and writing it to be.

Without anything further, this is the life and world of a boxing champion, New Orleanian, New Yorker, businessman, entertainer, and father. This is the life and world of Tony Canzoneri.

Ramon Antonio Vargas
March 22, 2023

CHAPTER ONE

"THEY USED TO CALL YOU DAGO"

———

Denise Canzoneri knew something terrible had happened when her maternal grandmother never showed up to pick her up from ballet rehearsal that day of December 10, 1959.

She headed home by herself and hoped against hope that her bad feeling was unfounded. But then she saw her grandmother, who looked bereaved. And her grandmother broke the news. Denise's father's heart had stopped. He had died at just 51 years old.

Memories instantly flooded the 21-year-old Denise's head, and blood rushed away from it.

He was the man who would take her to crowded restaurants for lunch dates and never have to wait for a table. The man who introduced her to Frank Sinatra and Tony Bennett. The man who had become the first to regain boxing's lightweight championship of the world after losing it. The prizefighter who had won championships in two other weight classes, including one which he bagged when he was a teenaged boy.

The curly-haired, take-no-prisoners pugilist who always charged forward after slipping on his mitts and did combat underneath the brightest lights of Madison Square Garden – the planet's most famous arena – more times than anyone else in his lifetime. The former butcher's son and shoe-shiner who earned enough of a fortune from his more than 170 professional bouts to buy an apple orchard and move his entire family onto it, even amid the Great Depression.

And now Denise had lost him for the rest of her life, just like that.

There was no denying Denise's dad was far removed from the peak of his powers. His Broadway showgirl wife, Denise's mother, had left him behind – and Denise, for that matter – in pursuit of a career in Hollywood. He had been forced to sell off the countryside resort that he had built next to the family farm, an estate so magnificent some of the most powerful men in New York's criminal underworld would vacation there, rubbing elbows with Denise's dad while unwinding over cigars and booze.

Denise's dad had chased the fame and fortune he once found in the ring after his retirement. He worked on stage alongside a nightclub comedian. He acted in a Broadway show.

But the nightclub gig had ended. The Broadway show's run lasted not even two weeks. His most successful projects involved guest spots in a handful of television shows and a bit role as a gambler in a boxing movie. Some of his steadiest income came from opening a liquor store and loaning his name out to a restaurant where he worked as a host, in the heart of the same world-famous New York theater district where his onstage career failed to launch.

Yet to Denise he remained a hero, and she was as sure as she was of anything that she would have much more time left with him. The rest of the world knew this man she had suddenly lost as the once-great Tony Canzoneri, swarthy, flat-nosed, and eternally smiling, win or lose, a member of the prestigious Ring magazine Hall of Fame.

But to Denise, he was just dad, who paid more attention to her than mom did. He was the man who treated her more nicely than any other had to that point and made her believe that she could turn her dreams of becoming a great dancer into reality.

Denise just could not grasp how it would take two days before anyone noticed that her father had never come out of the $21-a-week, midtown Manhattan hotel room where he had been living during the last year of his life. Neither could the veritable boxing publication Ring magazine, which would later observe in its March 1961 issue: "During this period there had been … no callers or inquiries for the man whom thousands had literally worshipped in his days of glory."

Denise couldn't comprehend that, when a bellhop unlocked her father's room and went in with a friend to check on him, they found her dad lying across a bed, in his underwear, alone and lifeless, having suffered a fatal heart attack.

"As the years went on, Canzoneri found himself with little left of the world's goods," mused one writer reflecting on Tony's passing.

Finally, an overwhelmed Denise could feel her spirit shatter within her. She fainted. "I was very, very close to him," Denise would say many years later. "I ... just ... did not take it too well."

In fact, had President-elect John F. Kennedy's personal doctor not made time to help her, she is certain her heartbreak would have killed her.

* * *

It was the turn of the 20th century, and leaving their Sicilian town of Palazzo Adriano had to have been a tough call for George Canzoneri and his wife, Josephine Schiro.

Their families' names were all over the community founded by Greek Albanians more than 300 years earlier – on storefronts, on buildings, and in the surnames of the few thousand people populating a place which a century later would become famous as the filming locale of the movie *Cinema Paradiso*.

The scenery was beautiful as well. There was the fountain near the center of the town's cobblestone plaza, and the street which hangs like a balcony over a westward valley, between mountainsides, olive groves and the occasional stone farmhouse. There were the vineyards, the church on a hill, the black cypress trees which shaded the cemetery, and the flume from which water fell melodically on the mill wheel belonging to George's father, Giuseppe.

But, to be sure, there were reasons for the couple's families to leave all that familiar scenery behind.

Southern Italians, for the most part, were impoverished peasants. They often owned little more than a couple of goats, a donkey and maybe a cart. They did not own the rural fields which they worked on and instead were the tenants of absentee, city-dwelling landlords. The landlords' overseers charged brutal rents – in some cases, up to three-fourths of what their tenants produced. And the property owners had little incentive to invest in revitalizing and refurbishing their lands. Instead, they preferred short-term tenants, whom they could evict at the end of their contracts while seizing any improvements that the renters had made on the grounds during their time there.

Meanwhile, droughts, earthquakes and malaria bedeviled farmers trying to make a go of it with their families in that part of Italy. And perhaps there may not have been a way out.

But thankfully for them, Louisiana – in the southeastern United States of America – was hungry for workers just like them.

Louisiana's sugar and cotton barons were looking to replace en-slaved Black laborers who were liberated after the Union defeated the Confederacy during the American Civil War a few decades earlier. Black people were leaving the region in large numbers during the Reconstruc-tion period following the war for a variety of reasons, ranging from reg-ular outbreaks of yellow fever to white supremacists who would try to intimidate Black voters out of participating in political elections. And while aiming to fill in the resulting gap in the workforce, Louisiana pri-marily targeted Italians.

The Pelican state perceived Italians to be self-sufficient and, more importantly, cheap to hire. Louisiana officials also figured Anglo whites – including those who would inflict often-deadly violence on Black Americans and other minority groups in the era – might be more will-ing to tolerate Italians than Chinese or Japanese immigrants.

So Louisiana officials published information touting their state's su-perior climate, fruit soil, industries, schools, job opportunities and – of importance to a pious people – churches. It also listed descriptions and prices of more than 6 million acres' worth of real estate properties which could be bought by folks who, in Italy, did not know what it was like to be in charge of their own land.

Other lifestyle perks in Louisiana hardly needed hype. Electric-pow-ered streetcars, called trolleys elsewhere, shuttled residents and business-people around. Residents living under sea level – in areas which new pumps helped drain out – were protected from flooding by an elaborate network of drainage canals and levees. Revelers had their pick of clubs where they could listen and dance to live performances from artists making their living on the city's vibrant music scene.

Italians in those days who were pondering a move to Louisiana "would've been somewhat conflicted," Tulane University history profes-sor Lawrence Powell said. "But there was that pull factor."

The recruiting efforts paid off. During a 30-year period beginning in 1898, roughly 70,000 Italians came to New Orleans on ships that would take more than a month to sail across the Atlantic Ocean. Many were part of a broader wave of 4 million Italians – the bulk of them Sicilians – who immigrated to the United States between 1880 and 1915.

As with many things in America, the reaction to the influx of Italians ran the gamut.

Many were confident that younger Italians would have no problem adopting American customs, especially as they worked closely with locals who were living there before them. A late 19th-century issue of the Political Science Quarterly ruminated how Italian immigrants proved themselves to be "extremely desirable settlers and ... good citizens."

"Fears ... they might introduce a lower style of living to the detriment of this country seem ... unfounded," the journal asserted, according to a 1986 paper from Louisiana State University's Roselyn Bologna Boneno.

Yet, as has happened throughout the history of the United States, some believed the only people who could ever truly be Americans were white Anglos. Those who harbored this mindset were bothered by Italians' accent, how they would address one another in their native language, and the way they formed tight-knit groups to watch out for each other. Their cuisine was different from the one in the U.S. at the time. For that matter, their clothes were different, too.

And some vociferously griped that there were white Americans who couldn't get even unskilled jobs because they were undercut by these immigrants from Italy who would agree to work longer hours for lower wages.

"They pay no taxes for our schools, they perform no jury duty, nor are they liable to; they do not perform any of the duties of citizenship, except the protection they get from the city or the state wherever they reside," Edmund Stevenson of New York, an emigrant commissioner, said at the turn of the century, according to Boneno's paper, "From Migrant to Millionaire: the Story of the Italian-American in New Orleans."

Stevenson further complained that, instead of spending their wages in America, "they" would remit the money back to their wives, children and parents in Italy.

Salvador Mandella, whose father used to make his living changing the wheels of old New Orleans streetcars after immigrating from Italy in the early 20th century, told Boneno the racial animosity was palpable.

"They used to call you Dago because the Italian people were always getting out front," Mandela said, referring to a slur for Italians. "They were always furthering themselves and the elder people were not. They were satisfied just the way they were. No one accumulated anything. They'd live from hand to mouth."

It wasn't just verbal. Dispatches in New Orleans's Daily Picayune newspaper conveyed little sympathy for arriving Italian immigrants, authors Anthony Maragavio and Jerome Salomone wrote in their book *Bread and Respect: The Italians of America*. One article chronicled the deaths of two children aboard the Elysian ship – which departed Palermo on September 28, 1890, and arrived in New Orleans 19 days later – as "dispassionately as if listing baseball scores."

Then there's the episode that's been narrated countless times for well over a century and saw New Orleans's anti-Italian xenophobia reach its nadir: the murder of the city's police chief David Hennessy and its even more violent aftermath.

Hennessy earned flattering news headlines in 1881 when, as a detective, he arrested Giuseppe Esposito, who in Sicily had allegedly helped kidnap Reverend John Forester Rose of England. After the kidnapping, Rose's family not only received a letter in the mail demanding a ransom. They were also reportedly mailed both of Rose's ears.

The U.S. deported Esposito following his arrest, and he received a sentence of life imprisonment in Italy for several crimes, including Rose's kidnapping and the murder of another person.

Hennessy was hailed as a hero for his standing up to Esposito. But, as can happen in policing, his reputation later took a hit. He shot a high-ranking colleague to death, but he asserted self-defense and managed to avoid being charged with murder.

In any event, one day in October 1890, someone gunned Hennessy down as he walked home from work and killed him. Nine Italian immigrants were tried the following year on charges that they assassinated Hennessy, and public agitation over the chief's killing boiled over when the jury acquitted the defendants.

The day after the verdict, a mob stormed New Orleans's jail and fatally shot, clubbed or hanged 11 Italians who were still being detained in connection with Hennessy's deadly shooting.

Prosecutors did not bring charges against members of that mob. Italy's government cut off diplomatic ties with the United States and even mulled going to war with America over the lynchings.

Nonetheless, "when the courts fail," one member of the New Orleans lynch mob wrote, "the people must act."[1]

There would be other traumatic episodes in the city within a relatively short time that would again particularly distress local Italians.

In 1896, "a determined mob of 50 men" attacked the jail in St. Charles Parish, which is several miles to the southwest of New Orleans. The group dragged six Italians out of the cells and hanged three of them. Newspapers at the time reported that local leaders may have participated in both the jail attack and the hangings, but what in essence was a grand jury determined that the slain Italians "came to their deaths by being lynched by parties unknown," said a 1982 journal article published by the North Louisiana Historical Association.

Nine years after that, a yellow fever epidemic infected more than 3,400 people, killing 452 of them. The first cases of that outbreak were detected in a mostly Italian section of the city, state public health officials concluded, which of course didn't help relations among newer and older New Orleanians.

There was at least one episode – albeit tragic – in 1907 which helped New Orleans reach a better kinship with its Italian community.

In June of that year, Walter Lamana, the 8-year-old son of a funeral undertaker who was originally from Italy, was promised ice cream from a nearby candy store but instead kidnapped by Italian criminals who hoped to get a ransom for the child's return.

The abductors demanded $6,000 in exchange for Walter, an amount that would have been difficult to collect for his father, whose undertaking business consisted of just a few mules and a funeral carriage.

Yet the father, Peter Lamana, managed to fill a sack with $6,000 in gold and rode 75 miles north to Bogalusa, with police trailing him. Unfortunately, either Walter's kidnappers spotted the cops or something else went awry, and no one showed up to collect the ransom.

Walter's captors strangled him. They wrapped the boy's corpse in

---

1   New Orleans Mayor LaToya Cantrell issued a formal apology to the families of the lynch mob's victims on April 12, 2019, in an effort to provide a measure of closure 128 years after the killings. The slain were fruit vendors Antonio Bagnetto, Antonio Marchesi, and Antonio Scaffidi; stevedores James Caruso and Rocco Geraci; cobbler Pietro Monasterio; tinner Loreto Comitis; street merchant Emmanuele Polizzi; fruit importer Joseph Macheca; ward politico Frank Romero; and rice plantation worker Charles Traina.

a blanket, hauled him out to a remote corner of a swamp, and dumped him there before he was found.

News of Walter's cruel slaying shocked the city. About 2,000 people packed the child's funeral at St. Louis Cathedral in the heart of the city's historic French Quarter neighborhood, including the mayor at the time, Paul Capdevielle. Some people went around and publicly grumbled that Italians had once again brought shame to the Crescent City.

But this time, there would be no deadly violence fueled by a general loathing of Italians. Instead, Italians and non-Italians came together less than a week after the boy's disappearance and pledged to work together to find those responsible for taking young Walter Lamana from his family. Newspapers supported the coalition's mission.

The group's members didn't manage to find young Walter alive. But the committee whose purpose was to bring justice down upon those who kidnapped Walter did identify the boy's killers and helped authorities capture them, which led to their conviction in court. One of Walter's captors was hanged. In a symbol of solidarity that would almost certainly strike modern sensibilities as unduly gruesome, Peter Lamana received the noose as a gift.

The execution of one of his son's convicted killers pleased Lamana, who endorsed it as a delivery of "just deserts," author Gary Krist wrote in *Empire of Sin: A Story of Sex, Jazz, Murder and the Battle for Modern New Orleans.*

"The Lamana kidnapping seems to have marked the turning point of bigotry against Italians," Boneno added in her paper. "[The aftermath] promoted a new spirit of cooperation between New Orleans and its leading ethnic group."

* * *

It was the same year that Hennessy was killed when Josephine Schiro immigrated to the United States. She settled with her family about 70 miles northwest of New Orleans: in Independence, Louisiana, a tiny community in Tangipahoa Parish[2], where Sicilians developed farms to grow strawberries.

---

2   Parish is the word that Louisiana uses for county.

The strawberries that these farms produced and distributed for the markets became world-famous, infused today in everything from milkshakes to beer when not enjoyed in their natural form.

Schiro's future husband, George Canzoneri, arrived from Palazzo Adriano at the Port of New Orleans on October 9, 1903. The author of Creole Italian: Sicilian Immigrants and the Shaping of New Orleans Food Culture, Justin Nystrom, doesn't think it was an accident that George came in the fall. That was typically the start of the growing season for citrus, which was another important crop at the time for the rural area generally north of New Orleans.

For a time, George Canzoneri ran a mill in Lumberton, Mississippi, about 85 miles northeast of New Orleans, a nephew of his named Robert Canzoneri wrote in a memoir titled *A Highly Ramified Tree*. But George, 12 years younger than Josephine, also spent time in Independence. And he and Josephine married and had several children.

One of those children, whom they named Antonino, was born on November 16, 1908, about 16 months after a heartsick city gathered to bury Walter Lamana. Named after George's mother, Antonina, "Tony" was born in the New Orleans suburb of Slidell, a quaint municipality about 60 miles east of Independence that was blanketed in pine trees and camellia flowers.

Yet, for their children's formative years, George and Josephine raised Tony as well as his siblings in a section of the city of New Orleans that many locals have long called Pigeon Town.

Carved out from the former town of Carrollton, Pigeon Town was dotted in shotgun, bungalow and Italianate-style homes amid pockets of small shops and other businesses. Some historians do not believe the moniker, despite its spelling, pays tribute to the bird species. Instead, they believe it is actually a somewhat disrespectful reference to that neighborhood's mix of residents over the course of its history – including formerly enslaved Black people and Italian immigrants – who spoke just enough imperfect, or "pidgin," English to buy something, sell something or get around the city.[3]

---

3   One of New Orleanians' favorite pastimes is to argue with each other and media reporters about what is the true name of any of the city's neighborhoods. Others will passionately tell you Pigeon Town's real name is Pension Town – referring to the military

Regardless, the Canzoneris ran a grocery store and meat market, as did many Italians who left an indelible imprint on New Orleans's cultural and dining fabric. Theirs was in a corner building at the Pigeon Town intersection of Dante and Birch streets.

At that spot, the Canzoneris were more than five miles away from what certainly would have been more comfortable environs in the lower portion of the French Quarter. The lower French Quarter – New Orleans's most visited neighborhood – became home to so many Italian immigrants that, for a while, locals referred to it as "Little Palermo," Nystrom said.[4]

Much later in his life, Tony recalled that running the business and household that they established in New Orleans was hard work for his parents.

"My father ... never had an easy day in his life," Canzoneri would later say in a June 1955 article in Boxing & Wrestling magazine. "He had a big family to support, and we all pitched in to help wherever we could."

Financially, though, there was no disputing New Orleans was more stable than Palazzo Adriano would have been.

"Life, on balance, is much better here for your average Sicilian" at that time, Nystom said.

The Canzoneri store and family abode was also as well located as they could expect, despite its distance from Little Palermo. Their complex stood eight blocks from a road and a levee running along the Mississippi River, a convenient route linking the city to adjacent, suburban Jefferson Parish. It was also two blocks away in the other direction from one of the lines where New Orleans's streetcars – which in those days were considered state of the art – had been running under a canopy of southern oak trees since 1893.

There could hardly be a better time for Tony and the other Canzoneri children to be growing up in New Orleans. Not only was the

---

pensioners and other war veterans who retired there – or simply P-Town. The city's planning commission, which delineates neighborhood boundaries, dubbed this neighborhood "Leonidas," drawing the name from the king who once ruled ancient Sparta.

4   The lower part of the French Quarter would be the areas of the neighborhood closest to Canal Street. The upper section would be closest to Esplanade Avenue, at the opposite end of the French Quarter.

general political climate becoming less hostile to – and, in at least a few ways, relatively more tolerant of – Italians. But also the Crescent City was crazy about the sport of boxing, and it was replete with residents who were captivated by bouts that could sometimes last more than seven hours. They seemingly couldn't get enough of the fights that on occasion were deadly.

All of those factors combined to blaze open a path to life-changing glories that neither Tony Canzoneri nor his loved ones could even begin to imagine then.

CHAPTER TWO

"I DON'T WANT TO WORK. I WANT TO BE A FIGHTER."

———

Often, there's more than one explanation for something that happened years and years ago. And so it is when it comes to precisely how and why Tony Canzoneri picked up boxing.

For one thing, according to Tony himself, his family's home in New Orleans was just three blocks away from where two-time bantamweight world champion Pete Herman was. Naturally, living so close to the boxing great meant Tony one day had the chance to set his own eyes on Herman and shake hands with him, immediately igniting dreams about one day replicating – and maybe even surpassing – the neighborhood legend's exploits.

"I think that first look at Herman made me want to be like him," Canzoneri remarked in the June 1955 issue of Boxing & Wrestling magazine of the retired boxing pro he had also described as "a fine man."

Additionally, at some point, Tony's older brother, Joe, began taking boxing lessons at the Gayoso Athletic Club run by a local man named Johnny Galway. Galway made his living digging drainage canals, building pump stations and eventually overseeing what became the agency which manages New Orleans's sewers and water service. But for years, his passion was teaching boxing to youths at the Gayoso, having previously attended both a public school named after real-estate baron John McDonogh[1] as

———

1   McDonogh's legacy in New Orleans is complicated. The failed U.S. Senate candidate donated much of his fortune to the cities of New Orleans and Baltimore, where he was born, so they could build public schools. But, more recently, people have fought to get his

well as a college run by the Jesuit Catholic religious order.

Galway sent the boxing teams he taught at the Gayoso all over the country, earning him respect among regional civic leaders and in national pugilistic circles. The Gayoso stood at a property that Galway also rented as his home in the 3000 block of St. Peter Street, in the neighborhood surrounding New Orleans's Bayou St. John, which was thought of as blue-collar at the time.

The gym wasn't exactly around the corner from the Canzoneris' meat market at 1538 Dante Street. The trek was about four miles. Yet, as is customary with little brothers, Tony – moon-faced and eager – wanted to imitate Joe. So he eventually started accompanying his older brother to his lessons and signed up to participate himself.

Joe pleaded with his younger brother to pick up another hobby and leaving boxing to him, as Tony would tell it many years later.

"Go on home, Tony," Joe would say. "This ain't no place for a kid." But Tony ignored his brother and persisted in going.

Though gradually fading, some lingering local resentment of Tony's parents' nationality may have also played a role.

Some tellings of Canzoneri's boxing origin story describe him as a frail-framed, 75-pound shiner of shoes when he was 11. Boys who were much bigger than him began picking on him ruthlessly, either because they were trying to lure away some of Tony's customers or because they were white, racist Americans who loathed Canzoneri's Sicilian background, reflected with his darker skin and hair.

Whatever the case, Tony eventually grew sick of them, so he accompanied Joe to Galway's Gayoso club and from there learned the skills that would help him beat back the ruffians who were terrorizing him in Pigeon Town.

"Tony learned to fight because they hated Italians," said Jay Honold, a maternal relative of Canzoneri, citing stories told to him by his uncles.

Canzoneri himself would later grow and speak glowingly about the vital lessons he learned from fighting off the bullies in his city. Just four pages into his seminal boxing book *The Sweet Science*, A.J. Liebling writes that Tony once confided in him that it wasn't until several years

---

name removed from those schools because he owned Black slaves and many of the schools' students have been Black.

An undated photo of a young Tony Canzoneri with one of his brothers. *Courtesy of Jay Honold*

into his youth that he even tried on his first boxing glove.

"Of course," Canzoneri coolly told Liebling, "I had some street fighting" before then. But it was nothing formal.

Whether to emulate and keep up with his big brother, shield his shoeshining turf from competitors, or protect his parents' Italian heritage, the butcher's son began mastering the art of punching. It started off modestly. Galway recalled that Tony's first ever boxing bout, when he was 13, was against a 75-pound Gayoso member named Milton Miles. Miles beat Canzoneri in a ring whose ropes were made with clotheslines at a small venue on the Pigeon Town corner of Maple and Dublin streets, according to Galway.

Nonetheless, eventually, Tony "became ... adept at beating older and bigger boys," and he spent most of his time working out at the Gayoso.[2]

In those days, in New Orleans and elsewhere, boxing clubs like the Gayoso enjoyed a spot in the public consciousness that their modern counterparts simply do not. It was one of at least five New Orleans athletic clubs which, nearly every night, supplied cards of high-quality bouts that attracted large crowds amid what was boxing's second peak in terms of popularity.

Those club cards were the spiritual successors of the state's earliest boxing matches, which Louisiana was the first in the country to legalize with a law passed in 1891, the same year as the assassination of New Orleans police chief David Hennessy and the anti-Italian sentiment which it spawned in some quarters.

"The law permitted the sport to be engaged in openly, with little restriction other than that gloves were supposed to be used," said a history on file at the State Library of Louisiana. But the requirement for gloves was about all that distinguished the sanctioned sport from the no-holds-barred, bare knuckled style of boxing that was the antecessor of the modern fight game.

Some New Orleanians still speak about some of that era's most legendary bouts. A boxing carnival hosted by the Olympic Athletic Club, along the Mississippi River, lasted for three days in September 1892. The storied, long-shuttered Olympic facility at 619 Congress Street in the city's Bywater section witnessed lightweight and featherweight title fights, but the tale about the carnival which New Orleans's boxing enthusiasts pass down to this day is James "Gentleman Jim" Corbett's dethroning of heavyweight monarch John L. Sullivan over 21 rounds. The money on the line for the fighters was as lucrative as it got in that era: a purse of $21,000 and a side bet of $10,000.

---

2   Another version of Tony's boxing origin story: an inconspicuous local fighter named Kid Gage, managed by relatively well-known New Orleans boxer Basil Galiano, spotted Canzoneri holding his own in a scrap and sent him to the Gayoso. There, Tony tendered an application to practice with the club's amateur boxing team, and it was accepted despite concerns over his diminutive size.

In typical boxing fashion, where the true champion at any weight class is often in dispute, a bout in New Orleans in April of the following year laid claim to being the longest-ever fist fight. Lightweights Jack Burke and Andrew Bowen tied after clashing for 110 – that's one hundred and ten – rounds, with 7 hours and 19 minutes elapsing between the opening and final bells.

It was the second time Bowen, a New Orleans native, had fought for at least 85 rounds in a bout. He scored an 85th-round knockout against an opponent named Jack Everhardt before his draw with Burke.

Medical records that might explain the irreversible punishment his body likely took during such marathon fights are beyond reach now. But, roughly 20 months after going the extreme distance with Burke, Bowen absorbed an 18th-round blow from George "Kid" Lavigne at the Auditorium Club[3] in New Orleans's Mid-City neighborhood and fell unconscious.

Bowen struck his head on the unpadded ring floor after falling and lost consciousness. He never woke back up. He died the following day.

Louisiana repealed its free-wheeling boxing law about the time of Bowen's death, which drew coverage from the US's most revered daily periodical, the New York Times.[4] The sport's popularity waned sharply in the wake of Bowen's killing in the ring. But then, Louisiana's Legislature passed a new law in 1920 which gave full governing power over boxing to a state commission made up of three gubernatorial appointees – and gave the sport a chance at a resurgence in the Pelican state.

The Gayoso and other clubs who similarly taught boxing's fundamentals to New Orleans's youth helped the sport find a foothold in the city, as did a broader revival of interest in the fight game after the end of the first world war. And, once exposed to those fundamentals, Tony found himself seduced by everything that the Gayoso had to offer, from teaching him how to repel the bullies who thought they were Pigeon Town's rulers to the rhythmic thumping sounds of gloves hitting punching bags to the smells left behind by a hard day's work.

---

3   This building was on the corner of Canal Street and Carrollton Avenue, one of the most prominent intersections in Mid-City.

4   The New York Times didn't know this at the time, but it would soon begin dedicating many column inches to Tony Canzoneri.

But many people were not at all charmed by boxing. And among them was one George Canzoneri.

Thinking about Tony spending so much time trying to learn such a brutal sport "was no fun for me," George Canzoneri once said.

He explained his main reason. Boxing made Tony scarce around the store whenever George needed his son to run errands, for one. And whenever Tony's parents caught him with mitts on his hands rather than the patent leather shoes and lace collared shirt his mother preferred him in, they would punish him.

George's wife, Josephine, loathed boxing as much as him, if not more. The couple implored their son to focus on his studies, first at Little Flower of Jesus School – a Catholic institution about two miles from the store – and later at the public Samuel J. Peters Junior High School[5] on South Broad Street, which was in New Orleans's Mid-City section and further away. Tony, though, remained committed to his sport and tried to work around his parents' reservations over his dreams of becoming a prizefighter.

George and Josephine unwittingly undermined their efforts to defuse Tony's interest in boxing when they moved their home and grocery to 3129 Palmyra Street in Mid-City. While it brought the family to within eight blocks of Samuel J. Peters Junior High, it also left them about three miles closer to the Gayoso than they previously had been.

Of course, the man in charge at the Gayoso, John Galway, was delighted at the move. It was obvious to him as he watched Tony pick up on his teachings that he had loads and loads of potential to become a boxing superstar one day.

"I saw in Canzoneri a real fighter – he was dead game and would fight any boy I matched him with," Galway once said. "He was not like most other boys who refused to meet this boy or the other. They all don't have the same fighting heart that Canzoneri has."

Tony went on bulk up from the 75 pounds that he weighed when he initially walked into the Gayoso, winning titles at the 85-, 90-, 95-, 100- and 105-pound amateur boxing divisions.

---

5   Named after one of the founders of New Orleans's public education system, it was later named after Israel Meyer Augustine, the first African-American judge elected to the bench of the Orleans Parish Criminal District Court nearby.

An undated photo of a young shirtless Tony Canzoneri and his brother Joseph.
Courtesy of Jay Honold

One three-round bout on October 17, 1923, made the local papers after pitting Canzoneri – fresh off a regional title win at the 100-pound weight class – against a champion fighter from another club named Henry Jungles. The 100-pound Jungles's strategy was to sit back and counter attack Tony, but the approach proved to be unwise.

Canzoneri overwhelmed Jungles with a variety of strikes. Jungles's defense soon tired, opening him up to more punishment, and Canzoneri earned a lopsided decision win that perfectly showed off his strengths in the ring.

"When Canzoneri fights, fans are certain they will get plenty of action," The New Orleans Item reported a couple of weeks later. "He is of the boring-in type and unless his opponent is an unusually good defensive boxer, they seldom go very far."

Reportedly, only one local New Orleans boy ever managed to get the best of Canzoneri once Tony hit his stride. That was Willie Bennett, who later fought professionally 13 times and won on eight of those occasions.

Canzoneri's successful amateur boxing apprenticeship translated into more than just trophies. He also "won more watches and suitcases" than U.S. presidents had headaches while they were in the Oval Office, Tony would later tell Boxing & Wrestling magazine. And those tokens of his success turned into money for his family when he sold them on the secondary market, such as there was one for a boy his age.

"I sold or hocked everything for whatever I could get, but when I got a buck for a watch I was doing good," Canzoneri once said.

Still, despite the proximity of Tony's family's home and store to the Gayoso, his obvious skill at the sport, and the infancy of the material wealth he'd one day accumulate, Galway said he had "the dickens of a time getting his parents to let him box." Doing that required him to call Josephine, more so than George, and beg her to let Tony come out to train at or compete for the gym.

"No," she would say for a while. "I don't want Tony to box."

Galway said Josephine remained an obstacle even after he began racking up trophies. The night that Tony became the Gayoso's champion at 100 pounds, Galway said, "I had to go over and all but get on my knees begging his mother to let him fight. She cried, saying her Tony might get hurt. I assured her that I would make him the 100-pound Southern champ and he could then quit the ring as champion."

At least Galway had one thing going for him at that point – George had gotten behind the idea of letting Tony see how good of a boxer he could be. George had started attending Tony's fights regularly, saying to friends, acquaintances and customers: "My little boy Tony is a champion fighter."

And Josephine eventually did cave, but that was only after she presented the men in her life with a compromise, as those familiar with the matter later told it.

The deal was this: if they were all so keen to let Tony get maimed in the ring, Joe would need to quit boxing.

"It's enough getting Tony killed," she would say to Joe. "I don't want you to fight no more."

Like his father at that point, Joe's belief in his little's brother's promise by then had grown. And Joe's belief that his little brother could hit it big was so strong that he, Tony, George and Galway all signed off on the terms offered up by Josephine.

Joe agreed to quit boxing. He agreed to quit so that Tony could fly.

* * *

With little fanfare, the Canzoneris had moved to Brooklyn by 1924, closing their meat market in New Orleans and opening another in the Big Apple. "Things were tough in New Orleans, and we heard New York was a land of opportunity where they had solid gold manhole covers," Canzoneri would say decades later in Boxing & Wrestling magazine.

Only George and Joe went up first. But then they later sent for the rest of the family to join them in a house that Tony once described as "nice, ... big and roomy."

Despite the relatively comfortable home, George and Josephine would say they didn't like New York City. It was too sprawling and overly crowded, and they found themselves often speaking about returning to New Orleans, which they considered their true home.

But many people who had moved to the United States from Italy also would speak about returning to their native country. Rarely did they do it. And the Canzoneris ultimately would neither fully make it back to New Orleans nor Italy, for that matter.

Perhaps sensing the unlikelihood that his family would ever truly return to the only city he had known and called home, Tony went to

Galway and asked him to become his legal guardian so he could stay in New Orleans. Galway would later say he contemplated the decision as seriously as he had contemplated anything. After all, Tony was his club's most talented member, and the boy had even started sleeping at the gym while his family was divided between New Orleans and Brooklyn.

Galway also had some things in common with Tony. The coach had been the son of immigrants, too – from Ireland in his case. And Galway's father was a grocer as well.

However, Galway and his wife, Hortense, already had children of their own – a few of them, in fact. And despite the glory and prestige which his beloved Gayoso club brought him, he paid the bills with the money he made from his time-consuming day job with what is now New Orleans's Sewerage & Water Board.

Galway ultimately decided he couldn't take Tony on as an additional mouth to feed. He told his star pupil that he should accompany his parents to Brooklyn, reminding him that New York – one of the planet's prizefighting capitals – would likely offer a world of opportunities beyond what Canzoneri's teenage brain could even comprehend at that juncture.

Tony was uncertain despite Galway's assurance and remained filled with trepidation about leaving New Orleans. But he relented and headed up to join his family in New York.

He later described how overwhelming his first step off the train at New York City's famed Pennsylvania station was. "I'll never forget how big that place looked," Canzoneri recalled. "Bigger than the whole city of New Orleans."

As the Canzoneri patriarch and matriarch would tell it, for at least a little bit, they thought that moving away from Galway and the Gayoso would extinguish Tony's passion for boxing.

Tony had gotten a job during nights operating the rolling machine at the cigarette manufacturing company Lucky Strike, and they thought that would likely eat up most of his free time. He was also going to school by day, though he was struggling and had even gotten held back a grade.

And yet, one day in their cellar, the Canzoneris caught Tony practicing boxing. George went in to scold him once again about needing to get serious about his future, but Tony deflected the incoming verbal volley.

"Papa, I don't want to work" the jobs George envisioned him having, Tony said. "I want to be a fighter."

The building which housed the meat market run by Tony Canzoneri's parents at 1538 Dante Street while his family lived in New Orleans still stands. Local musician Nick Sanzenbach now owns it and uses it as his personal residence.

The inside of the building which housed the meat market run by Tony Canzoneri's parents at 1538 Dante Street while his family lived in New Orleans. Local musician Nick Sanzenbach uses what used to be the store's front room as a living room. Sanzenbach says this space is original to the building, which was first built in 1857.

After initially running a meat market in New Orleans's Pigeon Town section, Tony Canzoneri's family moved their home and grocery to 3129 Palmyra Street a few miles away in the Mid-City neighborhood. It brought them closer to the Gayoso club, where Tony's career as an amateur boxer began. This photo shows the building at 3129 Palmyra much later when it was known as Rose Grocery in 2007. Flooding during Hurricane Katrina in 2005 after New Orleans's federal levees failed damaged the building, and it was later demolished. The lot where it sat remained empty as of spring 2023. *Photo by Karen Apricot, Flickr.com, Creative Commons license*

George took pride in the long days of hard work he put into his grocery stores and meat markets, and he was disgusted that his son told him he had no interest in that life. But Tony wasn't just offering simple recalcitrance. He also made a promise that struck George as particularly sincere.

"Papa," Tony said, "let me turn professional and I'll bring home plenty of money."

George pondered Tony's words. He knew his Brooklyn store was struggling. And that was disappointing to him because the only reason he had moved his family all the way to Brooklyn was because his New Orleans businesses had been faring poorly. And no one could seriously argue that Tony had done anything but thrive in the ring after he picked up boxing at the Gayoso.

George surrendered. If Tony wanted to see how far he could go as a prizefighter, he had his father's blessing, George said.

Additionally, George set up an introduction between Tony and a New Orleans friend who likewise had moved up to New York: a welter-weight boxer named Paul Doyle. Doyle and his manager, Joe Palazolo, often hung out with George and Tony's brother Joe. And during those meet-ups, the Canzoneri patriarch frequently would brag: "My Tony had lots of fights, and he won every one. Yep, Tony is a real champion."

Palazolo finally told George if that were true, there would be a ton of money to make in New York City. Finally, George arranged for Palazolo and Doyle to meet his son, but Tony didn't make all that favorable of an impression when he showed up in the lace collar shirt, patent-leather shoes and the short pants his parents liked him to wear in New Orleans.

"That's your champion?" Tony would later remember hearing Pala-zolo say to George[6]. "This must be some kind of joke. You said he was a champion."

Tony saw Doyle and Palazolo begin walking away while they con-vulsed with laughter, and he wanted to run away. But he stopped when he heard George loudly deliver what was then his clearest vote of confi-dence in Tony's prospects as a boxer.

---

6   To be transparent: the June 1955 Boxing & Wrestling magazine article refer-enced throughout says this occurred at Penn station when Tony first got to New York.

"Sure, he's a champion," George told Palazolo. "I know he's still young, but you wait – when he grows up, nobody will lick my Tony."

* * *

Meanwhile, back in Tony's former hometown, his old boxing coach Johnny Galway wrote a letter to Benny Lavine, who was in charge of New York's amateur fighters. Galway said he supplied Lavine with Tony's address in Brooklyn, introduced Tony as a southern region champ, and told Lavine that Tony was a rising up-and-comer on whom to keep an eye.

Tony ultimately signed up for the boxing team at Brooklyn's National Athletic Club. With his reputation in the ring having preceded him (and decidedly outweighing Palazolo's dismissal of his physique), National happily accepted Tony and unleashed his prowess on their opponents. He began bringing laurels back to the club almost instantly.

It was January of 1925 when Canzoneri earned some of the longest newspaper write-ups that he had up to that point. In what would be one of his earliest appearances at an imposing building named Madison Square Garden, Canzoneri powered through a field of respected bantamweight (118-pound limit) prospects at the state AAU championships. He toppled Henry Usse and Pete Burns in the quarterfinals and semifinals before advancing to the final against one Joe Scalfaro.

Scalfaro quickly learned why National was so happy to welcome Canzoneri. Canzoneri knocked Scalfaro down in both the first and second rounds, though Scalfaro got up each time and kept on fighting.

Scalfaro spent the third and final round desperately trying to close the points advantage which Canzoneri had gashed open with the knockdowns. But National's talented dynamo was too much for Scalfaro to overcome. Canzoneri – still in high school at the time – earned the decision in his favor, which was among the last to be awarded at that legendary building at 26th Street and Madison Avenue[7].

---

7   This 8,000-seat, palace-like building, the second to be named Madison Square Garden, closed later in 1925 and was demolished in 1926. The third iteration of Madison Square Garden, which was boxy and mostly resembled ... an industrial warehouse, reopened in 1926 at 8th Avenue and 50th Street, meaning it was actually located away from Madison Square. Tony Canzoneri was fated to become a household name in that third version of Madison Square Garden, whose most distinctive feature was an elaborate marquee at the front entrance. The Madison Square Garden where the New York Knicks

"Canzoneri is as full of fight as they make 'em and hits short and hard," Ed Van Every wrote in a dispatch for the Bristol News of Tennessee. With words that would prove prophetic, Van Every said of Canzoneri, "He will bear watching."

Tony Canzoneri headed to Baltimore on March 12, 1925, to face a local prospect named Sidney Lampe in the final bout of the bantamweight junior national championship. Their toe-to-toe exchanges throughout the fight's three rounds brought spectators to their feet multiple times. Those were good enough for Canzoneri and Lampe to win over one judge each, leaving it to referee Spike Webb to cast the decisive scorecard.

The good news for Tony was that Webb sided with him, and Canzoneri was crowned the country's best junior amateur at 118 pounds.

Tony then set his sights on the full – rather than just the junior – national amateur championship in Boston the following month. Canzoneri advanced to the second round of the tournament, but his run ended there after he lost a decision.

Despite the defeat, Canzoneri's confidence surged, and he figured the time for him to begin translating his skills into real money was fast approaching. All of his amateur bouts in New York – many of which were staged at the city's old Starlight Park along with other clubs – had created a buzz. Similar results in the pros meant big paydays.

He began mulling candidates to become his manager who would oversee his switch to becoming a professional boxer.

Canzoneri was not interested in starting small. Knowing he had plenty of prestigious hardware in his trophy and medal case, he coveted Billy Gibson, whose client list included the heavyweight champion of the world, Gene Tunney, and world lightweight champion Benny Leonard[8].

Yet it seems cosmic forces governing Tony Canzoneri's widening universe pointed him in the direction of Sammy Goldman.

Notably, the ex-champion and New Orleans-born boxer Pete Herman,

---

currently play, and which is also host to some of the biggest boxing matches today, is the fourth building to bear this renowned name. It opened in 1968 at 4 Pennsylvania Plaza.

8   Leonard would later offer high praise for Canzoneri, saying he developed a boxing style that worked for him while being very difficult to copy.

The Gayoso club where Tony Canzoneri learned to box stood where this residence now sits in New Orleans's Bayou St. John neighborhood. The property is a bit of a neighborhood landmark but not because of its association with Canzoneri's history. It is now co-owned by a woman whose son was murdered in 2001 and then painted an angel, flowers, people, trees and dancing silhouettes on the sidewalk as well as the home itself in a colorful tribute to him. Other parts of the tribute are a birdbath, a painted meditation labyrinth, benches and sculptures, including a miniature version of Michelangelo's Pieta, which depicts Mary holding the body of Jesus after he was crucified, according to a 2009 article in the Times-Picayune. Interestingly, a previous address for the other owner was about a block away from the Canzoneris' Palmyra Street store, property records show.

Credit: The New Orleans property tax assessor's website, top, and Google Maps, bottom

who had become familiar with Canzoneri and befriended him during his rise in the Crescent City, put in a word for Sammy Goldman.

A native of St. Louis, Sammy Goldman had once been a sports writer for The New Orleans Item newspaper and had broken into boxing by refereeing fights at the old Orleans Athletic Club on the corner of Bienville and North Rampart streets, on the edge of the French Quarter.

Goldman met a young Herman through his work at the Orleans. And along with many others worldwide, he followed along closely as Pete became the bantamweight champion of the world in 1917.

Having later moved to New York, Goldman went into business with Herman as his manager after Pete lost his bantamweight crown by decision at Madison Square Garden to a challenger named Joe Lynch. Herman, under Goldman's guidance, earned another shot at glory in 1921. He made the most of that opportunity, regaining the title from Lynch with a rematch decision win over him at the home of the Brooklyn Dodgers, Ebbets Field.

Herman lost his championship for good later that year. Blaming his ever deteriorating eyesight, Herman retired permanently soon after, moved back to New Orleans and opened a restaurant.

Herman in his retirement always credited Goldman with helping him enjoy a second reign as the world's bantamweight monarch, and he was forever on the lookout for the chance to repay his old manager.

"Maybe there will be another fighter as good as me around New Orleans some day," Herman reportedly told Goldman before they went their separate ways professionally. "If there is, I'll send him to you."

After Canzoneri stormed onto the scene at the Gayoso, Herman wired a telegram to Goldman. "Am sending a kid to you," it read. "He will be a great fighter some day."

But he didn't think it was just Goldman who could benefit from him partnering up with Canzoneri. Herman thought it would be equally helpful for Canzoneri to have Goldman on his side. And he told Tony that directly.

"He was," Herman once stated simply of his manager, "a great guy."

The recommendation meant a lot to Canzoneri. Not only was Herman a New Orleans-bred boxer, but – born Peter Gulotta – he was also of Sicilian heritage himself. Similarly, Herman's endorsement of Canzoneri carried weight with Goldman and caught his attention.

For his part, when he learned Tony was thinking of lining up Goldman as his manager, Galway wrote a letter to his old amateur champion's parents and told them that Sammy would be a great choice.

"I wrote ... that [they] would not make any mistake in letting Sammy Goldman manage him as Goldman was a New Orleans man and a good friend of mine who knew the game as well as anyone," Galway remarked[9].

Finally, the word of another relatively well-known New Orleans boxer named Basil Galiano also went far in nudging Canzoneri toward Goldman. Galiano, a lightweight championship contender, had seen the earliest days of Canzoneri's career and had such a favorable impression of Tony that he began calling him "the Italian Terror." Usually, whenever Galiano would call Canzoneri by his nickname for him, he would also playfully pat his head. But there was nothing fanciful about Tony being an Italian terror – it was perfectly accurate if you asked the ever-growing list of opponents whom he had bested.

After Canzoneri had moved to New York, Galiano was doing his preparations for an upcoming bout at a famed Big Apple gym run by trainer Lou Stillman. Canzoneri got the idea of taking the subway to Stillman's gym to meet Galiano. But, on the day Tony made the trip, the person working the door didn't know who Canzoneri was – much less who he would later be. And the doorman wouldn't let Tony in unless he surrendered a quarter that he would need to take the subway back home that rainy Saturday.

Canzoneri later recalled that he snuck past the doorman by walking closely behind a hulking heavyweight who showed up afterwards to train at the gym. The heavyweight's size hid Tony from the doorman as he skulked through undetected.

Once inside, there was such thick cigar smoke that Canzoneri couldn't immediately find Galiano. He wandered around for 15 minutes and nearly gave up to go home before spotting Galiano shadow boxing in an area behind the gym's rings that was off limits to anyone who wasn't a fighter, manager or trainer.

Eventually, Galiano walked out of that area and headed to the

---

9   Galway would later say he wrote this letter at Goldman's request.

dressing room, and Canzoneri made his move, cutting him off and blurting out: "Hi, Basil."

Galiano stopped as the boy who approached him continued: "Remember me, Tony Canzoneri from New Orleans?" It took Galiano a minute, but he recognized the name and the face.

"Sure," Galiano said, as Canzoneri would later recall. "You're the kid I used to pat on the head all the time."

"Yeah," a bemused Canzoneri answered. "That's me – Tony Canzoneri."

Canzoneri used his time with Galiano to tell him about the success he was having with National. He informed Galiano of his ambitions of turning pro – and asked Basil if they could ever spar.

Canzoneri was prepared to be turned down, but it didn't happen. Galiano said: "Sure, how about tomorrow?" Canzoneri agreed to come back around the same time the next day.

When Tony showed up to the gym a day later, Galiano introduced him to his trainer: Isadore Gastonfeld, better known to the regulars at the place as Izzy the Painter. Gastonfeld told Tony where to change, and then he sparred with Galiano for three rounds.

"Naturally, he's taking it easy, but I'm moving pretty good and getting to him with a left lead easily," Canzoneri would later tell Boxing & Wrestling magazine of the sparring session.

Gastonfeld called time at the end of the third round, declared "that's all for today," and Canzoneri started leaving the ring. Among the few people there that Sunday were three men smoking cigars and wearing white felt hats with black bands. They all circled around him and stopped him, with one saying, "Nice goin', kid."

He looked like he wanted to say more, but he didn't get the chance. Suddenly, Izzy's voice boomed from the ring: "Stay away from that kid. Sammy Goldman has got him."

Galiano then told Tony that Goldman had been watching them spar along with the others who approached him. Though Goldman hadn't yet said anything to Tony, Galiano made one thing clear. Galiano said out of everyone who had watched their sparring, Goldman was the one it'd be most worth getting to know somehow.

Tony later attended the fight for which Galiano had been training, and Goldman sat with him in the crowd. At one point, Goldman seemed skeptically amused when Tony wondered out loud if the fighters they were watching in a preliminary bout were really professional.

"Sure," Goldman said. "Why do you ask?"

"I could lick both of those guys in the ring and the four that went on before them, too," Canzoneri told Goldman, before realizing he was unsure how the remark might come off to the man who everyone thought should be his manager.

It came off well enough. After Galiano won his fight with a first-round knockout, Goldman invited Canzoneri to ride out of there in a cab with him, Basil, and Izzy.

"They talk fights from the minute they get in, and I sit with my eyes popping and my mouth shut," Tony would later say of the ride.

After that night, Canzoneri began regularly going to Stillman's gym to train with Izzy the Painter. He showed enough for Goldman to pay for Canzoneri to attend another Galiano fight in Philadelphia, covering his meals, hotel room and anything else that Tony asked on the trip.

As they returned to New York, Goldman and Tony traveled with one of that era's boxing promoters, Bob Levy. Goldman asked Levy when he was staging another card of fights at New York's Rockaway arena.

Levy thought quietly for a moment and then said he was having one on July 24th, 1925.

Goldman immediately replied: "Put Canzoneri into a four-rounder on that show. You pick the opponent."

Okay, Levy said. If that's what Goldman wanted, he'd get it. Just like that, Goldman had officially become Tony's manager.

At last, the moment had come. It was time to learn whether Tony could make good on his word to his dad that pro boxing was the ticket to better, more comfortable days – not just for him, but for their entire family.

CHAPTER THREE

THE BLONDE TERROR
OF TERRE HAUTE

———

If George and Josephine Canzoneri fretted about whether their 16-year-old son Tony could thrive as a professional prizefighter, their doubts must have started subsiding with his debut.

It wasn't the main event that day at the Rockaway beach arena in Queens – those, many of those, would come later, and at more storied venues. His opponent was also far from a household name. Jack Grodner had fought as a professional only once before, and he had suffered a fourth-round knockout defeat.

Nonetheless, Grodner was confident enough that he took his half of the $80 purse which the fighters split and bet it on his beating this newcomer, Canzoneri. The bout was on the undercard of a show featuring a contender for the featherweight world title.

And not even one full round into the bout which was scheduled for four rounds, Grodner learned his bet had been a drastic miscalculation.

As Sammy Goldman and Izzy the Painter watched him from his corner, Tony landed a left-hook, right-cross combination that knocked Grodner down to the canvas. Grodner was unable to regain his feet before the referee counted him out of the fight.

Tony, just like that, had collected his first win as a pro. And, according to information published by the online database BoxRec, Grodner never ever fought again.

"I must have looked like a big shot with all that high class management behind me, and believe me it didn't make me feel bad," Canzoneri would later tell Boxing & Wrestling magazine of his debut.

Such emphatic, debut victories[1] can send fighters' confidence sky high – to their detriment. Goldman made sure to nip that in the bud by teasing the bout's brevity.

"Sammy said he didn't have time to see if I could fight or not," Canzoneri would later say in jest about how short his first bout as a pro was.

Still, little by little, the boxing press found itself needing to dedicate more and more of its collective ink to this 5-foot-4 teenager, on some occasions billed to fans as a Brooklynite and at other times described to them as a New Orleanian.

In a clear indication of how times have drastically changed in the name of safety – let alone adequate recovery time – for athletes, Canzoneri fought and won 17 more times in the following eight months. Most of those victories were in New York, including one at Madison Square Garden, the venue where he had been crowned the Empire State's amateur champion a few months before introducing himself to the pro boxing world at Grodner's expense.

The bouts showed those who were paying attention that "Tony was a marvelous boxer-puncher with the quickness of a cat who could pinpoint a straight right with unbelievable precision," Ring magazine would write many years later in its July 1982 issue. He wasn't perfect, at least not yet, in part because he held his left-hand low while on defense and that left him particularly exposed to right-sided blows from his opponents. Despite that, the publication added, he "never [seemed] easy to hit."

Thirteen of those 17 triumphs – at both the bantamweight (118-pound limit) and featherweight (126-pound) division – came via decision.

That was an early sign that Canzoneri could rely more on volume and accuracy of punches to outpoint his opponents when the occasion called for it, whether in the low-stakes exhibitions that helped pay off a fighter's expenses and served as practice or for bouts where more prestige and pricier purses were on the line. That is, he could still triumph even if on any given occasion opponents didn't provide him the opportunity to win by knockout.

---

1   Canzoneri said he learned Grodner lost his half of the purse betting on himself when they ran into each other years later in New York City. In Canzoneri's words: "I bought him a meal and a couple of drinks to make up for it."

But there was no mistaking that Tony could also demonstrate fight-stopping power when the chance to do so was there. In one of those early victories, just before Christmas in 1925, Tony knocked out Danny Terris in four rounds.

Canzoneri understood that to be the first ever knockout in what at the time was the new rendition of the Garden, he would tell Boxing & Wrestling magazine in June 1955.

His slate of adversaries during this period ranged from young, unproven prospects like him to experienced boxers who had dozens of pro victories to their names but also ample supplies of defeats and draws.[2]

It didn't take long for questions to begin cropping up about just how high of a trajectory Canzoneri's career would have. He tied the 20th and 21st bouts of his career to unremarkable fighters named Mike Esposito and Benny Hall, whom he faced at bantamweight, an infamously low weight for many boxers to make. Pugilists who lose much of their natural weight to qualify for lighter divisions can in the process lose power on their punches, rendering them less effective. The effort to drop the necessary weight can also leave fighters overly tired by the time their bouts come around, weakening both their bodies as well as their chances of victory.

Regardless, Canzoneri bounced back with seven consecutive wins during a three-month stretch beginning May 28, 1926, including a trio of six-round fights that he won with three fifth-round knockouts.

Two of those knockout wins came in consecutive fights a month apart. Referee Jim Crowley stopped Canzoneri's June 25 fight with Archie Bell in Brooklyn's Coney Island Stadium after Canzoneri opened a deep gash over Bell's left eye. Then, on July 26, at Queens' Dexter Park Arena, Canzoneri landed rights that dropped Harlem's Manny Wexler once in the second and twice in the fifth round before Wexler was unable to answer the 10-second count.

---

2   Generally, in boxing matches where one fighter doesn't knock the other out, the winners are decided on three scorecards which keep track of who wins each round. Fighters who do better in a round than their opponents win by one point, with a knockdown adding an additional point. A fighter must have the advantage on two cards to win. Today, bouts have three judges, but in Canzoneri's era, the scorecards were kept by two judges and the referee for the most part.

But disappointing results would soon put the back-to-back knockout victories into proper perspective. He eventually posted another tie against a four-win, two-loss fighter named Georgie Mack, whose career eventually ended with twice as many defeats (10) as victories. Two decision victories followed over the next several weeks, including one avenging the tie with Hall. Yet again, any alleviation that may have come from overcoming Hall was fleeting.

That's because on his 18th birthday – November 6, 1926, a little more than a year after charging into the professional prizefighting ranks – Canzoneri endured his first taste of defeat.

The bout was against Davey Abad. The native of Panama had lost two of his previous six bouts and drawn one, carrying in an overall record of 31 wins, 12 defeats and nine ties. It was Canzoneri's first 10-round battle. It was also the co-main event of that particular fight card, indicating Tony's rising profile. And it went the full distance, four full rounds more than Canzoneri had ever boxed in an official match.

The judges rewarded Abad's flashy style with the decision, giving him a win on points over Canzoneri, whose record suddenly dropped to 28 wins and one loss, along with three draws.

Canzoneri, years later, came to view that defeat through rose-colored glasses. "The fight was very close, and most of the writers gave it to me," he said. "But it was good for me to know what it felt like to lose" a fight of that magnitude.

Anyone who had fought 32 times professionally before he was a day over the age of 18 was entitled to a bad evening. Furthermore, the loss to Abad came during a fight that tested his physical conditioning in a way no other contest ever had, meaning it was not quite time to panic.

Yet, to preserve his status as a promising contender, he had to recover and leave little doubt doing so. The good thing for Canzoneri is that he did just that.

After stopping Enrique Savaardo (then a putrid 3-34-11) midway through a 10-round fight a week later, Canzoneri stared down two stern tests that – if he failed – could have derailed the career which Goldman was helping him manage.

First up was a 12-rounder on November 22, 1926, against France's Andre Routis, thought of as a champion in waiting after he had won more than 40 pro fights. In front of more than 3,000 spectators at

Brooklyn's Broadway Arena, Canzoneri remembered making a less than stellar first impression.

Tony at this stage of his career had taken to reading up on the tricks old fighters would use to gain whatever edge over their opponents that was possible, and one that he was particularly keen on trying was what he called "the shoelace gag."

The strategy was simple: tell the opponent that his shoelace is untied and then waylay him if he looks down. Canzoneri tried it early, but Routis was unfazed.

"What the hell are you talking about?" Canzoneri then heard Goldman tell him. A flustered Canzoneri shot back, "I'm trying to get him to look down so I can belt him."

An annoyed Goldman, shaking his head, broke some news to Canzoneri that he hadn't even considered. "He don't understand you!" Goldman said.

Routis didn't speak English and couldn't understand what his American opponent was saying.

Canzoneri did get Routis to fall for the ruse during the next round by gesturing frantically at the Frenchman's shoes. Routis looked down and dropped his guard just enough for Canzoneri – who had quickly taken a step back – to land a right cross on the Frenchman's chin.

Only the move did little to influence the fight. Routis rocked slightly but kept his footing. Meanwhile, the crowd realized what Canzoneri had done and jeered him.

"I get the idea this kind of stuff ain't fair, and they don't go for it," Canzoneri would later recall[3]. "So I [didn't] do it anymore."

Canzoneri spent the rest of the bout wisely pressing his advantages in hand speed, height and reach to keep an otherwise conditioned, fearless Routis at bay. Tony was done with the trickery, to which he didn't ever really need to resort.

Canzoneri connected hard left jabs, stiff hooks and intermittent right

---

3   In the entertaining and informative June 1955 Boxing & Wrestling magazine article referenced throughout, Canzoneri told the piece's writer he had seen fighter Milo Savage replicate the move on Molly Mims on a fight televised that year. Mims fell for it, took a high right hand from Savage, but ultimately won by decision, according to newspaper recaps of that bout.

crosses, all from a distance, throughout the night. Routis, two pounds heavier than his opponent at 124 ½ pounds, concentrated on trying to break Canzoneri's defense down with body blows. Yet his strategy did not pay off. After the final bell, Canzoneri clinched the decision, eking out the edge on points.

New York Times boxing writer James Dawson, who covered the fight that night, held the result up as a formal notice that Canzoneri would be a problem for those plying their trade in the division just above bantamweight.

"Tony Canzoneri ... signalized his entrance in the featherweight class," Dawson mused.

There was hardly time to bask. Goldman had booked Tony a December 17 date in front of 9,000 spectators at Madison Square Garden against Bushy Graham, a 67-win, nine-loss and seven-draw fighter who was set to challenge for the world bantamweight championship early the following year.

Graham, at 4-to-1, was significantly favored by bettors in a fight that generated a gate of $22,390. That figure, of course, was much more significant in those days than it would be now. But, for Graham, it was pretty good for something he hoped would be just a tune-up for him.

Only it didn't work out like that for Bushy at all. Canzoneri said he diagnosed Graham's dancing style early in their bout, imitating it and then outpunching him with a methodical approach.

Faced with essentially a mirror image of himself, Graham stayed wed to a cautious, defensive stance throughout the match, keeping his speedy hands in reserve while he let Canzoneri pursue him for much of the bout. He went the bout's distance, but the judges were unimpressed.

Unanimously, they opted to award the decision to Canzoneri, who scored an upset victory that the New York Times called "startling" and "one of the biggest" of the year.[4]

"That," Tony would later say, "is when they began to take notice of me in New York."

_____

4   Graham lost his challenge against Charley Rosenberg on February 4, 1927, at Madison Square Garden.

Just like that, the sophomore year of Canzoneri's pro career was done. And it was clearer than ever to boxing's overlords that the setback against Abad was an outlier, the exception rather than the rule with this tough little New Orleans-bred Brooklynite.

They knew it was time to give Canzoneri a shot at a world title. It would be at bantamweight, rather than at the featherweight division where he was more comfortable. But still, there was no sense in delaying this opportunity for Canzoneri any longer.

And so Goldman, along with the rest of prizefighting's movers and shakers, plotted a course on which Tony would collide with a fighter from Indiana who more than did justice to his nickname: "The Blonde Terror of Terre Haute."

* * *

Indiana's Charles Bernard "Bud" Taylor began boxing in 1920, when he was 17 and Tony was 12. He commanded the respect of the profession throughout his career. At bantamweight, Ring magazine founder Nat Fleischer[5] considered him top five all-time, and the Blonde Terror of Terre Haute would ultimately earn induction into the International Boxing Hall of Fame.

The stamina Taylor counted on in the ring was unrivaled, and in both of his hands, he had one-punch knockout power. In 1926 alone, he beat respected contemporaries Jimmy McLarnin, Abe Goldstein, Joe Lynch, Clever Sencio and Pete Sarmiento. He previously had taken down another notable in Pancho Villa, the Filipino fighter who had become the first Asian to win the world's flyweight (112-pound) championship. All of that earned him the colorful Blonde Terror epithet by which the press referred to him.

The fighters' handlers hoped Canzoneri and Taylor would clash for the bantamweight championship – then vacant, or held by no one – on February 24, 1927. But Tony contracted a foot infection that forced the bout's postponement for more than a month.

Canzoneri had recovered by March 7 of that year, when he fought the Taylor-beaten Lynch for a final dress rehearsal at Broadway Arena in

---

5   Fleischer died in 1972. The ranking was dated 1953.

LEFT: Bud Taylor faced Tony Canzoneri for the world bantamweight championship in 1927. This photo from the Chicago Daily News which is in the public domain after the non-renewal of its copyright shows him in a fighting stance in Chicago in 1929. *Source: Library of Congress's National Digital Library Program, via Wikimedia Commons*

RIGHT: A portrait of Tony Canzoneri in a fighting stance in Chicago in 1929. The Chicago Daily News published this photograph and later didn't renew its copyright, allowing it to enter the public domain. *Source: Library of Congress's National Digital Library Program, via Wikimedia Commons*

Brooklyn in front of 4,500. Oddsmakers favored Canzoneri over Lynch, of California. But Lynch reported to the bout in top physical condition, and it showed.

Canzoneri piled up points with his steady attack, but Lynch was too strong to be knocked out. Time and again, Lynch absorbed the best and hardest Canzoneri could muster. Jabs, left hooks, right crosses to both the body and head – it didn't matter. Lynch kept charging forward, unabated.

One of the right crosses bloodied Lynch's eye. Another similar punch sent blood streaming down Lynch's head in the sixth round. Lynch's corner patched up the wounded eye – only Canzoneri reopened the gash in the eighth and then rocked his opponent with a telling punch to the chin in the ninth. Canzoneri followed up in the tenth with a thunderous uppercut-right cross combination. Yet a stoppage was simply not in the cards for Canzoneri. Lynch was standing toe-to-toe with Tony when the concluding bell clanged.

The judges' decision that day ultimately favored Canzoneri. But would that kind of fight from Tony be enough to topple Taylor later in the month and seize the bantamweight world championship that Canzoneri's friend from his old New Orleans days, Pete Herman, once held?

Many doubted it. For one thing, Canzoneri had not shown he could drop under the 118-pound limit at bantamweight and retain the punching power that could swing important bouts in his favor in heavier divisions. His win over Lynch was a testament to that. Both fighters were at 121 pounds, in the realm of featherweights, and Canzoneri was unable to put Lynch away.

The five fights before that were above the bantamweight limit, too, including what were arguably his highest quality wins, the decisions over Andre Routis and Bushy Graham.

"He has [class] and should go far with more experience," a sports wire service named Fair Play wrote about Canzoneri in a piece which The New Orleans Item ran. "But not as a bantam. He is too big for that division."

On the heels of Fair Play's commentary, the New Orleans Item predicted Taylor would beat their hometown product, Canzoneri, and prove – once and for all – that the Blonde Terror of Terre Haute ruled the world's bantamweights.

"He has swept all opposition aside in his bid for the bantamweight title," the Item's Fred Digby wrote of Taylor hours before he faced Tony in Chicago on March 26, 1927. "If Canzoneri cannot do 118 [pounds] and be at his best, he will rue the day he took this match."

Canzoneri indeed had his work cut out for him. The crowd of 7,000 at the Chicago Coliseum was not in his corner. Spectators cheered as a band, in the final moments before the bout, played "On the Banks of the Wabash," written by Taylor's fellow Terre Haute native, Paul Dresser, who offered the tune as a tribute to the childhood he spent along Indiana's Wabash River[6].

---

6   This is according to a description of the fight in the Bud Taylor biography, The Terror of Terre Haute, by John D. Wright.

Taylor was more than an inch taller than Canzoneri and had a slightly longer reach, which in theory would let him attack from further away than Tony could.

However, like Taylor, Tony had won five of his last six matches, though he drew one of those while Bud lost one. And it was the evenness of that stretch for both fighters which marked the day that they faced each other for the bantamweight championship of the world.

Taylor – aiming for the body – and Canzoneri, focused on the head, connected at a seemingly equal rate. They answered each other's pressure. For instance, in the seventh round, Taylor landed each hand on Canzoneri's jaw to back Tony into the ropes. But Tony survived the round and, in the following frame, used a long right to the ribs as well as heavy blows with each hand to the head to give Taylor a taste of his own medicine and corner him against the ropes.

Taylor missed on punches meant to counter and slow down Canzoneri, and in return he ate a left to the jaw as well as a right to the body that could have been trouble for him if the round didn't end when it did.

In the 10th and final round, knowing a world title was in reach for either of them, Canzoneri and Taylor planted right in front of each other at the center of the ring, aimed at their respective heads and went blow for blow. Their shots appeared to mirror each other – rights to the jaw, lefts to the head. The final bell clanged, and each fighter nervously awaited the result.

Those who were in favor of Taylor and thought he had done enough to win jeered when the decision came in. It was even – the pair had fought to a tie, the officials announced. No one would get the title or get to take home the diamond-studded championship belt – reportedly worth between $1,000 and $4,000 – which promoter Jim Mullen[7] had made for the occasion.

The fighters' camps furiously began working on organizing the rematch. They booked it for June 24, again in Chicago, only this time it would be in mythical Wrigley Field.

The crowd of 20,000 that showed up to witness the spectacle was

---

7   Mullen gave the belt a few weeks later to Taylor, who went into the fight with a bantamweight title that was not universally recognized. Canzoneri did not have a title of any kind at the time.

more than twice the size of the audience during the first-go round. The take at the gate – exceeding $65,000 in receipts – was more than four times larger than the $15,000 generated by the first edition. In other words, for the era, at a weight-class below the sport's more prestigious and heavier divisions, it was huge business.

Taylor, confident that he had figured out Canzoneri during their draw, took the fight to his opponent and didn't let up. Canzoneri began bleeding from the mouth during the first round, an inauspicious omen that he was in for a grueling night. He tried to keep his distance. But his shorter reach undermined that strategy, and he found himself often in the middle of the ring, needing to trade shots with the rangier, taller Taylor.

Taylor loaded up on points with both hands at Tony's expense. Canzoneri repeatedly managed to dance away and circle around Taylor in search of an opening to exploit. And, toward the end of the 10-round scrap, Canzoneri began finding success with long, left-handed punches. Canzoneri landed what was perhaps the punch of the fight when he connected a blow on Taylor's left eye, which splintered a bone over the optic nerve. That punch ensured the so-called Terre Haute terror would have a swollen, closed left eye to match Tony's when the concluding bell tolled.

In the Associated Press' estimation, those populating the Wrigley Field stands could hardly have asked for more of a spectacle just one year after Illinois legalized boxing.

"The two lads furnished the most thrilling action Chicago fight fans have seen since the sport was legalized a year ago," the Associated Press declared in one of its write-ups.

But the entertaining display from Tony did not clear the bar that the judges and the referee had mentally set for him to triumph on their scorecards. They unanimously awarded the decision, as well as the world bantamweight championship, to Taylor.

There would be no jeering this time. The result for which Chicagoans thirsted earlier in the year was finally at hand. Taylor was champion, and Canzoneri would have to keep waiting to be able to call himself a titleist.

Canzoneri would cap off his trilogy with Taylor nine months later, on December 30, 1927, in what for him were much friendlier confines at Madison Square Garden. The bout was not for a title. And Canzoneri came in four pounds heavier than Taylor at 125 ¼ pounds, just under the limit for featherweight.

Tony at one point knocked Taylor's mouthguard down to the ring canvas, serving notice that Bud's aggression and willingness to exchange blows would carry a price in a featherweight fight against Canzoneri.

But Taylor, whom Tony just could not get the best of, somehow again gave Canzoneri hell. Terre Haute's terror shook Canzoneri with punches to the body, head and jaw, disquieting more than 13,000 fans who had flocked to New York's boxing mecca in hopes of seeing their beloved Brooklynite exact revenge on Taylor.

However, to their horror, in the seventh and eighth rounds, devastating blows that Taylor landed on Canzoneri's body appeared to leave the Indiana fighter on the verge of a stoppage victory that would absolutely humiliate New Yorkers.

Only the heavier weight meant Canzoneri had more power in his punches than before. And he also had more energy in his legs, which better prepared him to weather Taylor's various onslaughts.

Eventually, a pinned-back Taylor struggled to parry quick, stinging left jabs from Canzoneri. Tony's backers at the Garden punctuated his more graphic scoring shots with approving roars.

When Taylor tried to shorten the deficit which Canzoneri created on the scorecard with a generally superior boxing technique, it was too late. The officials announced a unanimous decision for Canzoneri, and New Yorkers cheered lustily that Tony had gotten one back from Taylor.

It's true that Canzoneri had failed to capitalize on the chance to clinch his first world championship during his trilogy with Taylor. But Tony's triumph over Taylor at featherweight, while he was still a teenager, was a warning flare for those plying their trade in that weight class.

"Because he was a better boxer than his rival, Tony Canzoneri ... is a step nearer the world's featherweight championship, which is his goal," the New York Times' James Dawson wrote after Canzoneri at last conquered Taylor.

Another New York Times writer, legendary sports columnist Arthur Daley, could barely contain his effusiveness over the impression that Canzoneri made on him as Tony's career began to ignite. Dawson described Canzoneri as "buoyant," with a "grin [that] was big and warm," which complimented the style he used in the ring.

"He bubbled over with energy … [and] was bouncy," Daley said, the magazine Boxing Illustrated would report decades later. "He bounced impatiently in his corner as he awaited the bell. He bounced in swirling motion to the attack. He could box beautifully and, although a little fellow, he could hit in deadly fashion."

Furthermore, Canzoneri's rivalry with Taylor allowed him to get something unquestionably more important – and longer lasting – than a world title.

Canzoneri's share of the purse from the draw with Taylor was $10,000. He used those earnings to finish the purchase of a farm in the upstate New York community of Marlborough. In short order, Tony, his parents George and Josephine, and his five siblings were all living on that 144-acre property.

That meant Tony, at just 18 years of age, had delivered on the pledge he made to his father that he would use boxing to lift their family higher than the merchant-class lot that they had drawn in New Orleans and during the beginning of their time in Brooklyn.

"Papa, let me turn professional and I'll bring home plenty of money" was no longer just a promise. It was reality – Tony had made sure of it.

The Canzoneris maintained an apple orchard and vineyard on their bucolic patch in Marlboro. And they erected a country club there which drew larger-than-life guests who doubled as family friends and allies for life.

The resort resembled those further north in the Catskill Mountains which primarily catered to Jewish families, a social scene that was immortalized in *Dirty Dancing*, the Hollywood romance starring Patrick Swayze and Jennifer Gray.

This resort that the Canzoneris ran was aimed at Italian-American guests. But like any of its counterparts in the Catskills, "it was the place where everybody met," Canzoneri relative Jay Honold said.

As George and Josephine Canzoneri's children began having their own sons, daughters, nieces and nephews, the farm and country club would become the setting for some of their family mythos's most vibrant chapters. Tony would prepare there for bouts where the stakes were even higher than they were for the Taylor trilogy, which itself had brought the boxing world to its feet.

It would be a refuge, a fortress, where the Canzoneris and the world they were building could find shelter during an unprecedented economic depression that would soon erupt.

But first, that world of the Canzoneris – resting on Tony's shoulders – would get a whole lot bigger in the early part of the following year: 1928.

CHAPTER FOUR

"A WORTHY SUCCESSOR TO THE TITLE"

———

Champion boxers' journeys in some ways can resemble those of mythical heroes who are on quests to collect amulets scattered about the land. If they can beat each enemy guarding those amulets and gather them all, then they will earn recognition as the mightiest, along with all the fame and fortune that entails.

These days, boxing has four major sanctioning bodies, and each recognizes their own champions. An already confusing situation is made more so when those bodies crown multiple champions of their own in each weight class. Nonetheless, one sure way for boxers to be considered the undisputed champion of a weight class involves them collecting all the major sanctioning bodies' world title belts in that division.

In Tony Canzoneri's day, the New York State Athletic Commission – or NYSAC – and the National Boxing Association were the two rival agencies whose recognition pugilists sought to establish themselves as undisputed world champions.

Tony was just 18, in between the second and third episodes of his trilogy with Bud Taylor, when he secured the first piece of his first world title. On paper, the adversary standing in Tony's way for that title piece – the NYSAC's featherweight world championship – was as good as any he had faced.

Born Giuseppe Carrora, the boxer presented to fans as Johnny Dundee by then had fought literally hundreds of times while prizefighting for 16 of the 33 years he had been alive. The Italian-born, New York-based boxer had already clinched world titles at super featherweight

(130 pounds) and featherweight (126 pounds), the latter of which he secured by knocking down France's Eugene Criqui four times en route to a commanding unanimous decision in 1923. But, without ever being defeated, Dundee voluntarily relinquished his title – that is, he left it behind rather than defend it – to move up to a higher weight class.

The fighter who won a tournament for the right to succeed Dundee as champ also relinquished the title to campaign at a higher weight. And after that happened, as far as the NYSAC was concerned, the featherweight division had no champion and needed to crown a new one.

But after his successor moved up, Dundee agreed to drop back down to the featherweight ranks to face Canzoneri on October 24, 1927, at Madison Square Garden. The NYSAC, in turn, would recognize the victor of a showdown between those two as its featherweight class champion.

In one corner was the man who had once won the title and had never lost it in the ring. In the other corner was a young, promising contender who would be a worthy champion if he somehow could get the upper hand on Dundee.

As is often the case at the highest levels of boxing, Canzoneri and Dundee had worked out together before. Canzoneri later recounted that Dundee had taught him how to use his arms to tie up – or clinch – an opponent to slow down any attacks from close range. Dundee had also given Canzoneri some instruction on how to create distance between him and an opponent using head feints.

The relative familiarity bred a sense of confidence in Canzoneri as the bout with Dundee approached. Sure, as Canzoneri saw it, Dundee was the true world featherweight champion. Despite dropping the paper title recognizing him as such, "there wasn't anybody good enough to lick him," Canzoneri said.

That is, Canzoneri thought there wasn't anybody other than him who was good enough to lick Dundee.

"I respected Johnny for his greatness," he would later say, "but I wasn't smart enough to be afraid of him."

As was usual, Goldman and Izzy the Painter were in Canzoneri's corner for the fight. Canzoneri remembered his handlers seemed nervous in the dressing room before the match and acted as quiet as "clams." The loud round of applause that Dundee got when he was introduced to the Garden audience palpably unsettled Canzoneri's side, which could only hope that such enthusiasm wouldn't influence the judges who might decide the contest if Tony couldn't secure a knockout.

But then, Goldman calmed things down for his fighter. He delivered an instruction which made it clear he trusted both Tony and the confidence with which his young charge entered the night.

"Tony, I want you to do me a favor," Canzoneri later recalled Goldman saying. "When you knock Dundee down, I want you to pick him right up."

Canzoneri remembers spending the entirety of the ensuing affair trying to knock Dundee down so that he could immediately pick him up. "I forgot all about how good he was or those lickings he gave me in the gym," Canzoneri would later say of that encounter with Dundee and how Goldman's words had given him a way to block out an atmosphere that otherwise may have overwhelmed him. "I have only one thing on my mind – knock him down so I can pick him up."

Dundee fought bravely, withstanding steady blows that Canzoneri landed with both hands. He recovered each of the several times Canzoneri staggered him, including in the first round. He was too shifty to let Canzoneri put him down on the canvas any time he was off balance, too.

But Dundee had dropped 15 pounds in a month to make weight for the fight. The physical transformation sapped Dundee of his vitality by the time the opening bell sounded. His legs lacked vigor. His arms lacked strength. And, appearing at times to operate at half of his usual speed, Canzoneri dominated Dundee, leaving many of the 9,000 in the Garden to wonder why the referee didn't stop the fight before the 15th and final round.

Spectators were so sure that the outcome would favor Tony that many of the fans headed for the exits after the seventh round, the midway point. The crowd booed Dundee after the final round. And indeed, the officials in charge of the bout awarded Canzoneri a unanimous decision in his favor.

"The end, which marked the passing of [a] once great fighter, was more tragic than it was dramatic," James P. Dawson wrote in The New York Times after Dundee's defeat at the hands of Canzoneri was announced. "The great Dundee that was, has disappeared.

"In his place is only a shell, a harmless little old man ... [whose] heart and his courage alone carried him through the fifteen rounds, nothing else."

Canzoneri's win over Dundee, in time, would come to be viewed as one of the bouts that "made" Tony who he became, according to the July 1982 issue of Ring magazine. But Canzoneri quickly became frustrated with the contemporaneous media coverage of his dominant victory over Dundee.

He would later make it clear that he never forgot the headlines and articles which described Dundee as an "old man" – nearly twice as old as Canzoneri – whom Tony didn't want to hit out of embarrassment over their age gap. He was so upset he charged up to Goldman and asked, "How can those writers be so wrong?"

But Goldman was unbothered. Canzoneri would later say his manager just smiled silently and slapped his back.

The focus on Dundee's inability to live up to the moment, rather than on the achievement by a teenaged Canzoneri, is perhaps understandable. Despite having triumphed in nearly 200 fights, Dundee had lost in more than 60. He had taken more than a year off of boxing when he came back to battle with Canzoneri. And the age gap between the fighters was wide enough where sheer wear-and-tear erases any advantages that experience and savvy may have offered Dundee.

Dawson in his writeup questioned whether the NYSAC would even be able to keep a straight face as it tried to hold Canzoneri up as the world's featherweight champion. After all, he had not won a tournament like Dundee's successor – Louis "Kid" Kaplan – had before Kaplan left the title behind to step up in weight class.

Yet there was no denying Canzoneri was the only featherweight those days who could say he defeated Dundee in the division after Dundee became its champion in 1923. And he had as much of a right as anybody to face the man whom the National Boxing Association recognized as the world's featherweight champion, Benny Bass.

Bass had won a unanimous decision over Red Chapman in Philadelphia to claim the association's version of the world featherweight title, more than a month before Canzoneri routed Dundee. By beating the NYSAC's champ, not only would Bass humble Canzoneri. He would also pick up the second of two titles necessary to be recognized as the undisputed, best featherweight fighter in the world, the latest in a lineage passed down from Abe Attell to Johnny Kilbane to Eugene Criqui to Dundee.

If Bass lost, however, he would yield the division's undisputed championship to Canzoneri. And Canzoneri, at last, could silence some of the questions aimed his way about whether he was the real deal or if he was just the latest of the many pretenders who, to this day, come and go from boxing.

* * *

Bass's life story made him as compelling an opponent as Canzoneri would ever measure himself against. He was born in what is now Ukraine before his family decided to emigrate to the United States. The journey ended up being tumultuous, to say the least. The ship on which Bass's family first sailed out wrecked, and they had to be rescued at sea and brought to Ireland until they could arrange new transportation to the U.S.

The Bass family arrived in America in 1913 and settled in Philadelphia. Benny's father supported his loved ones by making and selling shoes. And once he was older, Benny contributed to the household by selling newspapers and working in the bindery department of a publishing company.

Bass met his first boxing manager at the publishing firm, and in due time his pedigree as a champion prizefighter emerged.

Pundits considered Canzoneri to have the upper hand in a number of key areas against the Ukrainian-born Philadelphian. Mainly, Tony's quickness helped him attack efficiently and defend himself cleverly, and that style could serve him well in the bout he set up against Bass for February 10, 1928, at Madison Square Garden.

Bass, however, was experienced, rugged and powerful. He had won 98 times, with 39 of those victories coming by knockout. Though he had lost on 16 occasions, many warned that Bass could end the fight against Canzoneri with a single well-placed, potent blow. And those issuing that warning weren't sure Canzoneri could do the same to Bass, having increasingly relied on landing more punches than his opponents, without caring how many they landed in return, a style that played well with fans and officials but which hadn't translated into all that many knockout wins.

While bookmakers favored Canzoneri to triumph, it wasn't by

much. They set the odds that he would win at eight to five.

Their logic was defensible. Though the 5-foot-4 Canzoneri was taller and fresher than the 5-foot-1, 24-year-old Bass, Tony had lost twice in 1927. One was his defeat to Taylor in their second of three fights, which let Bud secure the world's bantamweight championship. And then several low blows that were deemed illegal led to his disqualification on September 2, 1927, in round three of a 10-round fight against Cowboy Eddie Anderson, whom he had outpointed a month earlier.

Lastly, in a final tune-up in Bass's home city on January 30, 1928, Canzoneri lost on one scorecard, won on another and tied on the third to draw Pete Nebo, who would later contend for a championship in the junior welterweight (140-pound limit) division.

The disappointing result against Nebo snapped a six-match winning streak for Canzoneri that included his outpointing Taylor in the finale of their trilogy at the end of 1927. And it also seemed to shorten the odds for Bass to topple Canzoneri and come away from their encounter with universal recognition as the world's best featherweight boxer.

Canzoneri's manager, Sammy Goldman, acknowledged the slim odds throughout the training camp for Bass. He drilled the teenage phenom under his visage on quickening his hand speed even more while also buttressing his defense against left hooks, which Bass threw particularly powerfully.

Once the night of the fight came, it did not take long at all for Canzoneri to demonstrate the fruits of his and Goldman's labor in preparation for Bass. He nearly won the big showdown just three rounds in.

Having fended off attacks mostly aimed at his body, Tony charged in and unleashed both hands at Bass's head and body. Bass tried to answer the withering volley; but, in the last 10 seconds of the round, he started breaking down.

Bass tried in earnest to retreat, but he left his face uncovered in the process. Canzoneri noticed the opening and smashed Bass's jaw with both left- and right-handed blows. Bass tumbled to the ring in a heap and landed awkwardly.

The lapse was costly. After he hit the canvas, Bass broke his right collarbone, one inch from his breastbone.

The referee stood over the prone, pained Bass and began counting to 10. He reached eight – two seconds short of declaring Canzoneri the world's champion by knockout – when Bass regained his feet. The bell signaling the end of the round clanged almost immediately afterward, buying Bass critical moments to try to devise a plan to somehow turn the tables against a fighter who was not supposed to be the one with knockdown power that night.

Bass struggled to regain his composure at first, and so did the staff in his corner, who tried to convince themselves that Benny had not fractured anything. They insisted he had just bruised his shoulder, which they rubbed as he winced dramatically. "It looked as if Benny was through," Charles Leseman later wrote in the Ring magazine.

Canzoneri, hoping with everything in him for the night to end with his world championship coronation, largely dominated the next six rounds. He scored on punches to Bass's body at will and without pity, and a desperate Bass only managed to slow Canzoneri when he flagrantly punched him below the belt a couple of times. The crowd booed when the referee let Bass off each time with warnings rather than penalize him.

Still, there was a reason one of the sanctioning bodies recognized Bass as its champion. And that reason shone through in the 10th round, when the turnaround for which Bass had been flailing arrived, even as one of his eyes was so swollen it was nearly shut, and it was obvious to everyone that his shoulder was seriously bothering him.

Canzoneri felt well in control at that point of the bout and relaxed the guard against left hooks that he had spent much of his preparation on improving. Bass capitalized and landed two left hooks on Canzoneri's jaw, shaking him. Then, at the end of the round, Canzoneri ate a right-handed shot to the jaw to cap off a combination from Bass that otherwise was mainly aimed at Tony's body.

Canzoneri nearly fell to the canvas but somehow stayed up. Canzoneri was unable to answer, and Bass was again battering him when the round ended.

"I thought a brick wall had fallen on me," Canzoneri would later say about that string of attacks from Bass. "I'll never forget that."

Added New York Times boxing scribe James Dawson: "Bass, the weary battler, [had become] a savage, fighting maniac."

Canzoneri was still on wobbly footing when the 11th round started. Bass knew he had hurt Canzoneri, and Tony felt his opponent's confidence growing.

Bass landed punches on Canzoneri's jaw and head with both hands, again dizzying the precocious teenager standing at the edge of immortality. Bass's second wind let him keep up the pressure through the 14th and penultimate round of the fight while Canzoneri focused on merely surviving long enough to task the officials with going to their scorecards to decide the victor.

However, depending on the distribution of the scoring, Tony knew Bass's rally could be enough to deny him the featherweight crown for which he so desperately yearned. So he fired off both of his gloves with urgency in the final round.

Tony accompanied Bass around the ring rather than trying to retreat from him. He meted out punches and absorbed some in return. The message he was broadcasting was clear. Bass at this stage only looked like the stronger fighter, but it was a mirage. What Bass offered in the later rounds of the bout when he destabilized Canzoneri was too little, and it was too late, Tony's actions argued.

No one envied referee Arthur Donovan or judges George Kelly and George Patrick. The fight was close, with both fighters dominating each other at different junctures. "Both were great little fighters," Donovan would later say in the August 1955 issue of the National Police Gazette. "Bass was a good puncher. ... Canzoneri was a much better boxer."

Based on what Donovan saw, he chose Bass to win, rewarding the eastern European immigrant's courageous revival late in the bout.

But those who disagreed with Donovan's judgment noted how Canzoneri had inflicted a knockdown on Bass. And a handful of unsanctioned fouls from Bass had marred that portion of the bout, although it let him avoid being knocked out of the fight.

Kelly and Patrick could not overlook that. After the pair of judges turned in their scorecards, ringside announcer Joe Humphries declared that "the winner and new champion" was Tony Canzoneri.

It did not matter the decision that he earned was a split one. Tony Canzoneri – just three months after his 19th birthday – had conquered his first weight class as a pro boxer.

A few among the 14,000 at Madison Square Garden that night jeered when Donovan raised the hand of one of the few teenaged, undisputed world champions ever in boxing.

It was still boxing after all. And arguing that the guy who you wanted to win was robbed on the scorecards can often be as fun and fulfilling
as the fight itself.

Yet the vast majority of those in the Garden's stands could appreci-
ate what they witnessed that evening. With a thunderous, raucous wall
of clapping, stomping and cheering, they drowned out the boos and
hailed the new world champion.

The sights and sounds seduced Dawson, the New York Times writer. He dubbed what he was sent there to chronicle "one of the greatest
featherweight battles … in history."

The bravery with which Bass repelled a knockout by Canzoneri,
while nursing a broken collarbone for 12 full rounds, earned him admiration from supporters on both sides. Bass ended up at the hospital
that night, and the doctor who treated him "marveled that any fighter
could stay in such a furious battle with a broken collar-bone," according
to Charles Leseman's write-up for the Ring magazine.

Afterward, with a plaster cast holding his injured right shoulder in
place, Bass said even he doubted that he'd be able to go the full distance
once he was hurt.

"Every time I landed a blow after the third round was agony for me,"
Bass told Dawson. "It felt like the sting of a knife in my chest, and I had
difficulty shooting my punches straight. I'm glad, though, if the people
are satisfied I gave Canzoneri a good fight."

Then, in a tradition that continues to this day, Bass asked the rival who
had gotten the better end of a razor-thin decision against him for a rematch
at the soonest time possible. "I'd like," Bass slyly said, "to meet him again."

Bass's manager, Phil Glassman, echoed his fighter. "I am satisfied
now that Bass is a greater fighter than anybody ever before gave him
credit for being," he told Dawson. "I am confident, too, that he'll beat
Canzoneri in another match."

In his own conversation with Dawson, Canzoneri agreed that Bass
had fought well. "He certainly gave me plenty to do, particularly in the
late rounds when he made that finish," Canzoneri said.

And, indeed, Bass's wish for a rematch would come true. Nonetheless,
no matter how narrow the margin was during Bass's first encounter with
Canzoneri, that night unquestionably and justifiably belonged to the latter.

"The little New Orleans Italian who has adopted Brooklyn as his

THE WHOLE CANZONERI FAMILY: TONY,
the New Featherweight Champion, Who Won His Title
When He Defeated Benny Bass, Celebrates His Victory
With His Father and Mother and His Brothers and
Sisters.
(Times Wide World Photos.)

A cell phone photo of a newspaper picture cutout showing Tony Canzoneri, seated on the left, surrounded by his family after he won the world featherweight championship in 1928. Times Wide World Photos took the original picture.
Courtesy of Jay Honold

hometown [gave] a wonderful exhibition of boxing ability and an admirable demonstration of fighting pluck in the face of the adversity which threatened him in those closing rounds," Dawson wrote. "Canzoneri was ... a true champion, a worthy successor to the title."

That truth couldn't be more meaningful to Canzoneri.

"It's great to reach the top, and I hope I'll stay on top for a long time," he said to Dawson. "Not by hiding the title beyond the reach of any challenger, but by fighting and beating any challenger who wants to meet me."

Plenty of challengers stepped forward wanting to meet Canzoneri, in that division and heavier ones. They would produce mixed results in their attempts to cross Canzoneri, the boxing world came to learn.

Canzoneri's camp wasn't afraid of what was ahead. "That boy is a natural fighter," Izzy the Painter would later say of Tony. "He'll lick any of them. Mark my word."

Based on what they'd seen, journalists and fight fans had every reason to believe Canzoneri could turn Izzy's prediction into a prophecy.

Regardless, no matter what happened onward from the night Canzoneri had beaten Bass, nothing would change the fact that Tony and his loved ones – for the rest of time – had the right to invoke the phrase "undisputed, world champion boxer" as an adjective for him.

Decades later, in the June 1955 issue of Boxing & Wrestling magazine, Canzoneri would describe how he never forgot "oh, what a wonderful feeling it [was]" to have won his first championship. Perhaps his favorite part of that title was how proud it had made his dad, who had given his blessing to Tony's dream of making a go of it as a prizefighter in the waning days of their family's relative anonymity.

"My father ... walked around like he was the one who licked Bass," Canzoneri said in the magazine article. "Now he really could say, 'My Tony is a champion.'"

The hotel resort that his family ultimately opened on the farmland which Canzoneri had already used some of his career earnings to buy for them would make the absolute most of that reality. The reality was their Tony was a champion, and they saw it as more than fair to market his association with their resort in idyllic Marlborough, New York.

And, for several of the best years the Canzoneris ever had, figures on both sides of the law could not wait to visit the resort and be around the owners' history-making scion.

CHAPTER FIVE

"A CHAMPION RESORT"

—

Narrow roads winding through hills, under trees, over a stone bridge, along the bakery and past the variety store at the front of Marlborough, New York, led to 35 Lattintown Road. A silo, stables and an apple orchard atop a small mountain flanked the farm with which the Canzoneris supported themselves and their loved ones in their new town of only a few thousand people.

But anyone who became familiar with the place can't talk about it long without mentioning one feature in particular: a three-story building which dominated the grounds.

Out of that building, the Canzoneris ran their summertime country club hotel and resort. And after referee Arthur Donovan triumphantly lifted Tony's gloved fist while leaving Benny Bass's at his side that magical night when they had their lightweight world title fight in February 1928, the Canzoneri Country Club could truthfully advertise its slogan: "A champion resort!"

For the better part of the 1930s and 1940s, the Canzoneri Country Club emerged as upstate New York's "Italian safe haven," where "anyone with a vowel ending their last name" left city life behind for a few weeks each summer, according to a description in family member Deborah Burns's memoir, *Saturday's Child*.

Some of those guests were – for lack of a better term – ordinary people just trying to get a vacation closer to nature. But some of the other vacationers at the country club grew up with family patriarch George Canzoneri in Sicily before immigrating to the United States at

People gather around the swimming pool at the hotel and resort that Tony Canzoneri's parents operated on the farm that he bought them. The scene was photographed and put on a postcard. *Courtesy of Jay Honold*

the turn of the 20th century and were not exactly ordinary. They had made names and accumulated wealth for themselves bootlegging alcohol during Prohibition[1], and running guns to protect their enterprises.

The daughter Tony Canzoneri had later in life, Denise, recalls her first introduction to one of the latter kind of guests. The girl whose face bore a striking resemblance to Tony's was jumping around on a bed in one of the rooms on the sprawling property when one of her father's sisters rushed in and admonished her to be a lot quieter than she was being.

"Do you know who's next door?" the alarmed aunt asked Denise. Denise had no idea and stayed silent. The aunt answered herself curtly: "It's Joe Bananas."

Denise remembers asking whether she was supposed to be afraid of that man. The truth is many may have been.

---

1   Of course, this is the period in American history where the sale of alcoholic beverages was prohibited from 1920 to 1933, giving rise to a criminal underworld that tried to capitalize on illegal booze sales.

By the time Denise was growing up, Joe Bananas – nee Giuseppe "Joe" Bonanno – had served as an enforcer for New York mob boss Salvatore Maranzano. It was stressful work to say the least. Maranzano had violently clashed with another New York gang headed by Joseph Masseria in a street conflict colloquially known as the Castellammarese War because most of the belligerents were from the Sicilian community of Castellammare del Golfo.

The struggle culminated with the assassinations of both Maranzano and Masseria about three years after Tony won the world featherweight title against Bass. But Bonanno survived and, having inherited control of Maranzano's group, helped charter a commission by which New York's five major crime organizations – or families – avoided sanguine, deadly fights with each other that often drew unwanted attention from law enforcement.

It was a dizzying rise for Joe Bonanno, who started out as a foot soldier for a group tied to rackets, extortions, strong-arming of garment businesses, drug-trafficking and even murders, but was now its general.

In any event, the Canzoneris were among those who had standing permission to address that tall, physically imposing man by the playful-sounding nickname of Joe Bananas. Bonanno and his family spent enough time vacationing at the country club, Denise recalls, that she and his son regularly played baseball together on the grounds.

Denise recalls another of the country club's guests was the Neapolitan-born man who took the reins of Masseria's clique and became the first to actually propose creating the five families' conglomerate. The rest of the world knew this man as Charles Luciano. But Denise remembers he was introduced to her as "Lucky," who was there at the time with his wife.

"They were nice," Denise said of the interaction.

Denise admits that she had not gotten to spend all that much time with Lucky, who didn't show her the side of him that set up his former boss Masseria to be shot to death by a phalanx of gunmen working for Masseria's nemesis, Maranzano.

That would have been the same side with which Luciano preemptively and successfully arranged for the stabbing death of Maranzano, leaving Luciano in control of their organization.

Nonetheless, whether or not they dwelled in the underworld, affluent New York City men – primarily of Italian heritage – routinely sent at least their wives and children to while away summers cooling off in the hotel's swimming pool or lounging on the nearby deck chairs. The husbands and fathers would stay in the city working during the week and then join on weekends, visiting their loved ones or catching up with the other men – around the pool, during pickup games of handball, baseball and badminton, or in a dimly-lit cocktail lounge.

Other times, Denise said, some of those same important-looking men would come up not with their children or wives – but with the girlfriends they had managed to fit into their schedules. After finishing what they had gone there to do, they would head back to their lives, Denise recalled.

Whatever the reason for guests' visits, there was always one place off limits to wives, children or mistresses – and that was the country club's lounge. Hanging over the room was an oversized, framed sketch of Tony standing in a boxing ring, grinning and pointing a gloved fist at a crowd whose members wore gold chains and pinky rings. The lounge's chestnut bar ran the length of the room. Its stools were leather, and their color was maroon. Mirrors were behind the bar because its regulars were the kind of people who liked to make sure their appearances were in order – and to see if someone was coming up behind them.

Besides drinking booze and smoking, the lounge's patrons also listened to live musical performances. Sometimes that entertainment came from a breathtaking American redhead who sang and worked as a hostess at the lounge, Dorothy "Dotty" Adams. Sometimes it came from her husband and fellow musician, Jasper Canzoneri, one of Tony's three brothers.

According to Jasper and Dotty's daughter, Deborah Canzoneri Burns, and maternal relative Jay Honold, that illustrated how it took the whole family – immediate, extended and those added by marriage – to make the Marlborough country club run.

In addition to the farm in Marlborough, with help from Tony's earnings in the ring, the Canzoneris also bought land in a rural community roughly 15 miles away named Gardiner. More than a dozen relatives of Josephine Schiro Canzoneri, Tony's mother, settled at that secondary farm after they had loaded up a flatbed truck with all of their possessions and driven up from their first American home, which was in Independence, Louisiana.

Jay Honold said that included his grandmother, who was 16 years old when she got on a ship and endured the months-long, transatlantic journey from Italy to the United States. She married Josephine's brother – twice her age – and had 14 children with him prior to making the trek from Independence to Gardiner, without the benefit of interstate highways.

Their new home in the generally cooler climate of upstate New York came with more than a few strings attached, Honold said. They not only had to work and maintain the land where they lived in Gardner – they also had to staff the Canzoneris' farm and resort in Marlborough.

"They always owed them [for] the fact they had a new life in New York," said Honold, who was born in 1955 and lives in Gardiner. "They had to pay them back somehow, and that's why [the Canzoneris] always had the labor at their farm and the hotel."

Growing up and hearing his family speak of it, Honold sensed some Schiros felt like the Canzoneris transitioned a little too easily into regarding them – and treating them – as "the help." There were obvious differences, from the quality of clothes the different sides of the family wore to how they traveled. For instance, the Canzoneris got around by train whenever they had to go a long distance. There's no way they would have taken a cross-country trip on the back of a flatbed truck, Honold said.

"The feeling I got was the Canzoneris ... always had a nose up in the air over the Schiros," Honold said. "It was just a different class."

* * *

Deborah Canzoneri Burns, whose memoir titled *Saturday's Child* contains vivid descriptions of the country club and its history, tells a story of how even her mother's younger brother got into the mix at the resort.

Richard "Richie" Adams had primarily dedicated his youth to petty theft and was on the verge of serving a sentence at a juvenile detention facility after being busted one too many times. In a last-ditch attempt to keep him from being institutionalized, Richie's sister – Deborah's mother, Dotty – went to the judge presiding over Richie's case and pledged that she would personally make sure he became a productive and law-abiding citizen.

What Dotty meant was that, instead of letting him wallow in a chaotic environment where he was wasting his potential, she promised to make sure to fill Richie's hours with chores around the country club.

The tasks were menial. He was in charge of picking up gum wrappers and other litter around the pool. He would sweep the floor around the ping-pong tables.

One tale told by Deborah's husband, Bob Burns, sums up the unique environment where Richie landed. Richie couldn't swim, play baseball or participate in any of the other fun summer activities that the children at the country club enjoyed until he finished his daily chores. And one day, Richie confronted one particular boy who – on about a half-dozen different occasions – had left a proper mess around the pool.

"You're always making a mess here, and I gotta clean all of this up before I get to do anything fun," Richie told this boy, according to Bob Burns. The child simply shrugged off this agitated pool boy who had angrily marched up to him and interrupted his vacation.

A seething Richie did not take the boy's slight lying down and waited for the perfect moment to exact his revenge. When he felt that moment had come, Richie grabbed a BB gun which had been previously given to him as a present, waited for the messy boy who blew him off to come near him, and when the kid let his guard down, Richie fired a BB right into the boy's buttocks.

Richie couldn't deny the fact that shooting the boy in the butt was satisfying. But then Richie learned that the boy whose rear end he had thwacked with a BB gun was one Salvatore "Bill" Bonanno, the son and eventual successor of Joe Bananas.

And Joe Bananas, that same evening, sent word through the Canzoneris that he wanted to speak about this transgression with Richie – alone, man to man.

The thing was that Joe Bananas had been kind to Richie. For instance, there was one Christmas holiday which he spent up at the Canzoneri farm. He had been invited at the last minute, and other guests who had gathered at the compound and brought presents didn't know they needed to get one for him. So Richie was virtually empty handed during the gift exchange.

Richie was glum and moping in the corner of the room as the gathering's attendees opened their presents when Joe Bonanno – one of the guests of honor – came up to him, handed him a $100 bill and gave him a consoling pat on the shoulder.

Renowned mobster Joe Bonanno was a regular guest at the hotel resort which
Tony Canzoneri's parents opened on a farm which he bought for them. He
is shown here in an October 1964 mug shot. Source: *US federal government, via
Wikimedia Commons*

"He had never seen a bill that big," said Bob Burns, who was close to
his wife's uncle Richie later in life. "Him seeing this well-dressed, well-re-
spected man up there, he was totally taken – totally in awe – of this."

Now, though, Joe Bonanno wanted to understand exactly what it
was that drove Richie to shoot his son Bill in the ass.

Richie built up some courage and met with Joe Bananas as the mob
boss wanted.

"Why," Joe Bananas asked the fretful boy sitting in front of him,
"did you do that?"

Richie explained how messy Bill had been around the pool that
Richie had to clean up as part of his job at the country club. "I told him
to stop five or six times," Richie told Joe Bananas. "I figured I had to do
something to get him to listen, to take me seriously."

Joe Bananas listened quietly, keeping a stoic expression on his face.
When he finally spoke again, he told Richie: "I understand why you did
what you said you had to do. I'll talk to my son. He won't do it again. I
promise. But do me a favor – you don't do that again."

And thankfully for Richie's sake, that was it. That defused the drama, at least according to Richie[2], Bob Burns said. Richie got to keep his job at the country club, and he never again had a problem with Bill Bonanno.

As important as it was to those on the level which Richie and the other staffers occupied, the Canzoneri Country Club's most important job may not have been ensuring the rooms were clean, that the pool was pristine or that the bar was stocked. Their most vital task may have been making sure the resort never booked overlapping stays with guests who might be willing to spill blood to settle their differences and their business rivalries.

"There was all this protocol where ... they'd say, like, 'Bonanno's coming up for the weekend, but who else is coming?'" said Deborah Canzoneri Burns, a successful publicist whose memoir was honored with a gold medal during the 2020 Independent Publisher Book Awards. "So, it would end up where these specific two weeks would be Bonanno weeks, but maybe not these other two weeks because they had been blocked off for someone else."

Not every staffer at the resort kept their cool around some of the more hardened clientele. Deborah Canzoneri Burns shared one anecdote involving a Schiro relative named Vivian, who worked at the resort as a waitress and noticed a Bonanno family member eating in the kitchen with the hotel's chef, Lena Canzoneri, one of Tony's two sisters.

The man may have been eating in the kitchen to avoid someone in the dining room with whom he didn't want to speak, but whatever the case, he had a holstered gun. Vivian became alarmed at the sight of the weapon and scurried out the room.

_____

2   According to the Burnses, Richie became so enmeshed with the Canzoneris and their friends that he was basically at George Canzoneri's bedside as his health failed ahead of his death in 1946, fetching drinks and anything else George wanted. George repaid his gratitude by working with the Bonannos to get Richie placed with a family named Adamo after George's death.

Adamo's adulthood was turbulent as well, marked by robbing gambling games, Bob and Deborah Burns said. The pride of his life was his only son, Nicholas Adamo, who finished second in his class at New Jersey's Cliffside Park High School, graduated from Yale University, and played for the Bulldogs football team's offensive line as a walk-on. Richie was shattered in 1996 when 22-year-old Nicholas boarded a Piper Cherokee for a business trip and was killed when the small airplane crashed in Maryland. Richie died eight years after the crash. He was 66.

After the man left, Vivian cautiously approached Lena and asked – in a whisper – who the man was and why on earth he had a gun.

Lena quickly thought up an answer. "Well, he travels a lot by himself[3]," she said, according to Deborah, to hide the fact that he was a mobster and carried it to protect himself.

Vivian was satisfied with Lena's answer and let it go. Years later, Deborah said, "She realized ... that wasn't the truth at all."

* * *

There isn't much in writing that ties Tony Canzoneri or his family's country club to guests like the Bonannos or Lucky Luciano. However, in addition to Burns' memoir and Denise Canzoneri's first-hand recollections, there is an autobiography that Joe Bananas's son Bill co-authored in 2011.

Casually dropped nearly 300 pages into *The Last Testament of Bill Bonanno: The Final Secrets of a Life in the Mafia* is a black-and-white picture of Tony Canzoneri, dressed in slacks, a short-sleeved collared shirt that was tucked in, and a pair of boat shoes, with his arm cradling the lower back of Joe Bonanno.

Both Canzoneri and Bonanno – in an unbuttoned cardigan sweater – are smiling and appear to be holding cigars in a field, with a tree and a corner of the Canzoneri Country Club neatly framed in the background. The caption dates the photo as 1938, when Tony was 30, his daughter was 2 and he was nearing the end of his career.

Also, without explanation or qualification, the caption describes Canzoneri as "a Bonanno group leader."

As if he anticipated the reaction that such a claim about Tony Canzoneri might stir, Bill Bonanno dismissed as "myth" what many assumed was required of people who were welcomed into the Bonannos' inner circle.

"Conventional wisdom has it that before we admitted a member into a family, he had to make his bones," reads a part of Bonanno's book relatively close to the photo of Tony and Joe Bananas. "This has taken

---

3   In another rendition of the story, Lena answers that the man had the gun to guard to people, like a policeman, even if he wasn't a policeman.

on the meaning that he had to kill someone. Not true!"

Co-written with Gary B. Abromovitz, Bill Bonanno's autobiography makes it a point to note that "members from all occupations" were considered close associates of his family, including attorneys, dentists, directors of funeral homes, priests, firefighters, mechanics, dockworkers and grocers.

"We called upon them when we needed them," the book said. Yet, the book added, the Bonannos would never compromise whoever those professionals might have been because that would have put them out of service whenever they would have been needed.

Denise Canzoneri rejects that her father was "a group leader" of the Bonanno family despite what Bill claimed in his book. Citing what her father and grandparents told her, she said Bonanno, Luciano and their associates knew George Canzoneri from their days growing up together in Italy – "the old country," they called it.

Deborah Burns, Denise's first cousin, sounds less sure when she talks about their grandfather George. Until his death in 1946, George Canzoneri was in charge of the country club hotel that his champion son helped him purchase. And people who frequented resort had the habit of calling the Canzoneri family's patriarch "Don George."

In Latin cultures, "don" is a term of respect for older men, somewhere in between "sir" and "mister." Yet it's also come to be known as a term used to address powerful, high-ranking members of criminal organizations – especially Italian and Sicilian ones.

For instance, Joe Bananas wasn't Joe Bonanno's only nickname. Those who wouldn't dare call him by that benign-sounding but perhaps overly familiar moniker would opt for "Don Peppino," combining the title of respect with an Italian nickname for Giuseppe, or Joseph.

Deborah noted that her uncle Richie would only ever refer to Joe Bananas as "Don Peppino."

"Don Peppino – it was always Don Peppino," Bob Burns said of Richie.

Deborah Burns added that Don George was also not the only nickname applied to her grandfather. People would also refer to him as "the Sicilian Mediator" because he would often sit at a high-backed chair, with his Great Dane and two boxers at his side, and hash out disagreements of which most relatives weren't even aware.

The Burnses invoke another tale from the family storybook to drive home the level of respect that these larger-than-life contemporaries of George had for him. It's an apocryphal one (notably, the criminal it involves had just been sent to prison). But the Burnses aren't the only ones who have told it over the years.

It goes like this. Before the first of two fights he would later have against Barney Ross, an all-time great boxer, in Ross's hometown of Chicago, Tony frantically called George by telephone to report that two men claiming to work for the terrifying Windy City crime kingpin Al Capone[4] had stopped by.

As the story goes, it wasn't clear exactly what the men wanted beyond making it known that Capone called the shots in town. But George Canzoneri calmed Tony by telling him he would make some calls, and it would all be cleared up, according to the Burnses.

Whether George Canzoneri called Bill Bonanno or someone else remains unknown to this day. But according to the Burnses, it was said that Capone soon verbally reprimanded the men who had approached Tony, and once chastened, they let Tony be as he prepared to fight Ross.

There is no indication that the odd pre-fight visit at all influenced the result of Tony's ensuing fight with Ross.

For what it's worth, Tony's manager, Sammy Goldman, told a somewhat similar story involving Capone to his son. The son, Al Goldman, wrote a letter to The New York Times that the newspaper shared in 1979 which recounted how some people in Chicago approached Canzoneri's camp and attempted to pressure him to lose intentionally.

In that version, it was Sammy Goldman who called Al Capone directly because Goldman had heard Capone was a boxing enthusiast and an admirer of Tony Canzoneri.

"Capone told him not to worry, and that was the last he heard from the toughs," Al Goldman wrote in the letter, which New York Times writer Red Smith used as the basis for a column.

---

4   Capone was a sports fan. The timing of the story, as told by Burns, would have put this about four years after the St. Valentine's Day Massacre, in which seven associates of a Capone rival were killed in a north Chicago garage. Capone was suspected of orchestrating the killings but was never convicted.

According to Al Goldman, only one other time did boxing show its sometimes seamy underbelly during his father's run with Canzoneri. That was before another fight, this time in Philadelphia, and it involved "some muscle men" who approached Sammy and informed him that Tony would win the bout in three rounds if Goldman wanted.

"He refused to have any part of it," said Al Goldman[5], according to Smith. "I asked him – remember, I was very young – why what the other fighter was going to do had anything to do with it. He smiled gently and said perhaps next time they would come and say, 'Now, Tony will go in three,' and how could he then refuse?

"At any rate, they accepted his unwillingness to play."

Exactly what ties George might have had to the universe populated by Bonanno and others in his line of work has never been clear to Deborah Canzoneri Burns. But she has always wondered if Tony's mother Josephine Schiro may have been related to Nicolo Schiro, a New York mobster who was forced out of his group's top position by Salvatore Maranzano during the Castellammarese War.

Schiro relative Jay Honold also shared a story that he heard, though he repeatedly insisted that he could not vouch for its veracity. According to that story, a younger brother of Josephine named Tony Schiro was reputed to be so skilled at driving trucks across the United States that people who bootlegged alcohol during Prohibition often called him to avail themselves of his skills.

"Some of the pieces are missing, in how they got here [to America], in what my grandfather actually did for a living," Deborah said of the story about George Canzoneri and his family. "Some of it may be legitimate – like the grocery stores. Some of it may have been perfectly legitimate, and some of it may have been illegitimate. I don't know."

To be clear, historians have never cited any evidence which leads them to conclude that mob figures' proximity to Tony Canzoneri and family ever influenced the champion's results in the ring or his selection of opponents.

---

5   Al Goldman wasn't sure before exactly which fight this episode purportedly occurred, as Smith wrote. However, the younger Goldman speculated that it may have even been before a rematch with Benny Bass, which Tony granted him after Tony won the featherweight title.

Bob Burns, a boxing aficionado, elaborates on this point, saying Tony's Italian heritage and championship pedigree as a boxer only enhanced the esteem that George Canzoneri, his wife Josephine, and their family had earned from their neighbors and associates in their own right.

"The relationships, the admiration – it all predated Tony's fame," Bob Burns says. To argue otherwise is to assign guilt by association – namely, by association with people who looked up to George, Burns said.

Remarks from former Ring magazine editor Steve Farhood seem to support Bob Burns's take. Pundits regard Canzoneri's achievements as entirely legitimate. There is no evidence going beyond a reasonable doubt that foul play tainted any of Canzoneri's accomplishments.

And despite the color it added to Tony's life story, Farhood said having mobsters around him would not have been unusual in his time. New York's mob found it irresistible to be around boxers because people have always bet on boxing, even amid the Great Depression, which would unfold later in Canzoneri's career.

Large sums of money were always on the line for fights at Madison Square Garden[6], and no one at the time fought as often as Tony did at the building now affectionately known as MSG.

"Mobsters ... were always looking for an edge," said Farhood, an on-air analyst for boxing matches televised on Showtime.

Some may have believed the closer they could get to a boxer, the bigger the edge would be, theoretically because they would have insight into a boxer's true mental and physical state heading into a crucial bout. And sure, it wasn't unheard of for bettors to fix fights and pre-arrange their outcomes in their favor.

But Bob Burns knows the deal from speaking with his late father-in-law, who was Tony's brother, Jasper. Jasper Canzoneri always said no one had ever managed to penetrate the veil of legitimacy in which his brother Tony swaddled his career.

"When he won, he won," Bob Burns said of Canzoneri. "And when

---

6   Tony was destined to fight 28 times as a pro at Madison Square Garden, which – according to Farhood – tied him for most all-time with Emile Griffith, a welterweight, junior middleweight and middleweight whose prime was in the 1960s.

he lost, he lost. Period."

* * *

To be sure, Tony Canzoneri's featherweight championship gave his boxing career and his family's hotel business a measure of prestige that most of their competitors would have done a lot to get.

A fight promoter in New Orleans worked feverishly to book a homecoming for the newly-minted champion, who won a decision in an exhibition in Brooklyn just 13 days after defeating Bass for the world featherweight title. Tony got his tonsils taken out soon after[7], undergoing a surgery that people often get because of recurring throat infections.

Then, he took what – by his standards – was a relatively long break of three months.

Once out of his break, the promoter Frankie Edwards got Goldman to sign off on letting Canzoneri face a contender named Claude Wilson, from Birmingham, Alabama, during a May 28, 1928, exhibition at New Orleans's Coliseum arena.

The Coliseum represented a true return to Tony Canzoneri's Big Easy roots. Standing at the corner of North Roman and Conti streets in New Orleans's Mid-City neighborhood, the Coliseum was a little more than a mile from the Gayoso club where Tony learned the basics of boxing.

The prospect of Tony fighting for the first time as a pro in New Orleans excited locals, who flocked to the train station to greet him when he arrived five days before the bout.

Tujague's restaurant in the French Quarter hosted a banquet honoring Canzoneri and Goldman, who was also returning to New Orleans for the first time in what had been a while. Basil Galiano, the boxer who helped Canzoneri and Goldman meet, was among those feting the pair at the banquet. So was Pete Herman, the only other New Orleans fighter at the time who had been a world champion.

At one point during the visit, Goldman compared Canzoneri and Herman, the two most famous boxers whom he managed.

"Pete Herman was ... as capable a fellow as there ever will be," Goldman said. "Canzoneri ... is even more promising now than Herman was

---

7   An article in the July 1982 issue of Ring magazine contains this detail.

at Canzoneri's age.

"New Orleans can tell the world it has another native son who will make the rest of them sit up and take notice."

On the day of the fight, Canzoneri treated his hometown crowd to a dominating performance. Just one minute in, Canzoneri knocked Wilson down with a right to the chin. Wilson stayed down for nine seconds, resumed the fight – and then suffered a knee-buckling, left hook to his chin from Canzoneri.

Wilson hugged Canzoneri to try to slow the pace of the fight down. But once the fighters broke out of their clinch, Canzoneri connected on a left hook to Wilson's body and a right cross to his chin. Wilson fell to the ring with a reverberant thud.

He took another nine count and appeared willing to continue the fight. But Canzoneri apparently implored referee Ray Dolan to call off the rest of the bout.

Dolan listened to Canzoneri's appeal and granted it. The referee stopped the fight, and Canzoneri won, having scored a technical knockout at just about the two-minute mark of the first round.

Canzoneri's hometown debut as a pro was as resounding a success as he could have hoped. It was only the second time ever during Wilson's career that he had lost a fight by knockout.

"I hope New Orleans fans were satisfied," Tony said in the bout recap that was printed in the newspaper the next day. "I tried hard to please all my friends here."

* * *

As meaningful to Canzoneri as his featherweight title was, and as entertaining as his New Orleans homecoming was as well, neither would have been strong enough to give his name – or that of his family's resort – the staying power they wanted and needed.

That became especially true when, after a June 13 victory on points over Vic Foley in Montreal, Canada, he lost a decision in an exhibition to Harry Blitman in Philadelphia. Blitman, a Philly fighter who was undefeated with 35 victories and a draw, had been a test for Canzoneri that he failed just two months before he would defend his featherweight championship in a rematch against Andre Routis.

Canzoneri would later say in the June 1955 issue of Boxing & Wres-

Andre Routis is shown in a public domain press photo during training 1927. He had lost to Tony Canzoneri once in 1926 before challenging him for the world's featherweight title in 1928. *Source: Bibliotheque nationale de France, via Wikimedia Commons*

tling magazine that the loss to Blitman was one of the most decisive defeats that he suffered in his career. "Blitman gave me a terrible going over," Canzoneri told the magazine. "Busted me all up and cracked a couple of ribs."

Canzoneri admitted to being in less than optimal shape for the fight. And he said that was compounded with contracting the influenza virus before the bout and then fighting against Blitman despite not having shaken the illness.

After the defeat, Canzoneri developed pneumonia, and his illness was bad enough that rumors about it prompted a newspaper to publish a headline falsely declaring him dead.

Goldman, of course, wouldn't let his champion leave his mortal coil without putting up a fight. "Sammy got every doctor in town," Canzoneri recalled. "Goldman refused to let me die."

Within a couple of months, Canzoneri had overcome the flu and the pneumonia complication it caused, and he collected a knockout victory in an exhibition with a 68-win, 46-loss, and 12-draw fighter named Bobby Garcia. Maybe that KO win had given Canzoneri some confidence back a month before his clash with Routis.

But the truth was Garcia had won only one of his six previous fights, meaning he was in poor form when Canzoneri met him. And there was reason to fret Canzoneri wouldn't be able to carry that momentum over into the bout against Routis on September 28, 1928, at Madison Square Garden.

Routis, of Bordeaux, France, was a hardened challenger. He had become a respected contender after his father was killed in the first world war – news so distressing to Routis's mother that it triggered in her a fatal heart attack[8].

Even more concerning for Canzoneri, during the weigh-in on the afternoon of the fight, Tony came in a pound-and-a-half over the limit. Routis's manager, Joe Jacobs, began screaming for his fighter to immediately be named the champion and for the title bout to be canceled.

---

8   According to the narrative the boxing press advanced on Routis, Andre went on a bender after his mother died, guzzling white wine, getting into a fight with another boy who got cross with him, and won so handily he decided to see if he could make a living prizefighting.

But Goldman read the rule book to Jacobs: Tony had three hours to drop the necessary weight, according to the regulations. Jacobs had no choice but to relent.

Goldman and Canzoneri immediately got into a cab and told the driver to take them to a Turkish bath house. When they arrived, Canzoneri ran inside, wrapped himself in thick, heavy clothing and sat in the steam room for an hour. Yet he emerged still weighing the exact same, so they had him sit in an electric sweatbox.

The electric sweatbox did the trick. Tony Canzoneri sweated out the excess 24 ounces in time, got reweighed by the officials in charge of the fight against Routis, and avoided losing his title at the scales.

But the extreme measures that Tony Canzoneri took to cut weight came with an equally extreme physical cost. He was too weak to even raise his hands when he was done having to be in the electric sweatbox, he recalled decades later.

All he had the energy to do the rest of that day was have a glass of sherry with an egg in it, go to sleep, and wait for his title defense against Routis to start.

After the opening bell sounded, Canzoneri momentarily seemed as if he could overcome the physical exertion required of him earlier in the day and fend off Routis.

Two minutes into the bout, Canzoneri landed a right hook on the Frenchman that spun him around and plopped him down onto the ring. It was a dream start for Tony, who had gotten as good a fight as anyone had given him when he first encountered Routis nearly two years earlier. Routis got up before being counted out, but Tony dominated him for the rest of the first half of the fight and appeared poised to cruise to a successful defense of his featherweight throne.

But then the bill came due for the frantic effort he had to undertake to make weight and qualify to participate in the fight.

Fatigued, Tony's defense began breaking down. Routis targeted Canzoneri's head with short left hooks and then pounded Tony's body, exploiting opening after opening. A shaken Canzoneri barely answered Routis over the last four rounds of the 15-round bout.

One judge's ballot favored Canzoneri continuing as the champ despite his slump at the end of the bout. But the other judge joined the referee in voting to strip Canzoneri of his championship and to award it to Routis by split decision.

Tony's reign as monarch of the world's featherweights was over after a little more than seven months.

During that stretch, he had gone 4-1 in exhibitions and lost his only official title defense. Fred Digby of The New Orleans Item, which had effusively covered Tony's homecoming a few months earlier, turned on the fallen champ, saying his brief reign illustrated how mediocre the featherweight division was more than it showed anything else.

"Here isn't an outstanding 126-pounder at this time," Digby wrote. He added that he believed Bass, despite his loss to Canzoneri, may have actually been the class of the division at that moment. And he poked fun at Canzoneri's weight struggles, saying Tony's appetite could have just cost him the then-extravagant $50,000 guarantees which he had been commanding each time he fought.

"The little Italian has eaten himself out of a fat bankroll," Digby declared. "Spaghetti is a great dish but it has no place at the training table of a fighter."

Decades later, in the June 1955 issue of Boxing & Wrestling magazine, Canzoneri had no qualms about openly discussing how demoralized he felt after the defeat to Routis.

He considered it "a very close and tough" bout. He thought he had deserved to win because he had managed to knock Routis down, and he remembered many writers agreeing with him that he had earned the right to keep his championship.

But the truth was that it was the first time in his career he felt overly burdened by trying to maintain the necessary weight for him to compete in the division that he had briefly conquered.

"I trained all wrong," Canzoneri said. "Instead of reducing gradually over my entire training period, I waited until the last week to knock it all off at once."

If Tony Canzoneri was going to be remembered as more than a one-hit wonder, if his family hotel's patrons were supposed to be truly impressed about his affiliation with the resort, he would have to redeem himself. The loss to Routis forced him to realize that would require him to move up to what for him was a more natural weight: the lightweight class and its 135-pound limit.

The lightweight division has always been one of boxing's most prestigious weight classes. Throughout its history, it has teemed with elite fighters.

There was no doubt that the division offered Tony Canzoneri a ticket to immortality. It all would just come down to whether he could ever punch that ticket.

CHAPTER SIX

"HE WENT OUT LIKE A LIGHT"

———

After surrendering the only title he'd won until then to Andre Routis, Tony Canzoneri began fighting in the junior light-weight[1] (130-pound limit) and lightweight (135) divisions. The conventional thinking is that Canzoneri could claim a title pretty quickly at junior lightweight, a sort of in-between class above feather-weight but below lightweight.

There wasn't, however, much prestige in reigning at that division. The purses also wouldn't be as lucrative. So the plan Goldman hatched for his humbled former champion was taking tune-up bouts at junior lightweight while setting his sights on a challenge for the much bigger prize: the world's lightweight title.

Tony went on a tear after stepping up in weight. He won 11 of the 12 fights he took from October 29th, 1928, just a month after the defeat to Routis, through July 9th, 1929.

Amid that stretch, Canzoneri retaliated against Routis with a unan-imous decision victory in a junior lightweight clash in Chicago. That settled the matter: Canzoneri, at a weight more natural to him, was bet-ter than Routis. And he had now won two of the three encounters he had with him.

Tony also started demonstrating some punching power in his right hand that he had not shown in the bantamweight and featherweight

---

1   Colloquially, today this is referred to as super featherweight.

classes. He knocked out 108-win fighter Chick Suggs in six rounds. He recovered from being knocked down in the opening round against Armando Santiago to then knock Santiago out of the fight in the fifth round of their clash in Chicago. He scored a second-round knockdown and then a seventh-round knockout victory versus Joey Sangor.

And it was the power in that right hand which convinced Tony and Goldman that the fighter was ready for a longshot challenge against world lightweight champion Sammy Mandell on August 2nd, 1929, at Chicago Stadium.

Mandell, then 25, was undoubtedly one of the most skilled boxers Canzoneri, 20, had encountered up to that point. He was more experienced and held one of boxing's glamor championships, having compiled 115 wins, seven defeats and 11 draws. He was on a six-match winning streak. And at 5-foot-7, he was three inches taller than Tony and held a two-inch advantage in reach[2].

As Tony was working out on a punching bag at his makeshift camp set up at Chicago's Garden of Allah hotel, reporters asked him why he thought he had a chance against the Sicilian-born, Windy City-based Mandell.

"A massive right hand, propelled by muscles of steel, shot out like a flash and crashed against a sandbag" at that moment, according to an Associated Press account of the scene. Then, Tony looked over and said, "That smash has beaten a lot of good men and that smash is going to beat Mandell and make me what I always wanted to be – the lightweight champion of the world."

George Canzoneri made his way to Chicago from Marlborough to spearhead a cheering section that included the mayors of New York City – Jimmy Walker – and New Orleans, Arthur O'Keefe. Josephine was not there. She was still squeamish about seeing her son fight. And, when she listened to his bouts on the radio, she was never really entirely comfortable.

---

2   One way to measure a boxer's reach is to measure the distance between the fighter's armpit and the end of the fighter's fist. It can also be measured by measuring the distance between the middle fingers of each hand when the arms are stretched straight out, horizontal to the ground. It gives you an idea of how far away they can be from their opponent while still being able to strike.

But, in those days, George never missed any "important engage-ment" of Tony's, he told the AP. And, he told the wire service, he shared his son's confidence.

"He looks to be in perfect shape and if Mandell catches [Tony's] right once or twice, he will lose his title," George Canzoneri said.

Unfortunately for the Canzoneris, that perfect right never landed. The bout with Mandell went the full 10-round distance. One judge cast his decision in Tony's favor, determining that he won four rounds, lost two and tied the other four. But the other two judges, respectively, cal-culated that he won no more than two rounds. Meanwhile, they said, Mandell won six, drew the rest and therefore had earned the right to retain his title.

The outcome left Canzoneri's camp dispirited. Tony's record for ti-tle fights now stood at a single win, three defeats and one draw – which, all told, wasn't that impressive.

Yet, Canzoneri had outperformed Mandell on at least one score-card. And Mandell would one day be inducted into two of boxing's halls of fame.

So, at least in the immediate aftermath of the setback against Man-dell, it made sense for Tony and his camp to stay on the comeback trail.

That comeback journey picked up a sense of urgency after Tony's next fight, which involved a second homecoming to New Orleans.

Goldman worked with local promoter Frankie Edwards to stage a 10-round bout pitting Canzoneri against a 19-year-old prospect from Memphis named Eddie "Kid" Wolfe. Canzoneri thumped Wolfe from bell to bell, earning a lopsided decision. Fans who took in the fight at Heinemann Park at the corner of Tulane and Carrollton avenues[3] en-joyed the dominating display from the hometown boy. But then, things took a sour turn.

Immediately following the closing bell, Edwards ran off with most of the money generated by the show, including guarantees of $7,500 and $5,000 for Canzoneri and Wolfe, respectively. A motley band of boxing

───────────────

3   A minor league baseball team named the New Orleans Pelicans used to play at this stadium. It stood roughly where a self-storage facility converted from a hotel later stood, and in its old footprint these days stands one of the first Chick-fil-A fast food restau-rants that was approved for construction within New Orleans's city limits.

commission officials, police and seven businessmen who had put up a third of the expenses to stage the fight and its preliminary bouts frantically searched for Edwards. But, while their quasi-manhunt languished, he had made it to the train station and waited for a ride out west.

"Nobody except federal taxes and [undercard] fighters," whose compensation was paltry, "got paid," boxing expert Harold Buckley would later quip to sports columnist Howard Jacobs.

Eventually, some would have a laugh when looking back at the debacle. But Wolfe, who was newlywed when he clashed with Canzoneri, said the fight not only resulted in the worst beating of his life – but it also left him broke.

"Broken, dejected and badly in need of funds," he accepted an ill-advised fight against former world featherweight champion Louis "Kid" Kaplan in Chicago a month later. In the seventh round of that fight, Kaplan landed a thunderous right uppercut that cut Wolfe's mouth, loosened some of his teeth and left Wolfe unable to continue on with the bout.

In Tony's corner, George Canzoneri confronted Goldman and made the manager fork up half of what Canzoneri had been promised. That amounted to $3,750, not counting hotel costs, which were extra.

Nobody wanted to carry on like that forever. The life of a lightweight boxing champion could be complicated, sure – but usually it was less complicated than what they were putting up with doing business with the likes of Frankie Edwards.

Something even more momentous happened the day before Canzoneri[4] scored a unanimous decision in Chicago against Stanislaus Loayza on October 30, 1929, as part of a fight card promoted by former world heavyweight champion Jack Dempsey. Prices on the stock market collapsed completely. Billions of dollars were lost, and thousands of investors were wiped out, kicking off the Great Depression, which to that point had been the worst economic downturn in the industrialized world.

Over the next four years, almost half of the banks in the United States failed. Some 15 million people – 30 percent of the workforce –

4　　In two fights following his thrashing of Wolfe, Canzoneri beat Eddie Mack (67-5-7) in Chicago by technical knockout after an ankle sprain forced Mack after eight rounds, and then he outpointed Johnny Farr (39-28-12) at Madison Square Garden.

lost their jobs as employers desperately tried to cut costs in the wake of the stock market collapse. Breadlines, in which impoverished, starving Americans stood in line for free food, entered the public conscience in the aftermath. So did makeshift tent camps and shanty towns nicknamed "Hoovervilles," which were named after President Herbert Hoover and erected by jobless folks who had been evicted from their homes. A drought and storms ruined crops in the region encompassing Texas, Oklahoma and Kansas, or "the dust bowl," in the parlance of the day.

Boxing, though, remained popular, and fans continued flocking to the fights. Some of the sport's historians argue that was despite the consequences of the stock market crash and the Great Depression. Others maintain it was precisely because of those events that people chose to spend what little disposable income they had on the one thing that could take their minds off the misery which had engulfed the country.

"Boxing ... [was] an extension of the crucible of street existence," author Mark Allen Baker wrote in *Between the Ropes at Madison Square Garden*.

Everyone in the boxing business had the opportunity to capitalize on the demand – and the passion – for their product. They could all defy a reality most other Americans simply could not, depending on how kind their fates were to them as boxers, managers and promoters.

"Boxing is a whipping boy for a lot of people, but ... guys ... made something of themselves with boxing," Jimmy McLarnin, who unsuccessfully challenged Mandell in 1928, once said, in summing up the attitude of those who pursued careers as prizefighters during that era. "Look at Jack Dempsey. He was a bum, a hobo. And he became a champion, and a pretty decent human being."

Sure, if all else failed in Tony Canzoneri's case, he could return to the farm he bought his family. But, as he made clear to them in his youth, he hated the kind of work his parents did for a living. There was the hotel, but at best that would be seasonal, with many Americans in those days being simply unable to afford vacationing at a resort.

It was just not at all a good time for a boxer to give up on his day job and on his dream of becoming a champion in what has always been one of the sport's most competitive divisions. So Canzoneri and his camp had to press on.

Another championship would lift them into an economic bracket where each fight would be worth tens of thousands of dollars, sums that the millions of Americans who were unemployed in those days could only fantasize about.

Canzoneri knew he needed to complete the comeback that Goldman had plotted for him. He needed another championship in the worst way.

* * *

Canzoneri took the rest of 1929 off and then accepted a January 17, 1930, fight at Madison Square Garden against an all-time great: England's Jack "Kid" Berg.

Berg – at 74 wins, four defeats, and five draws – was in great form at the time. He had gone undefeated in his previous six bouts. He was also considered a contender for the world title at junior welterweight[5] (140-pound limit), so he was naturally bigger than a true lightweight.

Though the Great Depression was already well underway, nearly 19,000 people watched as Canzoneri nearly floored Berg in the opening round with a sequence of rights and lefts to the jaw. Berg survived the round but staggered in a daze into the arms of his handlers, who fretfully waited for him in his corner.

"The Canzoneri backers sat back and puffed their dollar Havanas," referring to a luxurious type of cigar, the boxing writer Stanley Weston would later write. But, Weston added ominously, "that was the last time Tony's entourage had cause to cheer."

Berg recovered in the second frame, discarding an upright stance he had used in the first round and changing to a windmill style that for him was more natural. "For the next eight rounds," Weston wrote, "it was all Berg with Tony just standing flat-footed and catching.

"Jackie never gave Canzoneri a chance to set himself. Throughout the rest of the fight Tony was on the defensive, never once given the opportunity to get his offensive underway."

Even though on the referee's scorecard Canzoneri had done enough

---

5   Some sanctioning bodies through the years have called this division "super lightweight."

to earn the victory that day, two judges overruled that decision and awarded a split win on points to Berg.

It was perhaps the worst and most demoralizing beating Tony had ever endured, as New York Times boxing writer James Dawson described it. Berg, Weston noted, "received one of the loudest ovations ever given an athlete in the Madison Square Garden."

The crowd had no problem with whom the officials picked to win the decision. "It was a fight New Yorkers will never forget," Weston wrote in closing. "Canzoneri will never forget that night either. His eyes were puffed and almost closed, and blood trickled from a deep wound on his left cheek."

Berg, Dawson reported, had likely put himself in prime position to challenge for the lightweight title which Canzoneri coveted but had already once missed out on. Yet, a month after dealing Tony the sixth defeat of his career, Berg moved up in weight to knock out Mushy Callahan for the National Boxing Association's junior welterweight title. He would defend that title four times over the following year.

As difficult as it was for Tony to stomach the loss to Berg, Berg's decision to campaign at junior welterweight meant he had not leapt over Canzoneri in the pecking order at lightweight.

Tony responded by again going on a tear. He won 10 matches in a row, including three knockout victories, of which two occurred in the first round as he continued to demonstrate flashes of punching power that each of his opponents would have no choice but to respect. One of those two opening-round knockout wins came against a 46-win, 13-defeat and five-draw Frankie LaFay, who was floored an astonishing six times by Canzoneri before the referee waved the rest of the bout off with six seconds left in the first frame.

During this stretch, Canzoneri gave Bass the rematch that the Philadelphian craved. Bass was unable to deliver on his promise of simply needing another shot at Canzoneri to prove he was the better man. Enjoying an edge in weight of nearly five pounds, Canzoneri scored a lopsided, unanimous decision win over Bass, who had kept their previous title fight – when they were both featherweights – a much closer affair.

Tony's winning streak ended in the Windy City with an unusually sluggish performance against a razor sharp Billy Petrolle, a lightweight contender whom the Chicago Tribune declared "looked like a million dollars" at a time when that amount of money was unfathomable to most Americans.

Tony blamed the fact that he lost a decision to Petrolle – albeit a split one – on having erroneously dismissed his opponent as an "old man" whom he could easily outslug.

The loss ultimately didn't block Tony from his plans to mount a second challenge for the lightweight title. But it probably did go a long way in explaining why pundits heavily favored his opponent, Al Singer, for a November 14, 1930, title bout at Madison Square Garden.

The 5-foot-6 Singer was two inches taller than Canzoneri. He had an inch-and-a-half advantage in reach and – at 134 pounds – outweighed Tony by a pound-and-a-half. All the natural physical edges were in favor of Singer, who had been nicknamed "the Bronx Beauty."

Meanwhile, Singer was also the only man whom Tony had not been able to beat in his first 11 bouts after Routis dethroned him as the world's featherweight champion. Singer had fought Canzoneri to a draw.

And, in what was perhaps the thing that Canzoneri's camp found most unsettling about him, Singer needed just one round to knock out Sammy Mandell on July 17, 1930, and take the lightweight championship of the world from him.

Fans of Canzoneri could not overlook how Mandell lasted all 15 rounds of the fight when Tony challenged him. Mandell, of course, had also managed to win and defend his title from Canzoneri.

But maybe bookmakers were too cavalier in favoring Singer with 9-to-5 odds. In a non-title fight a little more than two months before he was scheduled to face Tony, Singer had been knocked out and had lost to Jimmy McLarnin in just three rounds. Such an emphatic, decisive defeat can psychologically scar fighters. Would Singer have enough time to shake off losing in such a stunning manner before he clashed with Canzoneri?

Canzoneri's loss to Petrolle heading into the Singer fight was, to be sure, concerning to his supporters. Yet, "it had been close, hadn't it?" as the publication Boxing International put it much later in November 1965. "Besides, nobody was knocking Tony out, or even down. Wasn't that more than that Singer gang could say" about the fighter whom they supported?

EL PUGILISTA AL SINGER, NUEVO
CAMPEON DEL MUNDO DE LA
CATEGORIA PESO LIVIANO, CON-
QUISTO EL TITULO AL DERROTAR
POR K. O. EN EL PRIMER ROUND
A SAMMY MANDELL, QUIEN LO
POSEIA DESDE 1926.

After previously fighting Canzoneri to a draw, Al Singer faced
Tony Canzoneri for the world lightweight championship in
1930. El Grafico of Argentina published this photo of Singer
whose copyright expired and is now in the public domain.
Source: El Grafico of Argentina, via Wikimedia Commons

Also, in the ring, Canzoneri had the better power, footwork, hook,
right-hand punches, stamina and chin strength, which measures the
ability to withstand shots to the head from an opponent without being
knocked down. Skillswise, Singer's jab was really the only tool he had
which was superior to Tony's, as Boxing & Wrestling magazine saw it
while looking back in its April 1963 issue.

To members of the news media, Singer looked nervous and uneasy in his corner in the last moments before the opening bell. He cut a stark contrast to the man in the opposite corner. Tony was smiling. He bounced on the balls of his feet, looking fresh after a preparation that, by all accounts, was as thorough as ever.

Canzoneri and Singer circled each other for about the first 30 seconds of the bout, trying to coax one another out of their defensive crouch. Singer eventually jabbed Canzoneri in the nose – a wide target, as many accounts noted – and then connected a right hand to Tony's ribs.

Canzoneri, though, absorbed it all well, and he landed a right to Singer's body to retaliate.

Singer didn't answer the punch. Canzoneri seized on his opponent's reluctance and fired both hands at Singer's head. Singer parried the blows as best as he could and connected on his own right to Canzoneri's head. But then he began retreating toward Tony's corner, with Canzoneri – patiently but confidently – stalking Singer.

With his head lowered near his shoulder, Singer flicked out a left-handed punch. Canzoneri unfurled his own left-handed punch simultaneously. The strike was somewhere in between an uppercut and a hook. And Canzoneri landed it flush. Singer suddenly and awkwardly stiffened. He looked like he might collect himself for a moment. But what happened was that Singer tilted forward and fell on his face.

Singer caromed off the ring near Canzoneri's corner. He rolled himself over and ended up going under the ring's bottom rope. Shortly before referee Johnny McAvoy reached the count of 10, Singer stood up. However, while he was standing up, Singer was on the wrong side of the ropes and seemed as if he was about to fall off the edge of the ring.

Singer was, as the New York Times's James Dawson put it, "out of his head."

And the referee counted Singer out of the fight just 66 seconds into the first round. Singer's reign was done, having been knocked out in what was then the second-fastest time in a lightweight world title bout ever[6]. Tony, just like that, was the lightweight champion of the world.

Roughly 15,000 people at Madison Square Garden leapt to their

---

6   The fastest had come in 1902, when Joe Gans knocked Frank Erne out in 45 seconds, according to Boxing International.

feet, roared and applauded this 9-to-5 underdog who had ripped away the world's lightweight championship from Singer's clutches with lightning speed and in such stunning fashion.

"One of the most startling upsets of the modern times," Dawson called it.

Someone who was helping broadcast the fight over radio approached an elated Canzoneri amid the pandemonium and stuck a microphone in his face. With some of his first words as the undisputed champion of one of boxing's most prestigious weight classes, Tony chose to greet "grandma."

"I tried hard to put it over and I succeeded!" said Canzoneri, who was breathless because he was overwhelmed by what he had accomplished and not because he was tired from the 66-second fight with Singer.

Canzoneri then greeted the community where he was raised.

"Hello, New Orleans! Hello, my friend Pete Herman down in New Orleans – the one who taught me all I know about boxing," Canzoneri remarked. "I won the title, and I want my friends in New Orleans to know about it!"

It's possible Tony didn't realize his words would make their way back to the ears of his first boxing coach: John Galway, the master and commander of the Gayoso athletic club where Canzoneri first began his formal education in the sport.

An apparently offended Galway would soon speak to New Orleans's Times-Picayune newspaper and – in his mind – set the record straight on who was there at the Gayoso when Tony was first learning to box and who was not.

"I want to say that Pete Herman was never in my gymnasium in his life," Galway told the paper.

For his part, after leaving the arena the night that Canzoneri beat him, Al Singer sought seclusion in Lakewood, New Jersey. He reportedly contemplated retirement[7]. He just couldn't grasp that his time atop the lightweight class was over after just four months.

It's doubtful that the feelings of either Galway or Singer were anywhere near the forefront of Tony's mind right then. In addition

---

7   Singer did not retire then and continued prizefighting for a few more years.

to boxing's undisputed lightweight crown, he had gotten more than $7,250 for the bout. The deposed Singer got $21,760, giving Canzoneri's camp an idea of the bigger earnings that awaited them during Tony's impending reign as the world's lightweight champion.

A scan of this period's headlines show how demand to see Canzoneri in action exploded. Promoters in five cities outside New York wanted to bring Canzoneri to their towns.

Tony had already logged more than 90 bouts as a pro by then and had earned anywhere from tens of thousands to hundreds of thousands of dollars in his career as a prizefighter. Yet he was still just 22, and the consensus among boxing's literati was that Canzoneri's best days were still ahead.

Plaudits also rained down on Goldman. Sports columnist Harry Martinez of the New Orleans States newspaper hailed Sammy's decision to have Canzoneri skip campaigning at junior lightweight, the lesser respected division whose purses were less lucrative. That meant Tony had the shot to become lightweight champion much sooner than he otherwise would – and he could capitalize on that during a time when his country's economy was as anemic as it had ever been.

"Sammy has had more success with New Orleans boys in the East than any one we know of," Martinez added. "He has made lots of money for Canzoneri by getting him matches that attract the interest, and the little Italian has made such a hit since leaving here that Brooklyn and New York are claiming him as their own."

Goldman, of course, had no intention of losing momentum. Canzoneri doubled down on improving his skills in the ring while Goldman charted a path on which Tony would face some of the best competition boxing would ever have to offer.

Their bet was that, in exchange, they would get compensation that was heftier than anything to which they had become accustomed.

Goldman declared that Tony would take a brief break and then resume training after enjoying his respite. The manager offered both of the last fighters to beat Canzoneri – Petrolle and Berg – opportunities to challenge Tony if they wanted them.

Both fighters ultimately took Goldman up on the offer. Berg would come up first.

"Tony will fight for the title just as often as the public wants him to fight and against any challenger the public will support," Goldman said. Goldman reminded the public that Canzoneri already had experienced life as a champ, and he predicted that would serve Tony well in his new existence. "This is not a new sensation for Tony," Goldman said.

* * *

Canzoneri wouldn't fight again during the remainder of 1930. But then, he started the following year with a mini-exhibition tour which took him back to New Orleans, then to Jersey City, Boston and Philadelphia. He won three of the four matches during the jaunt, results which included a first-round knockout in Jersey City but also a loss by unanimous decision to a contender named Sammy Fuller.

Yet Goldman stayed true to his word that Canzoneri would not wait long to put his lightweight title on the line. With Goldman's help, Canzoneri secured an April 24, 1931, date for what was a mouthwatering bout: a 10-round rematch at Chicago Stadium against Jack Berg, who by then had won the National Boxing Association's version of the world junior welterweight championship.

The pugilists agreed the fight would be at lightweight, and it wouldn't be just Canzoneri's title up for grabs. Berg's NBA junior welterweight crown would be on the line as well.

That meant the victor would enjoy the rare feat of reigning atop two weight classes simultaneously.

"Two championships or none at all!" as the Associated Press put it.

Bookmakers again pegged Canzoneri as the underdog, favoring his English rival by 7-to-5 odds. "Little or no Canzoneri money [is] in sight," the AP added. "Berg is in super condition and his ability to set and maintain a terrific pace is expected to carry him to victory if the bout goes to the limit."

As the AP saw it, for Canzoneri to win, he would have to follow through on boasts that he would knock Berg out within five rounds.

The confidence of Berg's countrymen surged. Pundits across the Atlantic Ocean widely predicted that, by night's end, the lightweight championship of the world would belong to one of England's own.

Organizers had high expectations for the crowd, predicting they would have a sellout on their hands that would generate $136,000 in gate receipts.

That didn't materialize. A paid attendance of 11,780 produced a $54,990 gate. Nonetheless, those who went to the bout got plenty to talk about in return for having purchased a ticket.

That is because Canzoneri again made a mockery of the bettors and took firm control of the first two rounds. Berg initially tried to rush attack Canzoneri and pin him back on his heels. But Tony halted him in his tracks with two lefts to the body and a right to the jaw.

An undeterred Berg advanced again, following Canzoneri as Tony retreated to a corner. But then Canzoneri revealed it was all a ploy – he landed right uppercuts on Berg's jaw as the first round ended.

That made Berg realize he was in for a hard night. "My style of fighting was attack all the time," he would later say in a 1986 interview with author John Harding. "I used to love a man who runs because I could run after him. I hated a man who comes towards me and fights me. I like chasing a man, chasing him, hitting him."

Canzoneri's approach, therefore, "gave me trouble," he admitted. "When you go to him, he comes to you, and you have to back your way out of it. You have to do something to beat him, and it's difficult.

"Canzoneri was a good boxer, good puncher, good fighter, and he meets you in the middle and slugs it out with you."

In the second round, Berg tried to make Canzoneri pay for a missed right uppercut by landing a left to the New Orleanian's face. Canzoneri, though, was unaffected. He fired back with two right hands and two left hooks to Berg's jaw. Two more left hooks to Berg's head, and then a right cross to his jaw, left the Englishman rattled before the second round ended.

Sammy Goldman approached his fighter and suggested only one adjustment. You're hitting him too high with that right hand, Goldman told Tony.

That set the stage for a third round that would go down in history. Sensing he had lost the first two rounds to Canzoneri, and knowing he could ill afford to surrender a three-round advantage on the scorecards, Berg came out swinging. He threw both hands – in the middle of the ring – at Tony's body.

The Englishman then traded uppercuts with his rival and scored on two left-handed blows to Canzoneri's head. Soon, he angled in closer to Canzoneri and fired each hand at his body.

But, in his aggression, Berg left himself unguarded and exposed. Canzoneri exploited the lapse and cracked Berg once in the jaw with his right hand. Canzoneri quickly delivered the same punch a second time – and Berg fell on his back near a neutral corner.

In his interview with Harding decades later, Berg vividly described the moment and its difficult aftermath.

"Coming to my side of the corner I saw a shade, a vision – a vision of a man throwing a left and a right cross," Berg said. "I see him do that … and he hit me bang here on the forehead.

"My body stiffened, and I just fell. I didn't drop. … I bang my head on the canvas, and that woke me up."

Berg began regaining his feet as referee Phil Collins reached the count of eight. Then, he said, "I shook my head, and I crawl over … I never heard one, two or three. I hear four. So I crawl up on the rope, and I was holding the rope."

But, at that point, Berg fell back down again. Remembering how he suddenly found himself hanging from the third rope, Berg said, "I was helpless."

And, right then, Collins called off the rest of the fight. Berg was done, and it was over. Canzoneri was the winner by technical knockout, Collins ruled.

Berg's handlers came out to the ring to drag him back to their corner. He remembers how he began sobbing when he realized what had just happened.

A delirious Canzoneri leapt around the ring. The sight of a distressed Berg momentarily caught his eye. He paused his celebration, walked over to Berg, shook his hand and walked away as the British fighter's tears began flowing again.

Collins approached Canzoneri and raised his arm. Here was the fighter who remained the lightweight champion of the world. Here also was the new junior welterweight monarch.

Tony had just pocketed a $25,000 purse. He had also just taken his place at the very top of a profession he had made up his mind to pursue only a decade or so earlier.

Right then, unquestionably, Canzoneri was at the peak of his powers. He now had won three of boxing's lineal championships – so called because those particular titles had been passed down directly from the first fighter to win it.

Tony claimed each of them because he either directly faced and beat the boxer who was holding them at the time he challenged them, or he beat out the other very top contenders in the weight class after the prior champion left them vacant[8].

What's more is that Tony was holding two of those coveted lineal titles at the same time.

And maybe this was the best part of it all: While his mother wasn't there because she never had gotten behind the idea of her baby boy making his living in a boxing ring, Tony's father was in the building and had witnessed every second of it.

Tony lavished in the moment. Feeling as if he were gliding on air, he freshened up and changed his clothes. He headed to a cabaret party. There, he reveled. He sang. An orchestra under his direction backed his vocals.

Surrounded by his friends, and watching in sheer, unadulterated delight was the host of the celebration party: Al Capone.

Capone's close proximity to Canzoneri during Tony's post-coronation bash made some detractors ask loudly whether the fix was in when Berg, against the odds, went down in the third round.

But Fred Digby of The New Orleans Item dismissed the mini-controversy as sour grapes. He quoted one pundit who gathered that Berg simply planned the fight wrong, playing "right into [Canzoneri's] hands by walking into the little Italian."

"It was one of those terrific rights, tossed with Tony 'set,' that ruined the Britisher," the quoted pundit continued. "The knockout punch was one of the cleanest I ever saw."

Said Digby: "Some sports fans don't believe anything is on the level. To repeat an old gag: 'They wouldn't believe the Civil War was fought on the up and up.'"

Nothing suggests Tony paid any mind to the insinuations that Capone's presence at his party provoked. Not only did this victory end up

---

8   Such titles can also be won if lineal champions leave their weight classes and then one of the very top contenders still in the division beats another of the very top contenders. Lineal championships are considered by hardcore fans to be the truest because they are untainted by the politics of sanctioning bodies who may give a shot to one fighter while unfairly denying another. The websites linealboxingchampion.com and cyberboxingzone.com keep track of lineal champions in men's and women's boxing.

Tony Canzoneri celebrates as he becomes the lightweight boxing champion of the world after winning the fight against Al Singer following the first round at Madison Square Garden on November 14, 1930 in New York, New York. *Photo by: The Ring magazine via Getty Images*

being one of his favorite fights to talk about from that point on. He also had a simple explanation for his easily beating Berg.

"All you had to do with Berg was move back one step and then let the right hand go," Tony would later say. In fact, Canzoneri would add, he was so sure that he wouldn't have to go the full distance with Berg that he only did one day's worth of running while training ahead of the night that made him both the lightweight and junior welterweight champion of the world.

"I knew I didn't have to move," Tony said. "Just stand still, 'til he came in, step back once and let 'er go.

"I did, and he went out like a light."

Tony was in rarefied air. And he intended to stay there, breathing it all in, for as long as he could.

"AS POPULAR AS …
BABE RUTH"

———

W hen his crunching right-hand blow knocked out Kid Berg during their second meeting in the ring, Tony Canzoneri could legitimately argue that he had the same number of world championships as did his adopted hometown's most successful baseball team: the New York Yankees.

Legendary, slugging outfielder Babe Ruth had helped the Yankees[1] win three World Series in six seasons beginning in 1923. And in an observation that illustrated Canzoneri's standing at one point, journalists occasionally noted how Ruth's face resembled Tony's whenever they tried to contextualize the professional heights that the boxer had reached.

First-baseman Lou Gehrig had also made key contributions in the team's consecutive titles in 1927 and 1928. Besides Ruth's, Gehrig's was on the short list of names of sportsmen – in New York or beyond, really – whose celebrity could rival Tony Canzoneri.

It remained a time when boxing's popularity only slightly trailed – but perhaps even rivaled – that of baseball, then enjoying its run as America's favorite pastime[2]. That meant Tony Canzoneri, whose youth

———

1 The Yankees of course ultimately would overtake Tony in championships. They had 27 World Series titles entering the 2023 season.

2 Of course, for a plethora of reasons, this has changed. Popularity in other sports has steadily risen, including pro football and pro basketball, eclipsing baseball and boxing in the national conscience.

and status as a world champion boxer in three divisions, would get access to crossover opportunities that, to this day, remain reserved for the brightest of stars.

One of his more mundane ventures involved striking a deal to attach his name to a restaurant and watering hole just a few blocks from Manhattan's globally famous Times Square. At the corner of Broadway and 51st Avenue, Tony Canzoneri's Paddock Bar & Grill stood in the heart of New York City's bustling theatrical world, drawing in patrons who had watched, listened to, written about or even stood in the opposite corner during some of his most fabled performances in the ring. He worked as a host[3] for the establishment, which also provided his brother Jasper a job.

Along with a liquor store that Canzoneri opened on Atlantic Avenue in Brooklyn, the bar and restaurant provided Tony a stream of income – the use of his name came at a price – without requiring much, if any, involvement in the daily operations of the business.

Tony also built a portfolio of show business cameos. He appeared as himself in the 1933 film *Mr. Broadway*, where renowned comedian Ed Sullivan told jokes and listened to stories from patrons at the various spots that New York offered to its night owls.

After calling time on his boxing career, Canzoneri leveraged his fame in the squared circle into a gig feeding lines to comedian Joey Adams. He served as an on-stage partner of sorts, though the jokes that Adams cracked often came at Tony's expense.

Canzoneri in that role became known in his own right for his impersonations of actor Edward G. Robinson – who often started sentences with "see?" and ended them with "mmm, yeah" – and actress Mae West, who immortalized the seductive line "come up and see me sometime" in a song inspired by some dialogue in her movie *She Done Him Wrong*.

The makers of the comedic play *They Should Have Stood in Bed*, a farce about prizefighting, cast Canzoneri as a character named "Killer Kane." The production had a run at the Mansfield Theatre on Broadway, although it was brief, closing after just 11 days.

---

3   This is according to the July 1982 issue of Ring magazine.

Elsewhere, Tony participated in a cross-country nightclub tour with entertainer Lou Nelson, according to the February 1952 issue of Boxing & Wrestling magazine. He also landed a minor role in the fictional 1949 boxing movie *Ringside*.

Tony's character, "Swinger Markham," is a former featherweight champion as well as a hard-drinking, small-time bookie who tells the movie's antagonist, boxer Tiger Johnson, that his opponent, Joe O'Hara, hurt his eye in training. That leads Tiger to target Joe's bad eye in their bout and defeat him, setting the stage for Joe's brother Mike to quit his piano-playing career – which Joe wanted to support – and train to challenge Tiger himself.

The film had mixed reviews for reasons that went beyond Tony's acting abilities or relative lack thereof. Users of the Internet Movie Database have given it 5.5 stars out of a possible 10.

But there is no arguing that Tony's presence was a big deal to *Ringside's* producers as they marketed their film. He's smiling in the bottom right corner of the movie's promotional poster, wearing a brown fedora and a matching suit. And he is one of 10 actors[4] whose names are listed on the placard billing the movie as a "punch-packed drama."

Canzoneri later bagged an uncredited turn in 1952's *The Quiet Man*, which starred John Wayne as a retired Irish-American fighter and Maureen O'Hara as the redheaded[5] leading lady with whom he falls in love. Over that same year and the next one, he made guest appearances on three television shows. He had a guest role on a fourth show in 1955, which turned out to be the one that concluded his career as a thespian of the screen.

One can imagine himself or herself telling Canzoneri to stick to prizefighting given the relatively lean returns his ventures in the entertainment industry brought. He might have told himself that as well given how desperately he would seek to cling to his boxing career before he set off on life on the other side of the ring's ropes.

---

4   Joey Adams, Canzoneri's partner in their comedic act, also had a small role in *Ringside*. Tony is pressed up against him on the poster.

5   By all indications, the appearance in similarity to Tony's sister-in-law, Dotty Adams, was a coincidence.

But Tony's cousin Robert Canzoneri, in his memoir, *A Highly Ramified Tree*, described just how bright the boxer's star shined when he decided he would try his best to see if he could make a name for himself in something other than prizefighting.

"Tony ... was known, it seemed, to everybody," Robert Canzoneri wrote. Store clerks who came to know Robert's last name would frequently ask him, "Are you any kin ...?"

"We would answer modestly, 'First cousin,' [our] heart giving a little flip," Robert Canzoneri wrote.

"No kidding?" would be the usual response, the author remembered. He marveled at his lucky bloodline, writing, "How did we manage to be first cousins to the lightweight champion of the world, a real Italian, a New Yorker [many] knew only through pictures, newspapers, radio?"

In those days, the boys who would pick on Tony in New Orleans's Pigeon Town neighborhood all those years beforehand for being Italian – and a mere shoeshiner, at that – wouldn't dare now. In fact, many in both New Orleans and the Big Apple might have been willing to eat out of Tony Canzoneri's hand just to be around him.

Denise Canzoneri, the daughter Tony had with a woman[6] whom he married toward the end of his boxing career, saw the glamor her father had earned for himself from a much more intimate perspective.

She remembers she would be sharing a meal with her dad at his restaurant, and New York City's mayor would drop in just to say hello to him. Then, on some days, whether or not there was a special occasion to observe, Denise would dress up in fancy hats and gloves, and her dad would wear his finest suits, and they would go together to the best, most in-demand restaurants in town.

It never mattered if they had reservations or if the places had huge waits, Denise Canzoneri recalled. Her dad would just go to the front, talk to the person in charge of assigning tables to both patient and impatient diners, and get them seated right away.

Denise remembers Tony had a friend with a house in the Hamptons, on the affluent, eastern side of Long Island. The friend would let Tony

---

6   Many more details about her await later in this book.

and Denise stay at that posh house regularly, she recalled. And it wasn't just New York City that father and daughter explored together – Denise said he took her to what seemed like every part of the United States.

Sometimes, on their outings, Denise and dad would recognize some of the entertainment world's brightest stars. Just like when getting a table wherever and whenever he wanted, in those cases, Tony would take his daughter's trembling hand, march her to the front, and introduce her to whichever luminary he had recognized.

Here's Frank Sinatra, Denise recalls her father saying coolly once. This is Tony Bennett. Meet these countless other titans of the day's music and film industries, Tony would often say to Denise, who couldn't help but be starstruck each time.

Many times, Denise recalled, it was her father to whom people would come up, eager for an introduction. Tony would always stop to have a word and sign an autograph if those who approached him wanted that. Denise remembers one time a particularly large crowd surrounded her and her dad, and he wasn't satisfied until both of them had given their autographs to everyone there.

She didn't mind taking the time to do that because her father didn't. In fact, once, he said it was the part about professional boxing that he enjoyed most. It wasn't the championships, the getting to hit people for a living, or even the gratifying applause he would get whenever he did his job well. It was regular people getting excited just to see him while they were out and about.

"I often wonder whether it was worth it," he said one time[7]. "But I don't have to wait long for the answer. Every day, strangers stop me in the street and say, 'Aren't you Tony Canzoneri?' Lots of times, little kids who weren't even a gleam in their father's eye when I was fighting ask for autographs or just to shake my hand. It's a wonderful feeling to be remembered after all these years.

"Sure, it was worth it, every drop of blood and every stitch of it. I wouldn't have it any other way."

That's exactly how Denise remembers it, too.

---

7   This quote comes from a lengthy retrospective feature that writer Mike Casey penned for "The Cyber Boxing Zone" website. It is available at www.cyberboxingzone. com/boxing/casey/MC_Canzoneri.htm.

"He was always so loving, so caring, very humble," Denise said. "I was very privileged to get to see that. I always felt so funny about that."

* * *

But none of that had happened back at the beginning of the summer of 1931, when Tony was resting for two months after winning the junior welterweight crown. He returned to action with a tune-up fight against a 140-pound fighter. In that bout, Canzoneri nearly shut out 20-win, 20-loss and two-draw Michigan boxer Herman Perlick, winning nine of the 10 allotted rounds, according to the exhibition's lone official, the referee.

Then, a couple of weeks later, Canzoneri exposed the 140-pound title for the first time, going to Los Angeles's Wrigley Field to face Cecil Payne[8] on July 13, 1931.

Canzoneri, who at 132.5 pounds was nearly four pounds lighter than Payne, smashed the Louisville native early before a crowd of 20,000 people. A right-cross that Canzoneri landed on the Kentuckian's jaw dropped him within a minute of the first round.

With blood dripping out of his nose, Payne got up and would regain some of the ground he lost to Canzoneri as the champion fought at a deliberate pace. Payne began finding success with left-handed blows to Canzoneri's body and an occasional right to the head, taking advantage of a slight edge in height. But he tired in the later phases of the 10-round bout, and the rally he had started putting together wasn't enough to dethrone Canzoneri.

The referee raised Tony's hand, and an L.A. crowd which at junctures called for Canzoneri to show more – especially after the near-stoppage in the first round – applauded the outcome.

Nearly two months after defending the 140-pound title against Payne, Canzoneri granted Berg a chance to win that junior welterweight belt back while also simultaneously taking a shot at Tony's lightweight title. Controversy reared its head during this third match

---

8   Payne had lost to Canzoneri by decision less than two years earlier, amid a 12-match unbeaten streak that Tony went on following his dethroning as featherweight champ by Andre Routis. This rematch was in a minor league baseball stadium in Los Angeles that was separate and distinct from the famous ballpark in Chicago with the same name.

between Canzoneri and Berg, a 15-round bout at New York's famed Polo Grounds.

Tony notched another quick start, landing a right-hand punch to the chin that floored Berg midway through the first round. Berg took a nine count, returned to the fray and survived the round, hoping the break would be long enough for him to shake it off so he could then try to simply outbox Canzoneri and maybe win a decision.

But later on, during the moment everyone was talking about after the fight, Berg fell again. This time it was a left hook to the body which dropped Berg. To the 17,000 spectators packing the home of baseball's New York Giants, it was obvious the blow had come in below the belt, meaning it was illegal and should not have counted.

Protests rained down from the stands. If the blow had been bad enough that Berg couldn't continue, and had the fight taken place where it was originally scheduled, in Berg's hometown of London, Canzoneri would have been disqualified. He would have had to surrender his championships amid those jeers, right then and there.

Only the fight had happened in the territory of the New York State Athletic Commission, the sport's other major sanctioning body besides the National Boxing Association. And the NYSAC organization had recently changed its rules to eliminate the possibility of fighters winning or losing because of a low blow.

Furthermore, to add even more confusion to the situation, a foul should have been assessed to Canzoneri because of the low blow that sent Berg down to the canvas, and as a result he should have lost the round. But instead, the referee stood over Berg and started counting as if he had been knocked down by a legitimate punch.

So Berg had to stand up or the ref would rule him out of the fight upon reaching the count of ten. A distressed Berg regained his feet after taking a count of nine. But he was flustered and distracted, and his mindset was completely thrown off.

Berg offered little resistance the rest of the way against Canzoneri, who was clearly superior to the Englishman in a dozen of the fight's rounds. Berg struggled to even make glancing contact during the last five rounds of the bout as Canzoneri picked him apart with each hand, targeting both the head and the body.

Canzoneri cruised to a favorable, unanimous decision, and he retained the two titles he was holding. Yet if a champion's life implies perks, expectations from fans as well as sportswriters to dominate and entertain each and every time he would take the ring – from start to finish – were also a part of the package.

Media at the Polo Grounds were in no mood to congratulate Canzoneri for winning over Berg again. They asked him whether he avoided trying to finish off Berg after seeing how easily he went down in the first round.

Smiling, Canzoneri coyly replied, "I don't like to knock out anybody." He also addressed the confusion about the low-blow knockdown that seemed to take Berg completely out of the fight. "If I hit Berg low," Canzoneri said, "everybody knows I didn't mean to."

At least some members of the media were skeptical of that statement from Tony.

Elsewhere, in the defeated fighter's dressing room, reporters spotted Berg laying on a table and pleading with his manager to get him an ambulance. The scribes peppered him with questions about whether he was ready to hang up his gloves for good.

"Are you going on fighting?" a reporter asked. Berg struggled to reply: "I have to. I've got to win the title" back. He tried to argue that the fight turned on the low blow that doubled him over.

"I'll get even if I get him in there again," said Berg, whose 94-win, five-loss and five-draw record at that moment was still stellar. "I'll ruin him for what he did to me tonight."

As passionately as Berg spoke, few if any members of the press corps believed he had something like that in him. One writer went so far as to call Berg's statements "pitiful" and maintained that fight fans shouldn't get too carried away with this title defense from Canzoneri.

"Canzoneri may be a great champion, but he fouled a punching bag," that particular journalist wrote. "That was all Berg was."

But in those days, the fight game moved much more quickly than it does now. And not even three months later, people would be much more impressed with Tony Canzoneri after he delivered one of the most famous victories of his career – and the era.

CHAPTER EIGHT

"THE SURPRISE OF MY ENTIRE CAREER"

—

For as far back as the collective memory of boxing aficionados stretches, fans and pundits have said styles make fights. And after Canzoneri agreed to clash with the one they called "Kid Chocolate" in Madison Square Garden on November 20, 1931, casual and expert observers alike saw similarities between the two pugilists that had the potential of producing one of that period's most memorable clashes.

And they weren't wrong.

Writers relished the opportunity to document the humble upbringing that Kid Chocolate experienced in his native Cuba. Born Sergio Eligio Sardinas Montalvo, he helped support his family by working as a newspaper carrier, which echoed the childhood of the man risking his two championship belts in the bout, Tony Canzoneri. As they once did with Canzoneri, ring scholars couldn't help but hold high expectations for this 21-year-old who had slashed his way up the bantamweight and featherweight ranks to clinch the junior lightweight crown. They couldn't resist comparing his skill and appearance to Joe Gans, the first Black American boxing champion in the 20th century and ruler of the lightweight division for six years beginning in 1902.

Neither the two-belt champion Tony Canzoneri – who was coming off an easy, unanimous decision win over Philly Griffin in Newark – nor the challenger Kid Chocolate had ever been knocked out of a fight. And Sardinas, who had only lost to Kid Berg in the more than 70 pro fights to his name at that point, had gone down to the canvas in a single, solitary fight. It had been years since that had happened, too.

The so-called Kid Chocolate, Sergio Eligio Sardinas Montalvo, wears a three-piece suit and stands at the bottom of a staircase. He faced Tony Canzoneri in 1931 and 1933. Canzoneri later called him the toughest fighter he ever faced.

Source: The Los Angeles Times Photographic Collection at the UCLA Library. License: Creative Commons Attribution 4.0 International License

The odds slightly favored Canzoneri, with bookmakers telling bettors he had an eight to five chance of beating Kid Chocolate[1]. But no one was really sure of what the outcome would be, which was as exciting a proposition as there was those days, evidenced by the fact that Madison Square Garden's management – despite the ongoing economic depression – expected each of the arena's more than 20,000 seats to be filled for the first time in months.

The crowd delivered on expectations and packed the house. The belligerents delivered on expectations also. Through each of the 15 rounds for which the bout was scheduled, Kid Chocolate showed he had the resolve needed to answer every punch that he absorbed from Tony Canzoneri in kind.

Canzoneri was prepared for that possibility, and for the duration of the encounter he charged past withering shots from both of Chocolate's hands to drive his own blows into his Cuban opponent's body. Nonetheless, if accounts from that night are to be believed, those sitting ringside thought 10 rounds into the match that the crowd packing the Garden was in store for a changing of the guard.

Canzoneri, too, sensed things might not work out for him unless he changed the equation at that point of the bout. So he stepped up the pace over the last five rounds and began outlanding Kid Chocolate, connecting on telling shots to both the head and body, while making the Cuban miss as well. Kid Chocolate repeatedly, desperately clinched Canzoneri, and at different points in the thirteenth and fourteenth rounds let himself be chased around the ring. But he could neither keep Canzoneri away – nor make him miss for that matter.

Though Canzoneri seemed to be edging ahead down the stretch, at the start of the final round, he signaled to everyone in the mythic arena that the man standing before him was a worthy one. Tony Canzoneri reached his glove out to Kid Chocolate. Chocolate extended his own gloved hand and shook Tony Canzoneri's.

The moment of sportsmanship passed, and Canzoneri fired his hands at Kid Chocolate's body with abandon. Left hooks from Canzoneri were

---

1   For more on the nuances around Kid Chocolate's record, be sure to read the section on him in Chapter 12.

backing the Cuban up steadily when the concluding bell tolled, according to a recap of the fight published by the New York Times.

All eyes turned to judges Charles Mathison and Joe Agnello as well as referee Willie Lewis. Most of those in Madison Square Garden were palpably yearning for the decision that Mathison handed up: On his card, Kid Chocolate had earned the victory, edging the champion.

But, if that night that Tony Canzoneri and Kid Chocolate shared with each other had shown that styles indeed do make brilliant fights, then it's also true that to be the man one has to beat the man. And the five-round stretch that Kid Chocolate let get away from him at the conclusion of the match proved to cost him dearly. Both Agnello and Lewis judged their cards in favor of Canzoneri, who took the split decision and managed to escape with his belts by the thinnest of margins.

Public opinion was not on the side of Agnello, Lewis or the fighter they had chosen to keep on the lightweight throne. Full-throated jeers cascaded down from the rafters as Tony Canzoneri raised his arm in triumph[2].

"The champion of the lightweights still is Tony Canzoneri; but just as surely the heir-apparent to the throne is Kid Chocolate," wrote Herbert Barker of the Associated Press, almost certainly summarizing the emotion with which those who were disappointed in the result consoled themselves.

United Press's Henry McLemore echoed Barker[3].

"Whipped though he was, the kid made a magnificent battle of it, and still remains the prettiest boxer there is," McLemore wrote of Cuba's Sardinas. "The ring has nothing more thrilling to offer than the sight of that ... streak of lightning in the midst of one of his whirlwind flurries. Mercy me, how he can throw that leather, and goodness gracious how he can move in there and get away."

Canzoneri didn't take offense against McLemore, Barker and their ilk for their opinions about Kid Chocolate. He could see how pundits

---

2   Canzoneri weighed in at 132 pounds and Chocolate at 127.5. If Canzoneri had dropped two more pounds and still won, Chocolate would have had to surrender to him his junior lightweight belt, and Tony would've been the first boxer ever to win world titles in four weight classes.

3   Read ahead to see how Kid Chocolate continued on to a fine career but fell just short of this billing from Barker, McLemore and others in their industry.

were saying he had started slowly against Kid Chocolate and therefore had nearly lost.

"I wanted to show my friends I could outsmart Chocolate, who was a real clever fellow, and it almost cost me my title," Canzoneri later said[4].

Further, Canzoneri would also go on to say, "Kid Chocolate was the toughest guy I ever had to fight," which made his approach for that bout even more mistaken than it otherwise might have been.

Nonetheless, while styles make fights, they don't win them. Kid Chocolate had the style. But Tony, for those last five fateful rounds that night, harnessed the focused desperation and urgency which great fighters can summon when faced with the reality that they're on the cusp of losing everything for which they have spent their lives working. And that made the difference, whether or not writers and fight fans liked seeing Tony Canzoneri survive Kid Chocolate's attempt at an upset.

Lurking ahead was the painful lesson about how sometimes such desperate attempts to save everything can come up short. But, at least on that one legendary night in that most fitting of venues, Tony Canzoneri had come up very far from short.

* * *

What goes up must come down. The descent isn't always linear. And for Tony Canzoneri, who was entering 1932 at that point, it wasn't.

It began about two months after he denied Kid Chocolate the upset for which the Cuban challenger had fought so relentlessly.

Canzoneri had agreed to visit the 71-win, 18-defeat, four-draw Johnny Jadick in Jadick's hometown of Philadelphia and subjected his junior welterweight crown to jeopardy.

For his third defense of that title, Canzoneri put on about a half-pound to the weight he carried into the triumph over Kid Chocolate. But Jadick was an entirely different physical specimen with which to grapple, like Cecil Payne and Herman Perlick each had been for Tony in the summer of 1931.

At 136 ½ pounds, Jadick weighed a full nine pounds more than Kid Chocolate. And he, too, showed he could walk through Tony

---

4   This was according to the March 1961 issue of Ring magazine.

Canzoneri's best shots to set up some of his own damaging blows.

Canzoneri nonetheless surprised everyone by dropping Jadick to the canvas in the opening frame of the 10-round fight after connecting with a left to the jaw. But Jadick had jumped up and re-assumed his fighting stance before referee Leo Houck had even started counting, which sent Canzoneri a strong message that he would need a lot more than that to win the bout through a stoppage.

Jadick from that point answered everything Canzoneri had to offer and wouldn't let himself be backed up the way Kid Chocolate did. He scored points at will with a left jab that Canzoneri never managed to solve before the bout's last bell clanged.

Houck and the fight's two judges all saw a close fight between the two men. But all of them agreed Jadick had edged Canzoneri, with two awarding him the fight by a single round and the other by two frames. Jadick was now the junior welterweight champion of the world.

Canzoneri earned a return trip to Philly for a rematch against Jadick after compiling three 10-round decision wins and fifth-round technical knockout victory over the next several months.

That second fight against Jadick went better for Canzoneri in one sense as he tried to reclaim the title he had surrendered.

Tony persuaded judge Stewart Robinson to score the 10-round bout seven rounds to two in his favor, which means that particular official believed Canzoneri had routed the champion whom he was challenging. But Jadick had again used his trademark long left jabs to halt Canzoneri any time that Tony tried to charge forward. Neither Joe McGuigan nor Tom Walsh awarded Canzoneri more than three rounds, and Jadick consolidated himself as the world's junior welterweight champion.

Quite ironically, the boos which Canzoneri couldn't avoid on the night he bagged one of his career's most storied victories at Kid Chocolate's expense now rained down on Jadick. Seat cushions thrown by some of the irate, jeering fans also showered down in and around the ring after the final bell had revealed that Canzoneri would not get the junior welterweight championship back.

In a sense, the disappointment from Canzoneri's fans is understandable. Jadick had struggled against fighters who were "far inferior to Canzoneri," as the March 1961 issue of Ring magazine noted. But he was now undefeated in two bouts against Canzoneri and had abruptly, unexpectedly "proved a problem for the great champion."

Nonetheless, Canzoneri still held one of the fight game's most coveted and pursued laurels: the lightweight crown. And that was a salve to his supporters' wounded pride.

After two third-round, knockout victories in the fall of 1932, Canzoneri served notice that it would still take a special fighter to strip him of that title which remained in his collection. He scored a unanimous decision victory in a title defense at Madison Square Garden at the expense of the same Billy Petrolle who had outpointed him two years earlier.

There was no denying that, in front of 18,000 spectators mostly delighted with the outcome, Petrolle had gone the distance against a champion whom ringside observers "admitted … was worthy to stand alongside the lightweight giants of the past," as United Press put it.

But, on that night of November 4, 1932, all but a few of the bout's 15 rounds proved to be one-sided beatings in Canzoneri's favor, as the Associated Press somberly noted. And the price that Tony Canzoneri had exacted on Petrolle for the courage that the latter displayed was plain for all to see on Petrolle's badly cut, battered face and body.

Canzoneri[5] followed up with wins in three of his next four bouts, all during the first half of 1933. The sole defeat came on points against a 59-win, five-loss junior welterweight.

The last of those wins came at New Orleans's Heinemann Park against a fighter known to fight fans as Battling Shaw, a Mexican pugilist who had since beaten Jadick and swiped his world junior welterweight title.

The father of legendary New Orleans journalist Ronnie Virgets[6] attended that title fight and years later gave his son a first-hand account. Canzoneri didn't cut much of an impressive figure at the start of the fight, Virgets's father recalled.

---

5   Some may find it interesting that sometime after this Petrolle fight, a doctor named Harvey Wiggs made Tony a new protective rubber mouthpiece constructed from a cast of Canzoneri's mouth to ensure as perfect a fit as possible. Canzoneri showed the new mouthpiece off in a January 1933 photo available on Getty Images.

6   Virgets, with his deep, gravelly, distinctive New Orleans accent, often wrote about horse racing and was long a fixture at the city's Fair Grounds race course before his death at age 77 in 2019.

"Canzoneri looked a little puffy in the face, with noticeable scar tissue around the eyes and cheeks," Virgets wrote. "At this point, he had been fighting pro for more than eight years. ...

"But then he took off his purple robe, and he was like a thoroughbred. Small legs blossoming into shoulders you wouldn't believe for 132 or so pounds."

Canzoneri didn't treat his hometown crowd to any theatrics as he once had in the budding days of his career, such as when he tried to make an opponent think his shoelaces were untied to get him to drop his guard and punch him.

Instead, Canzoneri delivered as business-like a performance as he'd ever staged, fighting a mostly crouching Battling Shaw – born Jose Perez Florez – at close range all night. "There was no dancing, no wild punching," Virgets would later write, citing his father's recollections. "Just two guys throwing smart, sharp punches, blocking some, getting nailed by others. And they could both box and hit and take a punch. Once in a while, you'd see sweat fly or a head pop back from a punch, but they went right back together."

Virgets continued: "No flash, just the craft at its best. In a time of hard jobs, this was men in the hardest job and doing it wonderfully. You should [have heard] my old man tell it."

Canzoneri, in what would be his second-to-last bout in New Orleans, seized full control in the eighth round with a short left that "froze Shaw for an instant," Virgets's father remembered. "Then, [Tony] crossed over with the right, and Shaw's legs went out from under him and he went down."

Battling Shaw beat the count and made it to the bout's finish line. But Canzoneri cruised to a unanimous decision against Battling Shaw and had won back the world's junior welterweight title, securing himself at least one more spell as a lineal champion in two divisions at the same time.

That night, he also became the first boxer to win back the lineal junior welterweight championship after having lost it. And his performance lived on for the rest of time in the memories of Virgets's father, the journalist would later write.

"My old man always [imitated] this left-right combination in slow motion when he" recounted the moment in the eighth-round when

Canzoneri got the upper hand in the match and never gave it back, Virgets added. "This was textbook hitting so perfect that the visualization of it has burned across" decades. "He was so wondrous at his hard trade that made memories like that one for old men like mine to pass on to their sons."

It's impossible to know now exactly how many fathers told such tales to their children about Tony Canzoneri. But the recollections of Virgets's dad demonstrated how difficult it was to forget having seen Tony Canzoneri at his very best in person, even if it would turn out that there were fewer performances like that in his future than there had been in his past.

* * *

After he successfully challenged Battling Shaw and won his second junior welterweight championship of the world, optimism burned as bright as it had in decades across the US as Canzoneri set his sights on going to Chicago to face another of boxing's all-time greats: the New York-born, Windy City-raised Barney Ross[7].

President Franklin D. Roosevelt by then had signed the national recovery act meant to aid the US economy restart after the Great Depression. Breadlines were steadily thinning. The nationwide prohibition against manufacturing or selling drinking alcohol was about to end.

Times weren't totally better – melancholic songs like "Willow Weep for Me" and "Brother, Can you Spare a Dime?" blaring on radios and record players were evidence of that. But close supporters of Canzoneri, still reigning as champion, embodied the optimism one night while they were out with him during that period.

Canzoneri was late in joining them that night, having been caught up in conversation with a betting bookmaker who had a hot tip about a horse race the next day. But he arrived in time to hear friends talk about the matchup that he had scheduled with Ross for June 23, 1933.

"I hear that Ross is a helluva scrapper," one of Canzoneri's friends announced to him, according to the May 1964 issue of Boxing Illustrated.

Another in the group cut off the remark. "Naw," the friend said,

---

7   His first name was Beryl, and his family's last name was Rasofsky.

snorting. "He's just a kid – only a couple of years outta the amateurs. Tony will kill him."

"That," Boxing Illustrated noted later, "was the prevailing attitude in sports circles – at least in New York, where the flat-nosed Canzoneri was as popular as his giant-sized lookalike, Babe Ruth. Nobody felt that Ross stood a chance against Tony. And [Tony], basking in the idolatry of the faithful, agreed."

There was no question that, on that night out with Tony and his friends, Ross was being underestimated.

Having grown up with asthma in an impoverished area of Chicago, Ross purportedly learned to fight among Italians, Poles and Irish who occasionally would arm themselves with rocks, iron pipes, beer bottles and brass knuckles. "He was restless, on the go all the time, trying to make a buck to support his mother, left penniless with four other children" after Ross's father, a grocer, was shot to death by robbers, as recounted by Boxing Illustrated.

The ways Ross made a buck ranged from selling newspapers to running errands for his city's crime lord, Al Capone. That is all to say he had little interest in becoming what his father wanted him to be: a Hebrew teacher. And diminishing hopes of Ross ever becoming a teacher faded completely when he tried his hand at amateur boxing, tasted some success – including a New York Golden Gloves championship – and embarked on a career in pro prizefighting that now had him on course to lock horns with Tony Canzoneri.

Ross by then had used perhaps the flashiest style in boxing to build up a record of 44 victories, just two defeats and a pair of draws. If the fight went the allotted 10 rounds, Ross could lean on that silky, nearly impossible-to-decipher approach to outland Canzoneri and simply pull away on points. Canzoneri, despite his confidence, might need the knockout to ensure he would win if Ross came out in sharp form, some pundits seemed to think.

According to Boxing Illustrated, one conversation Canzoneri wasn't around to hear as he prepared for his fight against Ross was between Ross and Ross's co-managers, Art Winch and Sam Pian. It starkly revealed how hungry Ross was to reset the pecking order of the lightweight division.

Ross had long been impatient for his team to land him a championship fight with Canzoneri. His advisers tried to tell him Canzoneri had

Barney Ross challenged Tony Canzoneri for the world lightweight championship in June 1933. Here, he is shown in 1934. *Source: 1934 press wire photo in the public domain on Wikimedia Commons*

needed to show patience, more than once, before he achieved the status that he had attained in those days.

"Barney, it takes time," Winch reportedly told Ross. "How long do you think Tony went hungry before he finally made it?"

But Ross didn't want to listen to that. By then, he had fought three years in the amateurs and almost five in the pros waiting for a shot at a world title, as he told the January 1962 issue of Boxing & Wrestling magazine.

"I don't care about Canzoneri," Ross told Winch, according to the publication. "I need the money."

Ross knew he would be a handful for Canzoneri. The former Golden Gloves champ used his quick hands and feet to mount accurate attacks while also making himself an exceptionally tricky target to consistently strike. As the fight approached, he believed more and more that the championships held by Canzoneri were his destiny – if not his birthright.

Yet Canzoneri at that stage had been through everything, and he had always shown up when both glory and big money were on the line. For the Ross fight, the money was there for Tony – he was guaranteed $30,000 and then entitled to 40% of the $46,305 in ticket sales.

And so was glory. Fight fans from all walks of life were paying attention – including Capone.

This was the match later recalled by the Burnses where associates of the fearsome Windy City mobster allegedly visited Canzoneri's camp beforehand and casually reminded him who called the shots. This was the match for which Canzoneri's manager, Sammy Goldman, said he had to call Capone and report that some of Capone's colleagues had seemingly tried to pressure Goldman's fighter into losing intentionally, before neither Tony nor Sammy ever heard from those ruffians again.

There has never been any indication that the alleged visit by Capone's henchmen influenced the outcome of what happened next. And certainly nothing at all unexpected happened on Tony Canzoneri's account when he took the ring for one of his hardest, most unforgettable fights.

For starters, both fighters received a deafening ovation from the audience. Sure, the crowd felt Ross was theirs. But many still had warm memories of how Canzoneri had gone to their city and fought Bud Taylor to a draw during a title fight a few years earlier in the bantamweight division, where Tony was less comfortable than he would be at higher weight classes.

Canzoneri pressed forward throughout the bout once the opening bell clanged, eliciting loud cheers as he frantically searched for openings that Ross occasionally allowed him.

For the first half of the fight, Canzoneri blocked and neutralized the left jab with which Ross had become accustomed to piling up points. He also managed to slip a few uppercuts through Ross's guard, landing them on the challenger's belly and head.

Ross's mother was among those in attendance. And, decades later, Boxing Illustrated would describe how she shuddered every time Canzoneri pierced her son's defense, leaving Barney with cuts around his eyes and puffy bruises on his slender face.

However, in the sixth round, Ross himself had a breakthrough. He began to slip left hooks past Canzoneri's guard and land them on the champion's jaw repeatedly. And Ross often followed those blows up with powerful, short right hands.

The hometown fighter went on to outperform the titleist whom he was challenging in that round as well as the two which followed.

At that point, Tony Canzoneri began feeling like he did late in his fight against Kid Chocolate – as if it were all slipping through his fingers. He fired his hands with the same burning but focused desperation, seeing if he could quell the latest uprising bent on overthrowing his lightweight division reign.

"Through the sweat and fury of pounding gloves, he saw visions of himself as an 11-year-old boy in New Orleans, battling to protect his [shoeshining] business from bigger boys," Boxing Illustrated would later report. "But this was the world lightweight crown he was trying to save, and he tore into Ross, hoping for a knockout."

Yet Ross for long periods of that stretch met each of Canzoneri's blows with punches that were, at a minimum, equally effective. Eventually, Ross sensed the titles that Canzoneri was flailing to keep a hold of would go home with him as long as Ross was standing upright at the conclusion of the bout.

Ross let up for most of the fight's closing phases and retreated into the defensive shell that he had started the contest in. However, just before the final bell, Ross made the carefully deliberated – but undoubtedly risky –

decision to come out of that shell and deal Canzoneri a flurry of punches. That display of valor left the 11,000 in attendance yelling lustily.

The crowd was so hysterical it was difficult to hear the officials announce their decision, if recaps of the fight are to be believed.

Referee Tommy Gilmore – who, notably, was from Chicago – saw no reason to choose one over the other. He declared a draw, a result that meant Gilmore ostensibly believed that Tony Canzoneri deserved to retain his titles.

But Canzoneri had not similarly persuaded the two judges. W.A. Battyle and Ed Hintz awarded six- and five-point victories to Ross. Canzoneri's run as the world's lightweight and junior welterweight champion was over. Ross had officially deposed Canzoneri, and the latter man's title belts now belonged to the former.

As Ross raised his hand in victory, a dejected Canzoneri quickly turned and rested his head against the ring's ropes. "The decision was the surprise of my entire career," Canzoneri would later say. "Honestly, I thought I was so far ahead of Ross that I coasted in the eighth and ninth and did not extend myself in the tenth.

"I thought I'd won it easily."

Ross cavorted around the ring as his mother wept with joy. Boxing Illustrated wrote that Canzoneri also wanted to weep – but in despair – as Sammy Goldman screamed in the ring as loud as he could that the decision had been "an outrage! An absolute outrage!"

Some observers dismissed Ross's win as a hometown decision. Boxing Illustrated quoted one veteran sportswriter as having said: "When a Chicago referee gives a Chicago boy a draw, you can bet that the visiting gladiator won."

Whatever the case, for the first time in three years, thanks to that night, Tony Canzoneri was a former champion again.

* * *

Ross was bothered by the talk that he had won against Canzoneri largely because of a home-cooked decision courtesy of the officials in charge of the bout. It stung him to think that at least some in the public didn't think his win was entirely deserved.

"I beat Tony and fought just as I planned," he said afterward. "He was a great champion, and I am going to be a great one, too. He figured he was ahead? Say, I coasted myself in those closing rounds."

But he acknowledged how much Canzoneri had pushed him. Politically, it would be popular for him to quickly give Canzoneri a quick rematch, especially because Tony had fought Ross so closely.

Ross also didn't want to waste any time getting the opportunity to show that his win over Canzoneri was anything but a fluke. So, less than three months later, Ross signed up to once again face Canzoneri – only this time, he would go to Tony's territory and square off with him in New York City's Polo Grounds.

Fans rewarded Canzoneri's eagerness and Ross's courage with a lucrative gate. Nearly 30,000 people showed up, collectively paying almost $120,000 for the privilege. Canzoneri again fought as skillfully and frenetically as he perhaps ever had, this time convincing judge Arthur Kelly to award him a one-round victory.

One more card in his favor out of the remaining two would return him to his monarchy after an interregnum by Ross of just a few weeks.

But there was at least one important difference between the rematch and the first fight. The second bout was scheduled for 15 rounds instead of 10 like the clash in Chicago had been. And that added length seemed to work against Canzoneri, who after 10 rounds appeared to have the edge on the young champion that he was challenging.

Blood trickling down from his eye and cheek, Tony nearly knocked Ross down in the 11th round with a left hook that connected thunderously on the champion's jaw. Ross's knees buckled.

Canzoneri stepped back in anticipation as if he was bracing for Ross to fall, which would have at least won him that round. Of course, if Ross fell and didn't get back up, Canzoneri would have been world champion again.

But, after stepping forth just once, Ross straightened himself, and the bell marking the end of the round sounded.

Canzoneri had come tantalizingly close to seizing command of the fight that would give him back the titles he had lost, but he hadn't finished the job.

"Canzoneri couldn't believe it," Knockout Magazine's Dan Shocket wrote in a 1993 article on Ross, which described that fight. "The fight went out of him."

During the final four frames, Canzoneri faded in a way that was obvious to everyone watching. And ultimately, Judge George Kelly and referee Arthur Donovan cast their ballots in favor of Ross.

"Ross won the fight more on his courage than his skill, which was by all estimation remarkable," Shocket wrote.

The split decision had saved Ross's titles for him. And, at least for the time being, he had denied Tony Canzoneri's latest comeback.

Canzoneri was now left to ask hard questions of himself. The money for the Ross rematch remained good: nearly $13,800. But again, another grueling battle had pushed his body to its limits, it had reduced his face to a bloodied, bruised mess.

Right then, Canzoneri could have decided that he would leave the boxing ring behind once and for all, and he still would have gone down in history as one of the best to ever do what he had chosen to dedicate his life to.

Yet no one can say whether his primary feats – three years as champ of one of the most popular divisions in the game, and titles in three weight classes overall – would have stood the test of time. No one can say whether that resume alone would have propelled him to a life in show business and in the Broadway restaurant business.

It's what he did after the bitter, razor-thin defeats to Ross that etched his name in the history books alongside boxing's other immortals.

For men had tried to do it, to win the lightweight championship after losing it, but none could say they had done it – at least not until Tony picked up the pieces after the Ross rematch and started gluing them back together.

CHAPTER NINE

LAUGHING LAST

—

Having managed Tony Canzoneri throughout the fallen champion's career, Sammy Goldman knew a third collision with Barney Ross was the quickest way for his team to get back to the top of the heap at the lightweight division. So Goldman went to a matchmaker in New Orleans and tried to sell the idea of a third fight, only this time in the Crescent City.

It could be held either the night before a major football game or at the height of the local horse racing season. Sammy's proxy offered a guarantee of $30,000 for Ross. Goldman wanted so badly to pull the showdown off that he pledged to pay Ross's guarantee out of his own pocket if that was the only thing that stood in the way of the third match from happening.

Businesswise, the terms that Goldman was proposing were logical. The New York Polo Grounds crowd which took in Canzoneri's unsuccessful rematch against Ross paid a total of nearly $120,000 for their tickets. More than $36,000 of that went to Ross – which again, for those days, was a sum most Americans couldn't imagine earning through their work.

But, despite its generosity, Ross rejected the offer that Goldman had put on the table. And, for the next nearly two years, he lorded over the division which once belonged to Tony Canzoneri, doing so beyond his predecessor's grasp. There was absolutely nothing Tony or Goldman could do about it if Ross didn't engage with them.

While doing the best business they could, Goldman and Canzoneri otherwise gave his fans what they wanted by continuing to put him in the ring with the biggest names that they could get to play ball. Ahead of a December 1933 faceoff between Frankie Klick and Kid Chocolate for Kid Chocolate's junior lightweight world championship, each took a tune-up match against Canzoneri.

Canzoneri stared Klick down first in Brooklyn, bagging a unanimous decision win over Kid Chocolate's challenger in waiting. Then, after a few weeks passed, Canzoneri made the short trip over to Madison Square Garden to once again mix it up with Kid Chocolate.

This return engagement between Canzoneri and Kid Chocolate was much shorter than the first. In front of 12,000 people, in round two of a bout slated to last 10 frames, Canzoneri drilled a bone-rattling right hook into his Cuban opponent's jaw. Kid Chocolate crumbled forward and all but landed on his face.

Kid Chocolate tried to get back up on his feet about halfway through the referee's count. But he tumbled backwards, and the referee counted him out. It was the first knockout defeat – at a most inopportune time – that Kid Chocolate had ever suffered. And just a few weeks later, the Cuban dynamo would lose his junior lightweight title to Klick, who of course had taken Canzoneri the distance in what proved to be a more auspicious result than many first realized.

Nonetheless, from the night it happened until after their time in the fight game was over, Canzoneri's second victory over Kid Chocolate was one of his team's favorite to talk about.

When he was much older, Sammy Goldman's son Alfred wrote about how he cherished being there when his father pulled Tony Canzoneri close and shared the secret to beating Kid Chocolate.

"Kid Chocolate ... often went down into a very low crouch where he was hard to get at. [And] Dad told Tony that when Chocolate went down low, he was to go just as low and wait," Alfred Goldman wrote in a letter to The New York Times's Red Smith. "And when Kid Chocolate started to straighten up, then nail him. Which is what Tony did, and won the fight handily."

Tony, in an interview with a separate publication, recalled something similar.

"He had such a little head [so] he was hard to hit," Canzoneri once told New York's Newsday about Kid Chocolate, breaking things down bluntly, as he often did. "[And] I just kept hitting him on that little head."

Having put Kid Chocolate firmly and completely behind him, pundits were quick to declare that the Tony Canzoneri everyone knew was back. Readers could practically hear Associated Press sports writer Edward Neil panting in his recap of that fight, in which he wrote, "The crisp, shocking right hand that won brilliant little Tony Canzoneri the lightweight championship, then failed him in his title duels with Barney Ross, started him back tonight toward the ring glory he once knew."

Yet that path to which Neil alluded would neither be short nor straightforward. Notably, Canzoneri would go on to fight in 14 non-title matches during a 16-month period beginning in December 1933 before boxing's powers granted him a shot at pulling off the unprecedented: winning back the world's lightweight championship after having lost it.

He won 12 of those fights, dropping one decision each to two pugilists whom he defeated in rematches during this same run.

In the ring, that stretch against lightweight and junior welterweight opponents had its fair share of high moments.

For instance, he denied revenge to his former lightweight challenger Cecil Payne, knocking him out in five rounds in Cleveland. He victimized Klick again, stopping him in nine rounds. He also raised eyebrows again – in a good way – when, during this stretch, he traveled to Los Angeles and outpointed another of the boxing media's darlings: Mexico's Alberto "Baby" Arizmendi.

Arizmendi faced Tony at the lightweight limit but was preparing to try to win the New York State Athletic Commission's featherweight title in just a few months. Arizmendi's featherweight campaign culminated in his winning the NYSAC championship[1], a fact that in retrospect made Canzoneri's victory over him more impressive to many.

Additionally, in his final bout during this stretch, Canzoneri squared off in Pittsburgh against a fighter named Eddie Zivic. Tony overwhelmed Zivic and won by seventh-round stoppage while a 17-year-old boy who was about nine months into his career as a boxing pro watched on.

That rookie fighter was Billy Conn, who gave up his world light heavyweight championship to challenge all-time great Joe Louis for the

---

1   He never managed to win either the National Boxing Association title or the lineal title.

globe's heavyweight title in June 1941. As many might already know, Conn had a safe lead heading into the thirteenth round, but Louis knocked him out and saved his title.

Nonetheless, before all that happened and while he was still a newcomer learning his profession, Conn[2] took one look at Canzoneri on the night he beat Zivic and thought to himself, "That's the kind of fighter I want to be," according to the March 1961 issue of Ring magazine. "He looks like the greatest in the world to me!"

Yet myriad indignities can litter comeback trails like the one Tony was traversing, even if they were of a high enough quality to impress names like Billy Conn. And those in Canzoneri's camp could not avoid those indignities, despite the past glories that they had tasted.

That much became clear the time Canzoneri went to Kansas City and won on points over Pete Nebo in a 12-round rematch in 1932. It turned out the promoters were as many as $5,000 short of being able to pay Canzoneri's guarantee. And the choice for the former's champion's entourage was to either leave without their money or patch over the deficit in some other way.

Canzoneri's team chose the latter. So the promoters handed Sammy Goldman a $50 betting ticket, sent him to a thoroughbred race track in the area, and instructed him to place it on a particular horse.

"He was requested not to make any other bets," Goldman's son later wrote. "The horse won by himself and, if I remember rightly, the amount collected was [nearly] the amount owed."

Alfred Goldman said the entire episode – as obvious a fait accompli as there could be – convinced him to never make large, consequential bets at the racetrack.

Whatever the case, Goldman and Canzoneri were not sure how much longer they could carry on like that. Thankfully for them, it wouldn't be for much longer that they would have to. For the boxing gods granted their team an absolutely golden opportunity in April 1935.

---

2   Conn, who lost a rematch to Louis after the second world war, was the subject of one of renowned Sports Illustrated writer Frank Deford's most highly regarded profiles: "The Boxer and the Blonde," which – among other things – chronicled how he married his wife, Mary Louise Smith, despite her total disinterest in his sport and his feuding with her father.

By then, Barney Ross had also won – and subsequently lost – the world welterweight championship (147-pound limit). He wanted to win back that welterweight title, then held by Jimmy McLarnin, in the worst way.

Ross had also admitted to himself as well as the public that dropping enough weight to get under the 135-pound limit was something he simply could no longer do, at least not without compromising his ability to fight well enough to win. So he abandoned the lightweight crown that he had taken from Canzoneri and said he would begin focusing exclusively on campaigning at welterweight.

Without a doubt, the turn of events centering on Ross amounted to "another break for Tony Canzoneri," New Orleans States sports columnist Harry Martinez declared. Break or not, Martinez and many of his colleagues in sports writing conceded that Ross's decision to remove himself from the field at lightweight once again left Canzoneri, with his bona fides, at the perch of the division.

The New York State Athletic Commission, which at the time was still one of the sport's two major sanctioning bodies, moved quickly to refill the 135-pound division's vacated throne. Naturally, the commission gave Canzoneri the opportunity to reclaim his former belt. After all, he was the man who held it before the opponent who dethroned him departed for what he had hoped would be greener pastures.

But the panel needed someone to stand in Canzoneri's way to set up a fight that it hoped would generate some business. And for that, the NYSAC[3] tapped a stalwart of a contender named Luigi D'Ambrosio – better known as Lou Ambers.

Once he had been chosen for the fight against Canzoneri, Ambers told the world that just three years earlier he had hitched a ride from a stranger to Madison Square Garden to see Tony's first fight against Kid Chocolate. Ambers said he paid $1.10 for a balcony seat to watch Canzoneri win, though Tony left amid jeers from those in the crowd who believed Kid Chocolate had been robbed of a deserved decision win.

This time, Ambers would have a much closer view of Tony, whom

---

3   The title was vacant, and both Ambers and Canzoneri were considered top contenders for a shot at the belt, so this counted as the lineal championship.

he admitted had been his idol the night he stood in the corner opposite Kid Chocolate. And, Ambers said, if things went his way, he had a feeling that Canzoneri would lose the will to ever fight in the ring again.

* * *

The sports press couldn't resist setting up Canzoneri's showdown with Ambers as, at its core, a conflict between two men in different social and professional classes.

Bearing a nickname paying homage to his upstate New York home town that was famous for its gold mines, the "Hermiker Hurricane" was 21. Ambers was much younger and much fresher than Canzoneri, his fellow Italian-blooded warrior. To boot, he had also formerly served as a sparring partner for Canzoneri, another element that made the contest feel even more like a movie plot than it already did.

Canzoneri, for his part, was five years older and had been through what seemed like a thousand battles in the ring. He spent much of his free time at a farm that raised cows, sheep and horses, which he rode across the scenic meadows and acreage of an estate that he bought with some of his career earnings of about $200,000.

If Canzoneri ever had to get somewhere in a hurry, the veteran of 134 pro bouts could just hop into his fancy car and either drive it or get someone else to do it for him.

Ambers, on the other hand, did not have a comfortable, rustic retreat where he could get away from his trade's brutality. He didn't have a car, a horse – or even a bicycle, at that. He considered it to be splurging if he bought a bus ticket, and he worked in a factory to support his nine siblings and other family members.

Of course, when Ambers realized many brave, kindred spirits had improved their lots through boxing, he picked up the sport. He earned between $7 to $25 per bout in his early days as a professional. He earned his first $40 purse as a last-minute substitute for a fighter who had become sick. He won, pleased the crowd and was later invited back at a rate that was more lucrative for him.

Ambers erased his family's debt with a March 1935 unanimous decision victory at Canzoneri's home away from home, Madison Square Garden, over Sammy Fuller, who a few years earlier had beaten Kid Berg. Ambers's win over Fuller came during a nine-match winning streak that

Lou Ambers, on the right, spars with Marty Servo as Eristum Sams referees
– all three were boxing instructors at the Manhattan Beach Coast Guard
training station during the second world war. Ambers fought Canzoneri for the
lightweight world championship in May 1935. *Source: The Library of Congress*

he was carrying with him into the ring for the clash against Canzoneri.

"But if the Ambers family is out of debt, it isn't in the money," the
New York Times' John Kieran wrote just days before the Hermiker Hurricane was intent on delivering a direct hit on everything Canzoneri had
built. "Not yet. It's Tony Canzoneri who is the lord of the manor, the
owner of the broad acres. Lou would like a little of that for himself and
his numerous brothers and sisters."

The punditry saw it simply. There was a lot to suggest Canzoneri
might have quietly become the kind of self-satisfied fighter that his
harder, hungrier, younger form had cut down without mercy on his way
to championships in three weight classes. And now Ambers looked to
be every bit the second coming of Canzoneri – relentless, savvy, powerful, courageous, strong, and only getting more so with each outing.

Tony only ratcheted up the tension enveloping him and his opponent when he openly discussed the likelihood of hanging up his gloves for the rest of his life if he didn't hold his own against Ambers. After all, Canzoneri had his savings and the pleasures at the farm where he lived with his family to count up.

"I might just as well retire if kids like that are beginning to catch up with me," he said.

Taking note of such language, Kieran wrote of Ambers's chances: "It looks like a gorgeous opportunity for a poor boy who can fight."

That was especially true of a poor boy who, at most, gave away advantages to Canzoneri in power and in right-hand punches but was otherwise on equal footing, including in chin strength, jabbing, hooks and stamina, Boxing & Wrestling magazine would say many years later in its April 1963 issue.

Ultimately, the magnitude of the opportunity against Canzoneri may have been too much for the less-experienced Ambers to fully seize at that point of his career.

Canzoneri fought cautiously but dominated the first two rounds. By the third frame, that approach had convinced Ambers that it was a safe proposition to trade blows with Canzoneri in the middle of the ring.

Ambers was encroaching on Canzoneri – and shooting punches wide of the mark – when Tony fired a straight right from near his shoulder squarely into Lou's chin.

The loud blow tossed Ambers onto his back. Confusion, embarrassment and panic all washed over the Hermiker Hurricane's face as he tumbled to the canvas and nearly 18,000 voices roared approvingly at seeing him get knocked down.

He rolled over and bounced back up to his feet just three seconds into the referee's count. It might have been wise for him to take a few more moments to collect himself. But, in his rush to signal that he could still fight despite what had happened a few moments earlier, he sacrificed his chance at a slightly longer count.

When the fight resumed, Ambers sought to pick up where he had left off right before Canzoneri dropped him. Tony made Ambers pay dearly for that. Canzoneri again let his right hand rip violently. Once more, it barreled into Ambers's jaw. And, for the second time in the span of just a few seconds, Canzoneri had knocked his opponent flat onto his back.

Ambers had not learned his lesson from the first knockdown. Again, he jumped up to his feet unusually early in the referee's count, seeming to once again want to hide any hint of weakness amid the unforgiving din engulfing him. But then it sunk in for him that he had to change his plan if he was going to have any shot. This time, when the action picked back up, Ambers kept his distance from Canzoneri, bought himself some extra moments to recover, and got out of the round without taking any more significant damage.

Canzoneri sensed he had gashed open a significant lead on the officials' scorecards that Ambers would have a hell of a time overcoming if he didn't register any knockdowns of his own. Tony focused on defending that lead, staying careful not to expose himself to a blow that could take the fight out of his control as well as pacing himself to go the full 15-round distance if necessary. He scored at will on jabs while ducking, weaving and swaying away from the increasingly desperate strikes Ambers was throwing his way.

If Ambers still harbored any hope that he had somehow done enough to close the distance Canzoneri created between them early in the bout, Tony snuffed it in the final round. Another brutal right hand from Canzoneri knocked Ambers down to the floor for the third time in the evening.

There was no uncertainty in the air at all when the bell signaling the end of the match clanged. The officials unanimously declared Canzoneri both the fight's victor and the first in the lightweight division's half-century history to ever recover the world championship after losing it.

Once again, noted one sports writer who covered the fight, "the curly haired little battler ... manages to laugh last."

In the span of an evening, Tony's thoughts about possibly retiring had quickly left his head. He immediately began speaking about how a second reign as the lightweight champion of the world could pocket him another $100,000 from fight purses alone. He talked about yearning to measure himself against Jimmy McLarnin, who ultimately went 1-2 in a three-fight series against Barney Ross, he who had tamed Tony Canzoneri.

"Why should I [not]?" Canzoneri said. "I've never been hurt, I'm only 26, I love to fight and I even like to train. And where else could I pick up such easy money?"

Could anyone dispute that somehow, some way, when no one expected it, he had turned back the clock, resuscitated the best version of himself and humbled the guy who openly bragged about ending his career as a prizefighter?

Nobody could – even if, as it would later become clear, Canzoneri had not seen the last of Ambers.

* * *

Tony's cousin, author Robert Canzoneri, got an intimate look at the halcyon days that Tony, his loved ones and his professional associates enjoyed during his second reign as the king of boxing's lightweight division.

Tony ultimately won each of the 11 fights that he booked after routing Ambers. He won a pair of decisions over Frankie Klick, improving to 4-0 all-time against him. He tasted revenge by scoring a win on points over Johnny Jadick, who once swiped the world junior welterweight belt off Canzoneri and then later had beaten him a second time[4].

And he bullied McLarnin around the ring at Madison Square Garden for 10 rounds before earning a unanimous decision in his favor.

It's worth slowing down and taking a closer look at this bout with McLarnin, who was born in Ireland, grew up in Canada and trained out of New York. After the referee instructed Tony and his opponent – nicknamed "Baby Face" – to fight cleanly, Canzoneri inadvertently walked into the arena microphone hanging down from the rafters. The bump left Tony's forehead gashed, according to multiple accounts of the fight.

In Canzoneri's corner, Sammy Goldman asked Tony if he was okay. Canzoneri, at a minimum, was bleeding from a part of the body that can bleed profusely even when wounds there are minor. But Tony just nodded, over and over, that he was fine to continue.

Tony's corner subsequently sealed his cut and had him march into a clash with "one of the most dangerous welterweights in history," as the July 1982 issue of Ring magazine put it. And McLarnin spent the entire fight aiming many of his punches directly at the mic-inflicted cut.

---

4   When looking back at his two losses to Jadick, Canzoneri didn't make excuses – there was neither inadequate training, illness nor injury that kept Tony from being able to box better against him. "There was [just] something about that guy!" Canzoneri would later say, shaking his head, according to the March 1961 issue of Ring magazine.

Canzoneri started off slowly in the first round, getting bloodied up and punched into the ropes while essentially ignoring orders from Goldman to protect himself from McLarnin's right hand.

"What did I tell you?" an exasperated Goldman asked Canzoneri during the first break, as the May 1983 issue of Boxing Illustrated would report later. "Didn't I tell you not to let him hit you with his right hand? What are you going to do now?"

Canzoneri cleared his head, mustered up a grin, and sought to convey to his manager that he absolutely still had everything under control. "What am I going to do?" Canzoneri scoffed. "What is he going to do when I hit him with my right hand?"

Tony restored order in the second frame. He landed lefts on McLarnin's head and rights to his cheek that were there for the taking because Jimmy was so aggressively attacking the cut on Canzoneri's forehead. Tony also throttled McLarnin's chin with both hands. Canzoneri's withering attack ultimately dropped McLarnin to one knee, though he didn't take a count.

Eight more rounds ensued in which Canzoneri and McLarnin "fought as two kids would on a street corner, throwing aside everything they had learned in their years in the ring, intent only on knocking each other out," according to the Boxing Illustrated magazine's recap of the night. But there was never a point where Canzoneri had lost command over the affair, which his dominance in the second round had flipped in his favor.

Looking back at that fight years later, the featherweight champion Louis "Kid" Kaplan marveled at the grit which Canzoneri showed by choosing to stay in the contest despite gashing his forehead on the ring microphone before the bout began.

"The average fighter would have quit then and there," Kaplan would say, according to the Ring magazine. "Or at least he would have asked for time to recover his senses. But not Tony Canzoneri."

Tony celebrated his run of form against McLarnin and the others by jetting off to New Jersey to marry a Broadway showgirl whom he had met at the height of his fame. She was named Rita Goldberg[5], and her piercing brown eyes and devastatingly dark features must have sent

---

5   Some accounts also referred to her as Rita Ray.

countless hearts racing on sight, if observations from the era's writers are to be believed.

Meanwhile, it was after Tony had demolished McLarnin that his cousin Robert Canzoneri realized he was unable to go to the store in his hometown of Standing Pine, Mississippi, without clerks asking him if he was related to the famous boxer with the same last name. It was after his victory over McLarnin that the clerks started becoming envious of the fact that Robert could answer "yes" to that question.

When he and his family received an invitation to visit the farm run by his uncle George in Marlborough, New York, Robert Canzoneri himself had a hard time believing things. The invite could not have come at a more exciting time. During the time that Robert would be there, his older cousin would be preparing to defend his second lightweight belt in a rematch with Lou Ambers.

The visit to this vibrant place left an indelible impression on Robert Canzoneri, who was then about 11 and would later grow up to be an author and literature professor.

As he chronicled in his memoir *A Highly Ramified Tree*, Robert was brimming with boyish wonder when he piled into a new, wood-paneled, Ford station wagon that Tony's father George had sent down to Mississippi for the trip up north. Robert's dad, mom, sister, and two brothers joined him while Tony Schiro – one of the younger brothers of Tony Canzoneri's mother, Josephine – drove.

Robert's memoir assumes an awestruck tone as it describes the station wagon pulling up to the estate on the right-hand side of narrow, bucolic Lattintown Road. The pool in front of a low building, the majestic white summer hotel, the two-story house, the square stucco building where Tony trained, the horse barns – it was all nestled among rocky hills, orchards, and vineyards.

Then, there were the warm greetings marking the only time that the families started by George and his brother – Robert's father, who was also named Joe – gathered in their entirety.

"In some large room, they passed us down a line, hugging, kissing, crying," Robert Canzoneri wrote, describing his arrival to his family's famed resort.

Robert recalls being stunned by the beauty of Tony's new wife, Rita – "so dark and beautiful, so sleek and bold, so touched with lipstick and mascara that it would have been a sin to look directly at her if she weren't married to your cousin." Robert Canzoneri wrote that he never forgot how exciting it was for such a beautiful woman to speak to him, even if it was to tease him about being the only one who kissed her back during the greeting line.

All that Robert Canzoneri could remember from the moment was feeling mortified and how he sheepishly tried to defend his innocence, he wrote.

Robert, though, eventually got over it. And he says the following two weeks that he spent there were unlike any other in his life.

Days started at lunch time. Afternoons were for lounging in the hotel lobby, listening to the jukebox as it played tunes such as "Empty Saddles in the Old Corral," "It's a Sin to Tell a Lie" and "All the Jive Is Gone."

He recalls his aunt Josephine spending most of her time in the kitchen, using steaming pots that were as large as vats to make cheese. A seemingly "endless supply of young men, all relatives" poured the curdled cheese into woven baskets, pressed it, and tossed the resulting hoops into brined barrels. He vividly remembered how musty the curing cheese's odor and the aging wine kept in other barrels made the cellar where the goods were stored.

Dinner was at bedtime, and it was always a lengthy feast at a table for 20 in the hotel dining room. George sat at the head of the table, flanked by his family, Robert's family, suited men who had gone up there for the fight, and hotel guests, including a 3-year-old who sat so low at the table that he would cry in frustration because he couldn't get his spaghetti into his mouth.

Besides spaghetti, waiters served steaks, snails imported from Italy, fruits, nuts, and cheese – including an absolutely decadent "ricotta with a mild cherry jelly and flaky biscuits." Of course, many of the diners washed all of the offerings down with wine, but they would only do so after George raised his glass, waited for his guests to do the same, and offered cheers by saying, "Salut."

When the nights got even later, the sounds of voices and clinking glasses – as well as the smell of liquor – would trickle out from the hotel bar just off the lobby, which resembled a dark cave.

Robert wouldn't dare to venture there. He wrote that he had good reason to be wary of getting too close to the men.

At one point during the visit, when Josephine didn't have anyone close by who could help her store her latest batch of curdled cheese, she sent Robert to get her oldest son, Joe. Robert found Joe arguing with George in Sicilian, at a time when any intra-family tensions that existed could only have been exacerbated by the pressure surrounding Tony's upcoming title defense against Ambers.

Robert didn't understand what the argument was about. But he wanted to do what his aunt asked him and get her some help. So during a pause he spoke up and said to Joe: "Aunt Josephine wants you to come help in the kitchen." A seething Joe shot back, "Go get somebody else. Can't you see we're talking business?" Robert[6], chastened and embarrassed, slunk away.

A Highly Ramified Tree notes that neither Robert nor anyone else on the grounds used the much-loved pool. That's because the polio epidemic was sweeping through the country in those days, and health officials had ordered swimming pools closed in an effort to limit the spread of the illness, which typically occurred in the summer.

But Robert and other guests still found ways to pass the time, including by visiting the barns and riding the saddle horses, he recalled. They would sit in and pretend to drive an unused, Duesenberg limousine that someone who lost everything during the 1929 stock market crash had given to George because that person owed him money yet didn't have anything else besides the vehicle. They would get treats from an ice cream truck with nickels handed to them by Tony's longtime trainer, Izzy the Painter.

They took walks up the hills and into the orchards. They ran around the vineyards and took their younger cousins hunting for "snipe" – the nonexistent, made-up bird which parents desperate for a moment of quiet would send their kids after.

Guests went to the butcher shop run by one of Tony's brothers, Cyrus, who offered two kinds of sausage – one for American customers and another, cooked with red pepper and therefore much spicier, for Italians.

---

6   Robert writes that he again saw Joe 35 years later, while he tended bar at a bowling alley. Heart attacks had mellowed him out, and an otherwise genial personality made him so well-liked that business had tripled at the bowling alley after he started working there.

Robert Canzoneri at one point even visited the farm which George bought for the Schiros and which offered a view of the fabled Catskill Mountains. Robert Canzoneri marveled at how the low farmhouse and barn, held up by thick, hand-hewn beams, seemed older than a chapel in Clinton, Mississippi – near Standing Pine – that survived the Civil War.

Near the barn they scoped out a Revolutionary War-era fort that loomed over the Hudson River, across from a train worming its way along some railroad tracks.

As gorgeous as all that was to Robert Canzoneri, the star attraction there – of course – was Tony, along with everything that surrounded him.

Robert Canzoneri remembered he was in the main house one afternoon when Tony came over with Rita. She was complaining about how Tony would read newspaper stories aloud to entertain Izzy.

"I've done it for years," Tony told her. "You'll get used to it."

Then later, in the building where his cousin trained, Robert watched as Tony prepared himself to battle Ambers again.

"He would jump rope so fast [that] the rope was a blur, switching hands, crossing his feet, talking and laughing all the while with the people sitting in folding chairs a safe distance back from the ring," Robert wrote in *A Highly Ramified Tree*.

"He was trim, fast, good-natured; he had a wide spontaneous smile. One of his sparring partners was a redhead who'd begin to flush after a few minutes of being tapped in the face by Tony's gloves; suddenly he'd quit sparring and start to move in for the kill, only to land on his back in the same instant," Robert continued. "We believed that we couldn't even see Tony's hands move from where they were cocked low at his sides."

No matter how impressed Tony's first cousin was with his athleticism and hand speed, the reporters at the training camp were a tougher crowd. Reports persisted that Canzoneri would retire after facing Ambers a second time, but Tony countered with a bunch of reasons that he said he had to stay in the game.

"I feel that I have just about reached the peak of my career right now, and any talk that I am going to retire is a lot of wahoo," Tony told a reporter for the New Jersey-based Italian newspaper Il Messaggero. "Maybe that Ambers fellow wishes I would retire before we have our shindig."

Not only did Tony predict he would dispatch Ambers soon enough – he also dared to look ahead to a rematch with Jimmy McLarnin, whom he had beaten a few months earlier.

"I can gather the little Mick wants another crack at me," Tony said, invoking a slur for Irish people. "Well, Jimmy can have that little thing, but the result will be the same as it was in our last fuss."

For all the colorful scenes populating daily life at the Canzoneri farm, the place emptied on the day Tony put his lightweight title on the line against Ambers. The men accompanied Tony to Madison Square Garden to watch him defend the championship, nervous but confident that he would still be the world champion at the end of the night.

Robert stayed back with his mom, his sister, his younger brother and Tony's mom. They listened to the bout on the radio.

The book recalls how annoyed Robert was that the announcer repeatedly narrated how it seemed Tony was becoming tired.

"He kept saying ... that he couldn't keep his guard up, when everyone knew that was his fighting style," Robert Canzoneri wrote.

But the annoyance turned to fear when Robert heard the announcer mention a cut near Tony's eye and blood pouring down his face. Josephine pressed her hand against her own face, "giving little cries of pain," as Robert put it in his memoir.

The New York Times described a close fight, with Canzoneri in control at first but then losing ground to an Ambers who was swinging "from all angles." To make matters worse, the officials took a round away from Canzoneri because of a punch on Ambers that illegally came in below the belt line.

Avoiding the penalty may not have done much to help Tony keep his grip on the crown. In the end, the referee and two judges rewarded Ambers with a lopsided, unanimous decision victory, determining that he won 12, 10 and nine rounds on the scorecards they respectively kept for the 15-round fight.

The Canzoneri men were outraged when they returned to the farm, Robert recalled. "Tony really didn't lose," they assured. "He didn't look as though he had lost. The small cut on his face had no relationship to its bloody description on the radio. He was in good spirits, laughing and joking."

In fact, those men said, Ambers was so sure he had lost that he had squeezed himself through the ropes and was halfway out of the ring, heading for the dressing room, when the referee had to pull him back so that he could hold his hand up and present him to the crowd as the winner.

Ambers's victory was "to his obvious amazement," as the Canzoneri men put it after the fight, according to what Robert wrote.

Josephine accepted the defeat more calmly. When she heard the bell signaling the end of the 15th and last round, she finally appeared to be at peace again.

"She seemed to care only that the fight was over," Robert wrote, "not that Ambers was announced the winner and new champion."

Tony, too, took the setback in stride. He told reporters the defeat could be a blessing in disguise, the painful motivation that he needed to help him get as close to in-ring perfection as humanly possible.

There was no time to waste. Up next was a rematch against McLarnin. Up next was his latest shot at redemption, and he rushed back to the farm in Marlboro to sharpen himself for the opportunity.

But the McLarnin awaiting him at Madison Square Garden was not the same one whom Tony had pushed around in May. And, though it hadn't really been all that long since he beat McLarin, the Canzoneri who took the ring for that rematch – and other bouts afterward – was suddenly and brutally not quite the same either.

CHAPTER TEN

"PUT UP THE GLOVES"

—

Certainly, Tony Canzoneri had lost against the best before. He had withstood physical punishment, and sometimes he'd been dominated on the scorecards.

But even against the most skilled opponents that boxing had to offer, Tony looked like he belonged. And he just didn't look like he belonged in the same ring as Jimmy McLarnin in their rematch, and without much time for them to get used to the idea, those closest to him had to start worrying.

As the end of his second bout with McLarnin neared, Tony's nose had been gashed. A split lip he suffered while sparring in preparation for the fight had been bloodied, too. And the sight sickened more than 11,000 spectators at Madison Square Garden, many of whom pleaded for referee Billy Cavanaugh to stop the contest early and shield Tony from getting hurt or embarrassed even more.

Cavanaugh didn't do it. Canzoneri to then had never been knocked out of a fight, and Cavanaugh gave the ousted champion the chance to stay in there for the full 10-round distance which had been allotted. Tony indeed hung in there, but he never threatened to win the fight. All that he had with which to console himself was the ability to once again say he was still standing when another bout had gone the full duration.

He would not, however, be able to say he won or had even really come close to doing so. Along with Cavanaugh, judges Charley Lynch and Abe Goldberg had unanimously awarded McLarnin the victory, letting him even his score with Tony.

There was no denying it or point in even trying to hide it. It had been an inauspicious return to the ring for Tony since he had married Rita Goldberg, the Broadway showgirl who was 10 years younger than him. The defeat to McLarnin was his second straight after he lost his rematch against Ambers, which had not only cost him the lightweight championship of the world but had also snapped what had been a 14-match winning streak.

According to the May 1983 issue of Boxing Illustrated, Tony's performance against McLarnin was so moribund that a newspaper writer with whom the losing fighter was friends approached him and suggested to him that he hang up his gloves. He had to get real with himself after dropping two in a row against elite fighters as he was closer than ever to getting on the wrong side of the age of 30.

If he lined up a fight against another top talent, "I will put the blast on you," the writer purportedly told Canzoneri. "I will say that you haven't got sense enough to quit while you still have your health, your marbles and your money.

"The boxing commission should make you quit."

Tony replied: "I wish you wouldn't." He added that he had plans to take another shot at getting his lightweight belt back from Ambers.

"Well, I will [blast you]," the newspaperman firmly said. "By the way, what's the matter with Goldman?"

"Nothing," Canzoneri shot back, puzzled. "Why?"

"Does he want you to fight again?" the reporter inquired. Canzoneri had money, a restaurant, the farm and the resort on the property, and he was still as healthy as a prizefighter who was as active as he had been could hope to be. Did Goldman want Tony to fight until, as Boxing Illustrated put it, he was walking on his heels and hearing funny noises? What good would Tony's earnings serve him at that point?

No, Goldman didn't want any of that, Canzoneri confessed. "He wants me to quit, too," after both Ambers and McLarnin had outclassed him, Tony said.

"All right," the newspaper writer said, before Tony walked away from the conversation. "I promise that if you make the [Ambers] match, I'll blast the hell out of you."

According to the Boxing Illustrated piece, the writer followed through on his threat when Canzoneri went ahead and signed up for a rematch with Ambers, his third contest against the Hermiker Hurricane.

The piece supposedly went ignored, though Goldman later met the scribe and told him: "You're right. But there is nothing you or I can do about it."

"What does he want to fight for?" the writer asked Goldman. Goldman's reply: "Money."

The reporter didn't understand. What about the restaurant, the farm and resort, as well as all the previous purses?

Do you know "who eats in his restaurant?" Goldman rhetorically asked the journalist. "His friends, whose checks he picks up. What does he raise on his farm? Fruits and vegetables. Who eats them? Friends and relatives. Who stays at his summer hotel? Friends who don't pay."

Goldman revealed that Canzoneri had also taken to betting on horses but wasn't particularly adept at it. And "as soon as they hear he has a bet on them, [those horses] get tired. I don't care what he tries – he can get rid of money faster than anybody I ever saw. And how can he make money? Only by fighting. I hope this Ambers fight will be his last. But I don't know. I can't promise you."

Goldman had just one favor to ask of the writer before he left. "What?" asked the newspaper writer, who was seemingly amenable to granting the favor.

"Don't knock him again," Goldman said. "He knows you're right, but he can't help himself."

* * *

Having dropped two in a row to Ambers and McLarnin, Tony stopped his reputation's bleeding in the slightest way with three consecutive wins in tune-up exhibitions in April of 1937. Two of the wins were knockouts, showing perhaps that Canzoneri still packed a punch. Yet the following month, in the rubber match against Ambers, Canzoneri lost again – badly.

One judge ruled that Tony didn't win a single of the 15 rounds for which the bout was scheduled. Meanwhile, he won just two rounds on the scorecards turned in by the other judge as well as the referee.

Ambers had handed Canzoneri a shellacking that was like few – if any – he had endured as of then. It was his third defeat in the 11 months since his marriage, and he would never again fight for a world championship. The anemic performance brought out his detractors in the fullest of force.

"Tony ... was pulverized almost beyond recognition," New Orleans States sports columnist Harry Martinez recalled. No one thought "he would ever put the gloves on again," he added.

Canzoneri took the next 17 months off during what many assumed was the start of his retirement. But, Martinez wrote at the time, "Boxing is one game where a fellow never knows he is through. They all come back for that one last shot at the big money."

Canzoneri fantasized about squaring off with the Ring magazine's 1937 Fighter of the Year: Henry Armstrong[1], who won world championships at featherweight, lightweight and welterweight, and he made history by holding the three titles at the same time. Once again, Canzoneri thought, he would stage a comeback and make an absolute killing in the process at the expense of a living legend.

Goldman tried his best to discourage Tony given the beating he'd suffered at the hands of Ambers. Sammy reminded him that he had a wife. The manager told his fighter to worry instead about starting a family with Rita as well as kicking his feet up by the pool and relaxing at the farm in New York.

But Canzoneri made it clear that he intended to gun for Armstrong, with or without Goldman. And Goldman relented.

"I wouldn't let anyone else touch him," Goldman once told his son, Alfred. Alfred said that his father caved to Canzoneri because "he loved Tony and wanted to protect him."

On the first stop of that latest comeback tour, on October 17, 1938, Canzoneri showed why challenging "Homicide Hank" Armstrong was not a plan rooted in reality. It could hardly be called anything except the wildest of fantasies.

That day, Canzoneri lost on points to a fighter he had previously beaten by knockout: Eddie Zivic. Zivic came into their 10-round bout in Scranton, Pennsylvania, having lost his previous nine matches in a row. And Martinez, along with other pundits across boxing's landscape, were merciless after Canzoneri dropped the decision to him.

"Canzoneri ... is through as a fighter," Martinez said. He added that

---

1   At least at one point, Armstrong, Tony Canzoneri and Barney Ross were the only ones to hold two or more world titles simultaneously.

Goldman again pleaded with Canzoneri to quit, trying to do what is hardest for boxing managers, which is saving their fighters from their own selves.

But fight card promoters were in Tony's ear telling him he could still bring out a crowd and that there was money to be made from that for everyone involved. Yet such flattery was all just a polite way for the promoters to say that they thought they could still squeeze a few more dollars – if nothing else, a few more cents – out of Tony Canzoneri.

Tony's fight schedule at that phase of his career did nothing to contradict that notion. He fought 22 times in a one-year, six-day period that started a week after Zivic humiliated him.

He won 16 of those fights against a slate of veritable also-rans, including a rematch against Zivic that no one could have imagined that Tony wanted or really needed. The Associated Press greeted the occasion by noting that Canzoneri weighed in a flabby 141 pounds, too heavy for junior welterweight but too light to compete credibly at welterweight.

The wire service reported that Canzoneri couldn't avoid being cut under his left eye in the Zivic rematch. And the headline for the recap that the AP published was as unflattering as they wrote them: "Canzoneri, Fat and Thirty, Triumphs Over Eddie Zivic."

If Canzoneri thought getting even with Zivic would fool anyone, it didn't. There was a five-match stretch between late March and early June of 1939 in which he failed to win a single time, losing three decisions and drawing twice. One of the ties came at the end of what proved to be his last fight in New Orleans – in front of 7,000 fans at the Municipal Auditorium against local lightweight prospect Nick Camarata in the middle of May.

The business numbers were relatively decent. Tony made just under $2,000, and he also had his expenses – totaling about $500 – covered. But a photo in the New Orleans Item newspaper showed him take the ring with a loose belly and arms that had absolutely no muscle definition.

Nowhere to be found was the thoroughbred-like body "with shoulders you wouldn't believe" that local journalist Ronnie Virgets's father saw on Canzoneri when he beat Battling Shaw for his second lineal junior welterweight championship the previous time he had been to New Orleans. Nowhere in sight was the trim, speedy physical frame that

Robert Canzoneri remembered his cousin had when he was preparing to defend his second lightweight world championship in his rematch against Lou Ambers.

For spectators, the only thing less impressive than Canzoneri's physical shape was his performance against Camarata. Camarata's punches against Canzoneri kept coming in short, and the former world champion was the bout's aggressor and landed blows more consistently, as would be expected given his pedigree. But Canzoneri fought well only in spurts, and every time it seemed Camarata could be in trouble, Tony would ease up his attack by either dropping his guard or resting on his heels.

Adding to spectators' frustration was that there were moments where it was obvious Canzoneri was moving in for the knockout victory, "but the legs and arms wouldn't respond" for him to finish the job, as the New Orleans Item put it.

"The speed and stamina are gone," Item scribe Fred Digby wrote. "Only the spirit remains," at least in fleeting moments.

When the fight ended, the officials could not bring themselves to give Canzoneri the victory. Two judges ruled the bout a draw, ensuring that Camarata and Canzoneri each left their encounter with a tie on their records. The name of one of those two judges immediately jumped off the page of the evening's recap that the New Orleans Item published: Jack Galway, Tony's first boxing coach!

As for the referee, Ray Dolan, he thought Camarata had won, and his scorecard reflected as much.

"Tony should put up the gloves and retire," Digby wrote in the Item, adding that as far as he saw it, Canzoneri only avoided defeat because of a late rally that cut into Camarata's early lead on the scorecards.

Dolan's assessment of Canzoneri was even more biting in an interview that he gave to the Associated Press. The referee said that he believed Canzoneri should "retire before he goes blind" from being hit so hard and so often[2].

If Canzoneri decided he wouldn't be honest with himself and quit, Dolan added, "he'll be back on his heels." Someone who overheard

---

2   It's unclear if this was a reference to former Goldman client and ex-world bantamweight champion Pete Herman, who had reportedly started going blind years earlier following an injury in the ring.

Dolan's comment reportedly shouted at him that Canzoneri was "back on his heels now."

"I know it," Dolan replied, according to the AP. "But he'll be away back further."

Canzoneri's dressing room offered him no respite. A reporter approached Goldman while Canzoneri was nearby and asked the manager if he wanted his boxer to keep fighting. Goldman didn't hold back in his answer just because Tony could hear him.

"Well, no I don't, honestly," Goldman said. "Fighting is all right for a young man who keeps on a diet and trains. Tony doesn't keep on a diet. And he doesn't train much."

Tony Canzoneri waited quietly nearby for his manager to finish. Then, he said: "Me, I'd like to come back if the folks will have me."

No one knows how long Tony thought he might be able to stomach that lifestyle and its increasingly dire results. But, as Boxing Illustrated noted, there was really no way for him to avoid the reality that, more and more, he was "fighting in the small clubs, fighting nobodies" – and fighting badly.

* * *

Nothing, though, had been as bad for Tony Canzoneri as it got on All Saints Day 1939.

He was served up at Madison Square Garden that day as a test to an undefeated, 33-win fighter named Al "Bummy" Davis. Davis's punching power had made a splash in boxing circles, and the sport's shot callers were bringing him along and developing him as if he could be a star in the making.

"They were looking for a name to put on his record," Boxing Illustrated wrote of Davis. "So they matched him with Canzoneri."

Canzoneri did not arrive to face Davis in much better shape than what he was in when he drew against Nick Camarata. Most in the crowd who got a look at Tony saw "a puffy, fatigued figure ... [who] was a pathetic caricature of the lightning fast little pugilist who could turn on blasts of slugging fury with the same facility with which he could adopt a style of classic cleverness," as the March 1961 issue of Ring magazine later so floridly put it.

Nonetheless, there was no hint during the night's first two rounds that anything significant was brewing for Davis or Canzoneri on what was the 28th time Tony was fighting at the Garden. Eleven years older than his opponent, the 30-year-old Canzoneri relied on left jabs to Davis's jaw to dominate the scoring in the opening stanza. The second round saw him land two rights on Davis's jaw that wobbled the young contender's legs and for a moment had fans thinking that Tony Canzoneri may have at least one final vintage performance still left in him.

After all, "at his peak, Tony Canzoneri had everything," the Ring magazine would remark later. "He could pinpoint a straight right with atomic power and precision. His round countenance surfaced a steel chin. He was quick as a cat with hands and feet. He responded to pressure with more pressure. He was unique, in that he carried his left hand very low, but nonetheless [he] was a difficult target when he wanted to show his defensive skill."

But that idea – that hope, which was really more of a prayer, really – died in its infancy.

In the third round, Canzoneri inadvertently stepped into a left hook from Davis that floored Tony. Nearly 12,800 disbelieving sets of eyes watched as Canzoneri fell to the canvas. Many were unsure of what to even do.

Canzoneri could more than relate to the confusion that the fans were feeling. He got back on his feet at the count of four – about half of the time that he probably should have taken from the referee. But, if anything could drive home how unfamiliar what he was experiencing was to him, it was how quickly he got up from that knockdown.

When the bout resumed, Davis charged forward with something in his eyes that no boxer wants to see coming at him: fearlessness. Canzoneri had not recovered from the left hook that brought him down. He was still dazed, and he instinctively retreated until his back pressed against the ring's ropes. Then, just for an instant, he lowered his right hand.

It was the slightest of openings, but that's all Davis needed. He unleashed two bone-rattling lefts to Canzoneri's jaw that slipped through the former champion's guard unabated. Canzoneri slumped down to the canvas once more. He was sprawled out, nearly motionless, for several seconds. He managed to get up to his knees as the referee neared the count of six. And then Tony lumbered his way back to as upright a position as he could manage.

The fighter that referee Arthur Donovan[3] was gazing at right then was not one who could continue fighting. At two minutes and 13 seconds of the third round, Donovan ended the fight by declaring that Tony Canzoneri – for the first time ever – had been knocked out of a bout and could not continue.

The scene – what Davis had pulled off – did not bring the spectators in the Garden any pleasure. Hardly anyone cheered. They simply sat quietly, according to reports from the arena. They were still quiet when it was time to go, and they filed out to the streets of Manhattan in stunned silence.

Reportedly, few – if any – of those who were close to Tony had gone to the stadium that night. "Tony's friends stayed away from that one," as Boxing Illustrated put it in its May 1983 issue. "They knew what would happen and they didn't want to see it."

The only place quieter than the arena was Canzoneri's dressing room. None of the supporters or journalists who had gone there and surrounded Canzoneri dared to speak. Instead, they waited to hear what he would say.

Canzoneri, unsurprisingly, would come to consider his battering at the hands of Davis his worst defeat ever as a prizefighter. He could argue it was the only one that ended without him having at least the chance of winning. It was even worse than the decision loss all those years earlier to Harry Blitman, whom Canzoneri faced despite having the flu, only to come out from the other side of the bout with cracked ribs and pneumonia.

But against Davis, Tony had no flu excuse. He had simply gotten old. And, quite frankly, he had gotten his ass kicked. The "certain cocksureness" – as Ring magazine called it – with which Tony carried himself even when he was about to collide with some of his profession's biggest names was a memory as distant as the stars in the New York night sky outside the arena.

When Tony finally brought himself to speak in the dressing room, it was a mumble.

---

3   Donovan's son would not only go on to fight in the second world war, but he also played defensive tackle for the Baltimore Colts, helping them win two National Football League championships in 1958 and 1959. He earned induction into the Pro Football Hall of Fame in 1968.

"Well, it had to come sometime," he said, his lip cut and his right eye badly gnarled.

Did he have any plans about where to go from here? No, not yet, he said.

Was this it? Was this the last time that he would fight?

Tony stayed quiet for a few moments. Finally, he let out a deep sigh and uttered, "Gosh, I hope so."

This time, unlike all of the other times, there would be no comeback. There would not even be an attempt at one.

"Funny about things like that," read Boxing Illustrated's summation of the night. "Davis, by belting [Canzoneri] out, did more for him than all his friends put together, for Tony never fought again."

* * *

Among the many things Goldman was right about in his career was the purported guesses he would make about why Tony stuck with prize-fighting for as long as he did. For there eventually came a point in Tony's life where he never again had it as good out of the ring as he did when he was in it.

The fame which Canzoneri earned with each favorable decision and knockout victory paved his way to all kinds of opportunities that most Great Depression-era Americans could only dream about. He could pursue those opportunities while much of the rest of the globe dealt with the lead-up to and the aftermath of the second world war – and while his country geared up to wage the conflict in Korea in the 1950s.

But, it turned out, he just couldn't find a way to make many of those chances last or recur.

According to reports, *They Should Have Stayed in Bed*, the Broadway comedy in which he was cast just three years after turning in his walking papers from the ring, lasted on the stage less than two weeks. Making matters worse, his various television or movie appearances never translated into steady entertainment gigs.

Meanwhile, even some of his most faithful followers looked at opportunities like his role as the on-stage sidekick to comedian Joey Adams at a club in Midtown Manhattan with pity, something that was below a sportsman who had scaled the heights that he once had.

A 1993 article by Aaron Rose in the American Citizen, a New York newspaper, suggested Canzoneri only got that job because Adams was apparently the brother of Canzoneri's wife, Rita.

Adams would go on to publicly say that Tony "floored [the crowd] with jokes instead of fists" during their time working together. But, Rose said, for the 10 years that Canzoneri had the gig with Adams, the comedian humiliated him.

"Joey Adams smacked Tony during the act in order to elicit a few laughs from the audience," Rose wrote. The writer could say that with authority because he saw it himself on television on the variety show hosted by Ed Sullivan. "I ... winced each time Tony was slapped," Rose wrote. "It seemed inconceivable that a five-time champion was compelled to sink to this level for the purpose of earning a living."

The July 1982 issue of the Ring magazine contained observations that were similar to Rose, saying it was too kind to Canzoneri to say he was ever truly a partner to Adams. As the publication put it, "The truth is that Canzoneri was just a stereotyped punchdrunk fighter for Adams to slap and use as a stooge."

The sight of Adams slapping Canzoneri – by all accounts, without ever pulling the strikes back – was too much for some of the former world champion's most fervent supporters to bear, the Ring magazine reported in a separate March 1961 write-up.

"His one-time worshippers found [it] so distasteful," the magazine added, "[that] their threats caused its discontinuance." The publication didn't elaborate.

Canzoneri, of course, made some passive income through the liquor store in which he had invested by then as well as the bar and grill to which he licensed his name. And for a long time he had his family's resort, which provided a lifetime of memories for so many of its guests and his loved ones.

For a while, that was enough to project an outward image of someone who was thriving. He moved Rita, himself, their daughter, and his in-laws into a sprawling, six-room apartment in Manhattan's Upper West Side.

He treated his brother Jasper to a wedding extravagant enough to attract some truly larger than life guests when his sibling married Dotty, the mother of Tony Canzoneri's niece Deborah Burns.

One of those guests was a dog who acted in movies and otherwise performed tricks. Jasper's best man was one Giovanni Morale – better known as Johnny Burns[4] and frequently at the same side of Joe Bonanno, the famed mobster and Canzoneri family pal.

But, with the passage of time, Tony's name meant less and less to the general public. Regulars at the country club gradually thinned out. It was hardly noticeable at first, but eventually, it was impossible to ignore the plummeting number of reservations. Guests that did book stays began making them for just two weeks, then only one, instead of the entire summer, as had once been normal.

George Canzoneri tried to recoup some of the lost earnings by selling off what he could of the acreage surrounding the resort, sensing "the years were washing over the hotel like water eroding rock," as Burns poignantly phrased it in her memoir, *Saturday's Child*. There were too few guests left, old or new, to earn even half of what the hotel customarily made.

Emotional blows also accompanied the slow unraveling of Tony's economic fortunes. His father George Canzoneri died in 1946. His mother died seven years later. If losing the parents for whom he did so much might have sparked a desire for him to reconnect with Jack Galway, his first boxing coach whom he once asked to essentially become his guardian so Tony could grow up in New Orleans after his family had decided to move to New York, it was too late. That is because Galway had died in 1948.

Tony and his three brothers by then all had families leading very "different, expensive lives" that left them little time to focus on turning a profit at the farm which had meant the world to their parents. They also took on and shared the responsibility of caring for their two sisters, who never married and at one point lived with Jasper and Dotty, too, according to Burns.

Eventually, Burns's mother, who kept the resort's fiscal books in order during the dusk of its existence, forced what was left of the Canzoneri clan to sit down together and grapple with the fact that the only way forward most likely involved selling the perennially deteriorating resort.

They heard Dotty out and agreed with her. Ultimately, the Canzoneris sold off their country club to a family which was committed to running the property that once billed itself as the champion resort in

---

4 Johnny Burns is no relation to Debbie's husband, Bob Burns.

the most dignified manner that they could, Burns said.

Burns said she formed countless childhood memories at that reincarnated resort, leaving the city and going there for the summer almost immediately after each school year let out. But, to a generation of Canzoneris and some of their lifelong friends, selling off the country club marked the end of an era.

Elsewhere, whether or not you believe in this sort of thing, Tony's return to the ring after marrying Rita was as bad as omens get. He lost three times in less than a year after his wedding – and then he suffered a fourth defeat after an extended layoff that some later came to interpret as a trial retirement.

Indeed, as Rose put it in his 1993 American Citizen article, Tony's marriage to Rita was "not a successful union."

Though she was one of the key people in Tony's corner at the time that he was trying to figure out what to do with his post-retirement life, Rita once confided in Burns's mother that every project he had going on was "small potatoes." Her husband may have been done with his career, but she wasn't done with hers, and she long yearned to move to the West Coast to try her hand at acting on the movie screen as well as on television.

Denise Canzoneri, who was born in 1938, the penultimate year of her father's boxing career, doesn't remember her parents bickering with each other all that often. "My father may have punched everybody in the ring but to every other person he was as gentle and kind and loving as he could be," Denise recalled once.

Yet, speaking with sadness in her voice, she said it became obvious that everything was far from perfect when her dad asked to speak with her one day in about 1954, when she was 16. He told her, nervously and glumly, that he and Rita were getting a divorce.

Denise had hardly been able to process the news before Rita packed up, headed for Los Angeles, and left her daughter to finish growing up with her maternal grandmother in the apartment on the Upper West Side.

Burns recalls Tony refused to live with his former mother-in-law, so he moved in with Jasper[5] and Dotty at their place in Queens, staying in

---

5   According to Burns, Dotty's first date with her father Jasper – Tony's brother – was at Tony and Rita's sprawling, six-room apartment in the Upper West Side. Tony and Rita's daughter Denise was 10 then, dark-haired, almond-eyed, tentative. It seemed Denise

a bedroom that he later surrendered to Burns when she was born.

Soon after his split from Rita became public, Canzoneri tried to cheer himself up by accepting "the attentions of a very pretty and affectionate" brunette, according to a report on the 14th page of the New Orleans States newspaper on February 21, 1953.

He would also occasionally take out Dotty as his date, particularly when Jasper worked as a maître d' at various clubs that Tony became involved in or where he was still considered a big deal.

Newspapers which dedicated some of their column inches to rumors about celebrities couldn't pass up the chance to report that Tony was out and about in the town while accompanied by this pretty redhead who, it turned out, was his sister-in-law.

Despite the scandal that the celebrity rags tried to stir up, Burns said she is certain Dotty and Tony kept things platonic. It really just came down to Jasper never attaining the fame that Tony did despite his having some musical talent. And Jasper also made ends meet primarily by working nights.

Nights were when Tony, eager to keep his mind off Rita, went out to the kinds of lively night spots that famous boxing champs could access – which were also places that Dotty loved being at if only someone could take her.

So Dotty would tag along with Tony because he was just glad to have the company, and she was glad he could get her into places she was interested in being. And she was also glad to be out while in the company of someone who would keep her safe without having any expectations – including expectations of sex – because they both loved Jasper, Burns said.

"There was a fondness and a safeness between the two of them, and they both had a mutually beneficial [arrangement of], 'Hey, we're going out, and we can do it safely because we're both together,'" Deborah Burns[6] explained.

---

would revel at whatever attention her ambitious, aspiring actress mom gave her, but it wasn't much, and Denise appeared to be closer to her already famous dad.

6   Burns's book does mention that Dotty at one point had an extramarital affair with another man outside the family, but her and Jasper's marriage survived the infidelity.

The outings with Tony were also a way for Dotty to mend her own broken heart, though hers was for a different reason. At the time, she was grieving the loss of a son that she was expecting with Jasper. The miscarriage was later on – about six months – in Dotty's pregnancy. "We were going to name [him] George after your grandfather," Burns recalls her mother once telling her, making it clear that she was still grieving the lost baby after all those years.

While Tony had people who could help him take his mind off his failed marriage, Denise for much of her life did not.

Burns always recalled how her cousin Denise seemed to have an eternal "wound, an emotional frailty," at least in part because of her parents' divorce. There were unfulfilled aspirations of hitting it big as an actress and dancer like her mother had dreamed for herself. Denise would later say that all stemmed from a desire for approval from her mother after Rita left Denise with Denise's grandmother as Rita headed out west to California, where it later became clear that she found some professional success.

Denise said she and her mother did not have the same kinds of fond memories that Denise had created with Tony. She did not speak of any magical moments where they got dressed up to go out to lunch at packed places whose lines they could simply skip. There were no long nights out at the movies or at dance clubs together.

Burns recalls the pain between her cousin and aunt was all laid bare one time when Burns – then nearly 17 – met Rita.

Denise and Rita shared a meal with Dotty and Burns that day. Denise was about 36 at the time, and in front of her aunt and cousin she told Rita during the meal: "I could have gone to college ... if you hadn't pushed me into being an actress."

Rita told Denise to not say such things in front of those who were in their company that day, adding: "You're a grown woman. You're embarrassing yourself."

"You mean I'm embarrassing you!" Denise shot back, as Burns recounted in her *Saturday's Child* memoir.

Denise eventually accused Rita of leaving her with nothing. "It's all your fault – all of it!" Burns recalled Denise saying.

"That is your own fault," Rita countered. "Stop blaming me."

When Dotty tried to stick up for Rita by drawing some similarities between them, Denise sarcastically assured Dotty, "You're nothing like her."

Then, glaring at Rita, Denise scoffed, "You don't know how to be a mother at all," according to Burns's recollection.

"If I don't know how to be a mother," Burns recalled Rita saying, "you sure as hell don't know how to be a daughter."

Before the quarrel ended, Denise challenged Rita to admit that Rita never loved her daughter, according to Burns. In turn, Rita said, "You wonder why I don't come to see you? This is why."

Yet, as painful as that episode must have been to everyone there, that wasn't the sharpest blow that life dealt Denise. The deepest wound that life inflicted on Denise involved her dad, who to the rest of the world was the five-time champion boxer who reigned at that most famous of arenas, Madison Square Garden.

However, to Denise, the great Tony Canzoneri was just dad. And, in her 20s, her dad died – alone and without any warning for his loved ones.

Denise, Tony's last closest living relative, would never forget how her father's death almost robbed her of her will to live.

CHAPTER ELEVEN

"ONE OF BROADWAY'S BRIGHTEST LIGHTS ... BURNED OUT"

———

The night of January 23, 1959, in Shreveport, Louisiana, was perhaps one of the last times in Tony Canzoneri's life that he got to feel like a VIP again. The Louisiana Sports Hall of Fame was inducting Canzoneri – a member of the Ring magazine's hall of fame since 1956 – as one of just three members in its inaugural class.

Canzoneri's fellow guests at the ceremony being hosted by a local country club were as distinguished as Louisiana sports history could offer. Mel Ott, who was born in the New Orleans suburb of Gretna and helped the New York Giants win the 1933 World Series, was another inductee. Rounding out the class was the Louisiana State University football program's first unanimous All-America selection, Gaynell Tinsley.

For a long time before that night, Canzoneri didn't think he would be able to get away from his business in New York and make it down to the event. His fellow New Orleans-raised world boxing champion Pete Herman, who had just narrowly missed out on getting inducted himself, had accepted an invitation to collect the Hall of Fame plaque on Tony's behalf. But the more Canzoneri thought about it, the more he wanted to be there. So he made arrangements to be able to make it.

Tony's first cousin Robert Canzoneri from the neighboring state of Mississippi was there too, according to his memoir, *A Highly Ramified Tree*.

"He still had the wide smile, and although he was overweight, he still moved so lightly that it seemed his feet didn't quite touch the floor," Robert Canzoneri recalled of seeing his famous first cousin again.

162

Men accompanying Tony handled everything for him. One of them introduced himself as a member of one of New Orleans' richest families, according to Robert, who – along with the author's father – got a fleeting moment with Tony, the man of the hour.

Robert Canzoneri never forgot how taken he was by Tony's ex-wife's beauty, so he asked about her. Tony replied that Rita had remarried after leaving him and departing New York for Hollywood. "She's happy," he added. "And so I'm happy."

Robert noted how Tony's polite smile as he relayed the news seemed strained and that he only held it briefly. He also broke eye contact and shifted his gaze to the side after saying he was content that Rita was happy without him. Tony kindly excused himself from the conversation after that. After all, he had to get in front of the gathering, accept his induction plaque and warm the crowd up with a joke – one about carrying a grandfather clock to the shop while a drunk asked him if he was doing that because he couldn't afford a watch.

The night had to have been a nice change of pace for Tony. In those days, he was living in a room at the Hotel Bryant, which was on the corner of Broadway and 54th Street. It was just three blocks from the bar near Times Square that for years paid him to carry his name.

People who found themselves close enough to get to the bar couldn't resist their curiosity in seeing how Tony was getting along all those years after he had stashed away the boxing gloves and other tools of his profession. They had to look as closely as they could to detect signs of the man who had once won five world boxing championships.

One of Tony's fiercest rivals, Jack "Kid" Berg, was one of the visitors to Tony's namesake bar a few years before his hall of fame induction in Shreveport. "He had a big board outside, and a picture of the people he fought and won and lost" against, Berg recalled.

In a 1986 interview with author John Harding, Berg said it was hard to see Canzoneri so obviously beyond his prime. He got the impression that Tony was financially broke or close to it. Berg, who had often fought in New York City, also couldn't help but notice that at least some of the bar's patrons that day were men whom he knew to be gangsters.

Tony and Berg bantered about their trilogy of fights before they parted ways, according to Kid. Berg told Canzoneri that he had won the first of their fights, fairly lost the second one and asserted that he should've won the third. Canzoneri didn't argue with that opinion.

Berg said he brought up how Canzoneri fouled him with at least one low blow in the final chapter of their rivalry. According to Berg, Canzoneri purportedly brushed off that comment by cheekily remarking: "Where [else] could I hit you to win the fight?"

Though Canzoneri seemed engaged once the visit started, at the very beginning of the conversation, it seemed to Berg that Tony was bewildered, confused and as if he needed a moment before realizing exactly who this unannounced visitor of his was. "He had a lot of fights, took a lot of punishment," Berg said in reference to that moment.

Another person who paid a visit to Tony at his bar and grill was a writer for the National Police Gazette in 1955. The scribe recounted that he was sitting at one of the establishment's tables contemplating how the Bummy Davis who rocked Canzoneri into retirement would've been no match for any of the championship versions of Tony when Tony himself strode up to the writer that day.

"Hiyah, kid – how's tricks?" was Tony's greeting, as the writer recalled. The writer replied: "Tricks are pretty good. How is it with you? How's the ... restaurant?"

Tony said he was optimistic that the establishment would do well so close to the Broadway theaters before the writer set him up to do the Edward G. Robinson impression that many by then had known Canzoneri for.

"You look more like Edward G. Robinson nowadays than Robinson himself," said the writer.

"Oh yeah? Think you're a wise guy, eh?" Tony shot back, sounding and looking just like the movie mobster.

The writer shifted the conversation to boxing with a compliment – "you were one of the greatest fighters, pound for pound, I ever saw" – and a question: "Tell me, what was your toughest fight, the one that stands out in your memory above all others?"

Other times, Canzoneri had singled out an opponent like Kid Chocolate. But on that visit – for whatever reason – it was Benny Bass, on the night Tony won the world featherweight championship, his first lineal title, through a split decision.

"I thought I had the guy stopped in the third round – but he fooled me," Canzoneri said of Bass, who had broken his collarbone at that point of the bout yet forged on. "He came on in the later rounds to give me plenty of trouble."

The writer went on to provide a detailed reliving of Tony's win over Bass under an article flatteringly headlined "One of the Greatest Little Men in Ring Annals: Canzoneri Had Tough Time Winning First Title." But, the writer couldn't help but note that on the night he met him, Canzoneri – despite his willingness to relive the glory days – appeared as if he were "a shell of his former self."

In any event, whenever he would get done with working the room at the bar and grill, Canzoneri would lay his head down for the night at his room in the hotel which also had once been home to another Italian icon of the era.

Revered actor, singer and comedian Dean Martin moved to the hotel in June 1944, and the entertainer's manager Lou Perry lived there at the time as well. But by no means was the Hotel Bryant the beloved "Dino's" first choice of living accommodations. He had checked in there because it was cheaper than the opulent Belmont Plaza Hotel where he had been staying, and he was trying to save a little on expenses.

The rate which Canzoneri paid for his room at the Bryant was $21 a week. And the staff grew accustomed to seeing him coming and going.

But they weren't the first to notice when a couple days had passed and Tony had stopped coming and going. The first who noticed were at Tony's bar.

* * *

Outside Tony Canzoneri's Paddock Bar & Grill that day on December 10, 1959, a crowd of early Broadway theater showgoers streamed by. They marveled at a 50-foot water tower in nearby Times Square and at how the Empire State building which hulked over the city could shine a light 25 miles out to the sea. They ignored a man selling balloons out of a suitcase that were made to look like a boxer and were attached to a cardboard base that would make them bob up again whenever punched.

Inside, the bar's regulars gathered for plans centering on rehashing old bouts, analyzing the fight game's modern boxers, and generally longing for the return of better times that had gone by, never to come back again, said a description of the scene in Ring magazine.

New York boxing matchmaker Carmin "Dewey" Fragetta was

seated at a table when he noticed Tony wasn't there yet. Usually, by that time of day, Tony would be there. So Fragetta called out to the bartender: "Tony's late. Think he's coming in tonight?"

The bartender said, "Who knows? He wasn't here all day yesterday or the day before."

Seated at Fragetta's table was Al Singer, at whose expense came the first of Tony's two lightweight championships of the world. Singer frowned when he heard what the bartender said.

"Tony's gaining too much weight," Singer, thinking out loud, said to Fragetta. "He must be up around 160 now – about 30 pounds more than that night he beat me for the title."

Fragetta sighed and brought up how the former world heavyweight champion Max Baer had also gained a lot of weight after retiring. "Look what happened to him," Fragetta added, alluding to the fact that Baer had died from a heart attack only a couple of weeks earlier.

Another bargoer joked about how the balloons outside were like Tony was those days – "round and soft." But the group soon composed itself and afforded their friend the respect he had earned over the course of his entire professional career. As Fragetta put it, the balloons would come right back up again after each and every time they were hit – "just like Tony."

Jokes about having become fat probably wouldn't have bothered Tony too much, if the June 1955 issue of Boxing & Wrestling magazine was any indication. "Maybe I did put on a few pounds," he said to the publication as he looked back on his career and opened up about how he still followed the profession that he gave up after 14 years of pursuing it.

"But," he joked to the magazine, "I can still shadow box without getting hit." He added, in a more sincere remark, "You never lose your liking for the sport."

After Fragetta's comment about Canzoneri's resilience, someone at the bar then mentioned that – come to think of it – Tony's daughter had come by the place a little earlier looking for him and "seemed worried." That person said it was unusual for Canzoneri to not be at the bar "for two whole days." But Fragetta encouraged his companions to keep calm.

"Stop worrying," Fragetta said, according to Ring magazine's description of the scene. "It's still early."

"Yeah," agreed Singer, whose picture was among those hanging on one of the bar's walls.

It's said that absence makes hearts grow fonder. And finding himself to be missing Canzoneri, Singer started showering his one-time rival with compliments. "He was great," Singer reportedly then said. Even in his earliest outings, it was easy to see that Tony would be "simply great," he continued.

"A good manager can spot it every time – almost," Fragetta added. "Tony had it more than anybody I knew."

They talked about how young Canzoneri was when he got his start in prizefighting, embarking in the profession at an age where some children are still just barely trying out activities like the Boy Scouts. They admired how tough Canzoneri had fought Jimmy McLarnin back in the day, and they laughed at how – before the first of those bouts – he bumped his head on the ring microphone, which was hanging over him. "He was seeing stars all over the place before the fight even started!" joked former featherweight champion Louis "Kid" Kaplan, who had joined the group that day.

Eventually, the conversation once again turned to Baer's death and weight, and how many pounds all of those at the bar had been gaining themselves. "You lead an active life till you're thirty, thirty-five, and then you quit," Fragetta said to the group. "You quit and go soft. The heart just can't stand all that extra weight without some exercise. None of us gets enough exercise."

Then, they quite suddenly realized it had gotten dark outside. And out of nowhere, a friend of theirs named Billy Lustig[1] walked in. He was pale.

Staring blankly ahead, Lustig said loudly but emptily: "Tony's dead."

A deafening silence gripped the bar before Lustig elaborated on the news he had just rather coldly dropped. He explained how a friend of Tony's named Norman Schwartz noticed that he had not heard from Canzoneri in days, and he had become worried. That was so unusual for Canzoneri. So Schwartz went over to the Bryant hotel to ask the staff there if they had seen Tony. They hadn't in a couple of days, they said, so

---

1   Information online describes him as a gang leader and labor racketeer.

Schwartz asked them to go to Tony's room and check on him.

A bellhop entered Tony's room and found him lying across the bed, in his underwear and lifeless. Tony had been dead for about two days, medical authorities would later say. There were no signs of forced entry or a struggle that would suggest he died from anything other than natural causes.

"He called me, all excited, and I went in," Lustig said of Schwartz. "Tony was on the bed, all blue."

His shoulders sagging and his eyes welling with tears, Lustig added: "I knew he was dead but I shook his arm just the same, trying to wake him up."

No one in the bar said much of anything. They were all having a hard time believing what Lustig had just told them. Over the stillness, they could hear the balloon salesman outside trying to offload his merchandise. They could hear how he punched the balloons and how they would pop back up again.

They all wished their dear friend could get up again one more time, too. But, they knew they had to start coming to terms with the fact that he couldn't and wouldn't.

"The talk of gawking out-of-towners mingled with the honking taxi horns and the cop's whistle," read the Ring magazine's description of the end of that sorrowful night. "The million lights along Broadway made the place look like a fairyland.

"There was no hint, except in the little bar ... that one of Broadway's brightest lights had just burned out."

* * *

It's impossible to know now whether Tony's hellacious schedule as a prizefighter – on average, fighting more than once a month for the duration of his 14-year career – shortened his life. As his friends repeatedly remarked at the end, he had also put on an amount of weight that was unusual for him and that, to them, seemed unhealthy.

Being knocked out of a fight just one single time doesn't mean Tony's career otherwise spared his cranial health. The concussion crisis that engulfed the National Football League decades later taught the public that it wasn't the few particularly violent hits that wrought havoc on the health of athletes in contact sports – but rather it was the accumulation of smaller, steady blows over the span of a career that took an unforgiving and sometimes fatal toll.

They also say that stress is a killer. And as American Citizen newspaper writer Aaron Rose alluded to in a 1993 piece, there were numerous stressors for Tony Canzoneri outside his medical health that could have been detrimental to him in his post-boxing life, both personally and professionally speaking.

Divorcing Rita, seeing her get remarried, allowing himself to endure the degrading experience of being slapped on stage just to get a few laughs during a comedic performance "must have led to an emotional upheaval" for Canzoneri, Rose wrote.[2]

According to some of his closest loved ones, by all indications, Tony indeed died of one of the heart attacks that his friends all feared he – or they – would have, as they made clear shortly before the Bryant hotel staff discovered the former world champion's body.

None of that prevented the spread of rumors that Tony had possibly died by suicide or had maybe even been murdered, especially given some of the associates he and his family had. After all, there's nothing more American than a good conspiracy theory.

Yet there's never been anything credible suggesting that Tony Canzoneri's untimely death was anything other than a natural one.

Denise Canzoneri remembers only bits and pieces of that heartbreaking day when she – along with the rest of the world – learned her daddy had passed away. She remembers she was 21 and had ballet practice that day, and her maternal grandmother had made plans to pick her up from her training session when it was over.

Yet her grandmother never showed up, Denise recalled. She remembers the terrible feeling that something had gone wrong which she got when she realized her grandma wasn't coming to get her. But she still hoped for the best as she decided to leave from practice by herself.

As soon as she got home, she learned she would never see her father again.

Denise remembers fainting when someone gave her the news that

---

2   It's important to note that Rose's article is almost entirely about Canzoneri's successes and makes clear that he thought very highly of Canzoneri. The piece's concluding line is: "In my mind, he will always remain a great man."

her father had died. When she remembers becoming aware of her surroundings again, people told her she had been sitting for what had essentially been entire days inside the Campbell funeral parlor on Madison Avenue. The place had held the wakes of countless celebrities. Now, it was Denise's dad's turn, and she couldn't bring herself to leave.

"That was a trauma in itself," Denise said of how she virtually shut down after learning of her father's death.

Denise's dad's funeral, held six days after the discovery of his body, was fitting of the stature he had achieved as someone who had five times been champion of the world.

More than 400 people packed the chapel where longtime minister Norris Tibbets conducted the service honoring Tony's memory. Joey Adams eulogized the fallen prizefighter whom he would slap as he tried to shock their audience into laughing.

Barney Ross led the roster of honorary pallbearers, having dethroned Tony as the world's lightweight champ, having gotten the better of him again in their rematch, but always speaking of him respectfully despite their intense battles.

"What a Canzoneri would do these days," Ross[3] later told Boxing & Wrestling magazine. "He could stay at [lightweight] and beat most of the welterweights around."

Other mourners included former world featherweight champ Abe Attell, world middleweight titleist Rocky Graziano and Ruby Goldstein, the boxing referee and one-time contender for the world lightweight belt.

Then, an undertaker who would go on to inter the Grammy-winning entertainer Judy Garland buried Tony at Mount Olivet cemetery in Maspeth, New York.

The dignitaries and the tributes all did very little to console Denise, who said she wondered throughout whether she would ever get past her grief alive.

Denise's mental and physical health took such a steep nosedive that

---

3   Obviously, the respect was mutual, or Ross would not have been an honorary pallbearer for Canzoneri. But, according to the March 1961 issue of Ring magazine, Tony later in his life would not agree with the notion that his defeats to Ross were deserved, and he would say: "He never really beat me!"

her loved ones arranged for her to see Dr. Max Jacobson, the German physician many in the public simply knew as "Dr. Feelgood."

Jacobson was what society would now call a celebrity doctor. His client list was packed with stars and reflected just what Tony Canzoneri's name came to mean to American culture.

Those who worked with Jacobson included John F. Kennedy, the U.S. president-elect when Tony died; Jacqueline Kennedy, then the first lady in waiting; Marilyn Monroe, the famed Golden Globe-winning actress and reputed mistress of JFK; New York Yankees star Mickey Mantle; and renowned literary author Truman Capote.

Other heavy hitters who turned to Jacobson were Nelson Rockefeller, then the governor of New York; Academy Award-winning film director Cecil B. DeMille; actress Ingrid Bergman, herself an Oscar winner; and entertainer Eddie Fisher, whose daughter Carrie would grow up to play Princess Leia in the Star Wars film series.

Jacobson's career ultimately ended in disgrace when an explosive investigation that the New York Times published in 1972 found that the secret of Dr. Feelgood's success and popularity was his injecting amphetamine – colloquially, speed – into his patients' veins. The state medical board nixed his license to practice in 1975, having concluded – as The New York Post once put it – that he made "unknowing drug addicts out of a long list of the famous and distinguished."

But, even years after the revelations about Jacobson, Denise said she thinks back on the doctor more fondly than many others who only read about him. She maintained that she had more than enough good reasons for that.

For one, the counseling she received from him helped her clear the fog that enveloped her life after the unexpected loss of her beloved dad, she recounted. And sure, yes — the medicine that Jacobson had given to Denise in those days helped, too, she said.

Simply put, "he saved my life," Denise, who later became a ballet instructor, said of Jacobson.

Yet that was only one of at least two crucial interventions in Denise's life for which Jacobson was responsible before his death in 1979, she said.

The second of those interventions came during Jacobson's first marriage. His wife had a cousin – he was 6-foot-4, handsome, worked as the

New York Heart Association's director of public relations, had a father who was an architect and had a mother who was an interior designer. And Jacobson's wife got the idea to introduce Denise to her cousin – who was ironically nicknamed "Tiny" – and to see what happened from there.

Alfred G. Freeman was 23 years older than Denise when his cousin introduced him to the famous prizefighter's little girl. From the first time they met, Tiny treated Denise like "a queen," she said. Honestly, Denise said, it reminded her of how Tony was with her.

In 1966, just seven years after losing her dad, Denise married Alfred. News of the nuptials, conducted by a Yonkers justice of the peace, landed in the New York Times. The first person mentioned after Denise in the brief report was the boxing phenomenon who had raised her and doted on her, another reminder of his significance not just to the bride but to her city.

"I really think she sought a father figure to replace what she had lost," said Christopher Freeman, the son who Denise and Alfred later had.

As heart-wrenching as it was for Denise to see Tony separate from Rita and then die as prematurely as he did, Christopher said she sought above all to ensure her son grew up in a loving environment after he was born in 1973.

Mom succeeded, Christopher said. And, in spite of all the ill emotions that her move to Hollywood caused among some of her family members, Rita showed a side to Christopher that Denise admits she didn't get to see too often.

As Christopher grew, Rita had already hit her peak as an actress, having landed roles on episodes of the television shows *The Untouchables*, starring Robert Stack, and *Perry Mason*, whose cast was helmed by Raymond Burr.

Acting under her stage name Rita Duncan, she portrayed a mobster's mistress named Rita Rocco on *The Untouchables'* first-season episode "The St. Louis Story." In the "Treacherous Toupee" episode that served as the fourth-season premiere of the legal drama *Perry Mason*, Rita depicted a Fresno, California, beauty salon owner named Flo. Flo was questioned by Mason's private investigator Paul Drake about whether she remembered a particular customer while the titular attorney and

Rita Duncan, Tony Canzoneri's ex-wife, appears in an episode of the legal drama *Perry Mason* in 1960. *Source: Paramount Plus screen capture*

the PI investigated the customer's sudden disappearance.

"I'll have to think about it," Flo says in the episode to Drake, who's played by William Hopper, before making him hand over cash to get her talking. Wearing a blonde wig, she ultimately introduces Drake to the missing customer's husband in an episode whose leading guest star was Robert Redford, who would later win Oscars as a filmmaker and actor.

A sense of mystery seemingly always surrounded Rita. Notably, when remembering Tony and Rita, some of those in their family made it a point to bring up a story from when – at some point – she worked at a club run by the late New York mobster Bugsy Siegel.

During one of her shifts, a drunken gambler apparently propositioned her for sex. Rita turned him down. But the matter didn't end there. Purportedly, soon after, the boorish man showed up dead at the foot of a bridge from which officials claimed he had jumped off intentionally.

Relatives are careful to not draw any conclusions from that story (for the record, at least one published newspaper article mentioned it). They offer it up more so that listeners can make up their minds about the kind of people that often came around Rita, Tony and their ill-fated marriage.

In any event, life's pace slowed and things did settle down for Rita out in Hollywood eventually. After her move, she remarried, having wed the screenwriter, playwright and novelist David Chandler. And once her days as a thespian were behind her, she started her own talent agency, representing writers and actors.

Christopher's suspicion was that Rita in the end did grasp what she ultimately had to sacrifice in terms of her relationship with Denise as she embarked on her quest for success in Hollywood. And, perhaps to compensate for the strain that caused her relationship with Denise, Rita showered Christopher – her only grandson – with affection, attention and affirmation, he said.

Rita never lost her signature sense of glamor and zeal for passionate argument, both Denise and Christopher said. Christopher said Rita presented herself to him as if she were a white, Jewish version of Diana Ross, the glamorous lead singer of the lifetime Grammy-winning Supremes. She would sometimes engage in "vicious arguments" with David that Christopher would do his best not to overhear, but he did on occasion. It made him wonder if his grandmother had the same kind of verbal clashes with the legendary grandfather he never got to meet.

"You know, she was such a marvelous woman," Christopher Freeman said. "And by all accounts, my grandpa – though a tiger in the ring – was a gentle soul outside of it. I can see how they balanced each other."

For her part, Denise never tried to interfere with the relationship that Rita sought with Christopher but was never really ever able to establish with her.

"My grandmother was terrific to me," said Christopher Freeman, who now works in office managing and personal training after having written a screenplay. "She gave me the world."

The Freemans, as the years passed, remained close to the Canzoneris. That didn't change even after the Canzoneris' most famous scion was gone.

In another colorful chapter of a family lore bursting at the seams with colorful chapters, Tony's brother Jasper turned to Denise's husband Tiny after a couple from Dutchess County, New York, kidnapped Jasper and demanded $200,000 from Dotty as a ransom.

The entire saga revolved around an innkeeper named Ramazan Katouri and his wife, Manda, who wanted to make money quickly by giving their rare coin collection to Jasper so that he could then sell it and give them the proceeds.

Jasper, then 55, had trouble finding a buyer, and the Katouris lost their patience with him. They summoned him to a restaurant in Brooklyn the night of September 27, 1971, and handcuffed him after he arrived.

Then, the Katouris spirited Jasper over to an apartment about 70 miles away in Beacon, New York, and telephoned Dotty to demand the money for his safe return.

Dotty heard out what the Katouris wanted – and she immediately called the police. Investigators figured out where Jasper was two nights later, kicked down the door, rescued him and jailed the Katouris. Officers ended up seizing three loaded pistols at the apartment where Tony's brother was being kept, but thankfully, no one was shot.

The whole ordeal left Jasper traumatized and distressed. A couple of weeks later, after testifying before a Brooklyn grand jury weighing kidnapping charges against the Katouris, he wrote separate letters on the same day to New York police commissioner Patrick Murphy and Kings County district attorney Eugene Gold asking them to provide him protection. He claimed Manda Katouri had pointed him out to three Albanian men while he was at the courthouse, and he was worried they were plotting to kill him.

"I fear for my life," Jasper wrote in letters his daughter later inherited.

Yet the Katouris never took it further, and when Jasper calmed down, he thought his experience might make a good story that he could sell to a book publisher or filmmaker.

For help with the project, Jasper tapped Tiny Freeman, who typed up two manuscripts.

Though the manuscripts never resulted in a book or a movie, Jasper's daughter Deborah Burns chronicled the entire saga in her memoir *Saturday's Child*. The pair of scripts also give a glimpse into a horrifying experience most people never find themselves needing to survive, describing how Jasper overheard Manda saying she wished she could just cut off Jasper's ears and nose as well as remove his heart from his body.

"Even now, ... I wake up at night in a cold sweat, the result of a repeating nightmare in which two cocked revolvers are pointing at me, one at the middle of my forehead, and the other at the back of my neck," one of the manuscripts about Jasper's ordeal said.

But, as it had once in her early 20s, the steady, unrelenting forward march of time again would take from Denise some of those closest to her.

Tiny died in early 1999, almost four decades after Denise had lost Tony. He had just turned 85.

Then, in June of 2000, Denise lost the mother who had blossomed into this attentive, gracious grandmother to her boy, for which Denise would always be grateful. Rita by then had been living at a nursing home in San Gabriel, California. And she had closed her talent agency about 12 years earlier.

Of course, as she did four decades beforehand, Denise leaned on family and trusted friends to survive the heartbreak. Christopher takes care of his mother to this day, and Deborah checks in with them regularly.

They were all going to get together, along with Canzoneri cousin Jay Honold, in the spring of 2020 to celebrate Tony's induction into a sports hall of fame on Staten Island, New York, where he collected the second-to-last win of his career. The event was postponed following the coronavirus pandemic, which swept across the United States and within a few years had killed more than a million people throughout the nation. None of the relatives could wait for the induction to be rescheduled because they wanted to revel in one last victory for the great, indefatigable Tony Canzoneri.

They got their night when the Staten Island Sports Hall of Fame held its banquet in 2021. Denise, unfortunately, said she couldn't go to the event because she couldn't move around as easily in her 80s and in a post-pandemic world. But Freeman went to accept the induction on behalf of his family, and he even gave an acceptance speech and took a picture with Deborah Burns.

During his speech, Freeman shared that he'd once heard that the one-time trainer and manager of boxing legend Mike Tyson – Cus D'Amato – had shown the former heavyweight champion clipped news-reel-style videos of some of Canzoneri's fights as part of his training.

"An unending source of pride for me was learning that Cus ... would show clips of my grandfather to a young Mike," Freeman said that night in a speech that Burns recorded with her cell phone. "So when I'm watching highlights of Tyson, I like to think a little bit of Tony is in every uppercut."

Freeman reiterated how much his mother adored her father, and how – as he put it – "his death [had left] a permanent hole in her heart." He alluded to how she found the mildest of comforts in seeing how her father's funeral drew celebrities, mayors and governors. It also drew fight fans who weren't as famous as some of the other attendees – but whose admiration for Tony was just as intense, if not more so.

"He was universally loved," Freeman said of his grandfather that night of the induction in 2021. "And thanks to all of you here, he will never be forgotten."

As likely was the case for the rest of those who went to the event to toast what Freeman called "an incredible honor" for Tony and his survivors, Christopher never got to see his grandfather fight in person. Of course, for that matter, neither really did his mother, who was born the year before Bummy Davis knocked Tony Canzoneri into retirement.

But Denise always said she felt lucky that one day her uncles – like Cus D'Amato reportedly did with Mike Tyson – showed her some home films of her old man when he was in the shape of his life, in his prime as a prizefighter, sitting at the very top of the boxing world.

Having never really grown to care about the profession that vaulted her family's last name into global fame, Denise doesn't remember much of what those clips showed. She remembers not understanding much of what was going on. And she also remembers that she couldn't stop herself from excitedly yelling out at one point: "Punch that bastard out, daddy! Just punch him out!"

Denise, sighing, chuckled at the memory when reliving it decades later. Of course, she knew the fighters could not hear her, she said. And she also knew that – every single time that he could – her daddy did exactly what his little girl was asking him to do.

Tony Canzoneri's niece Deborah Burns, left, and grandson Christopher Freeman attend his induction into the Staten Island Sports Hall of Fame in 2021. They hold up a plaque that lists Tony's accomplishments and has a photo showing him in his prizefighting prime. *Courtesy of Deborah Burns*

ABOVE: Denise Canzoneri married the love of her life, Alfred Freeman; raised her son, Christopher, in a loving household; and smiles here in October 2019. But the death of her father Tony Canzoneri left "a permanent hole in her heart," according to Christopher Freeman. *Courtesy of Christopher Freeman*

LEFT: Deborah Burns and Bob Burns. *Courtesy of Deborah Burns*

CHAPTER TWELVE

"TONY ... DUCKED NO ONE"

—

Besides watching the actual bouts themselves, there might be nothing that boxing fans and historians – self-styled or otherwise – love to do more than debate where prizefighters are ranked among the greatest ever practitioners of the sport they call the sweet science. And that's if the prizefighters even belong in the discussion in the first place.

Tony Canzoneri, without a doubt, belongs in the discussion of the greatest ever lightweights – and, if you ask many, the list of all-time, pound-for-pound greats.

Renowned boxing writer Nat Fleischer, who was Ring magazine's editor-in-chief for 50 years until his death in 1972 and owned the publication for much of that time, at one point ranked[1] Tony Canzoneri as the seventh-greatest lightweight in the sport's history.

Meanwhile, a 2015 article from Mike Lockley of Birmingham, England's, Sunday Mercury newspaper – which included more modern legends – made the case for ranking him as the sixth-greatest lightweight boxer of all time.

---

1   In Fleischer's view, Canzoneri demonstrated throughout his career that his ability to take a punch without going down – his chin – and his right-hand strikes were his best assets. His power, footwork, hooks and stamina were all good before the end, and his jabbing ability was above average. None of the six ahead of Canzoneri in Fleischer's ranking or the three behind him were fighting during Tony's era, making it clear that Nat thought Tony was the best lightweight of his day.

In other words, Lockley reasoned, Tony trailed fighters such as his number one Roberto Duran – a champion in four weight classes who successfully defended his lightweight crown 12 times – and number four Pernell Whitaker, a three-division titleist who triumphed in eight challenges to his lightweight throne.

However, in what can only make Italian-American hearts soar to the skies with pride, Lockley's list placed Canzoneri four spots ahead of the fighter many consider to be the greatest from Mexico's long, proud lineage of boxing champions: Julio Cesar Chavez[2], whose reign as a lightweight champion lasted three title defenses but may have been the peak of his unforgettable 115-bout career. Canzoneri was also two spots above the pride of Nicaragua, Alexis Arguello, who racked up four defenses of his lightweight title.

Nonetheless, many others ponder how Canzoneri would've done getting into the ring against any of the division's all-time best. Duran, Arguello, Chavez and Whittaker were some of the fight game's brightest names not just in the 1980s and 1990s – they were some of the best ever, pound-for-pound.

Some argue that Tony's fists' being forever in motion would have given him a shot for at least a victory on the scorecards over anybody – on any day – on the strength of work rate and points. Others scoff at the mere thought of him standing a chance against today's crop of men's title holders and contenders at lightweight, noting that guys like Devin Haney, Vasiliy Lomachenko, Teofimo Lopez and Gervonta Davis knocked out their opponents about 52, 65, 72 and 93 percent of the time. Canzoneri's rate of victory by knockout was much, much lower: about 25 percent.

It's all a harmless and fantastic thought exercise to conduct over burgers, beers or even stronger sustenance and spirits. But, boxing's leading minds caution, it is truly impossible to know how Canzoneri would do if he ever clashed with the likes of Haney, Lomachenko, Lopez, or Davis, because today's fighters – for medical reasons, marketing purposes and a plethora of other motives – would not subject

---

2　　　Saul "Canelo" Alvarez has had a say about this, winning championships in four divisions, from super welterweight to light heavyweight.

themselves to the grueling regimen that Canzoneri undertook a century or so beforehand.

It bears repeating again that, on average, Canzoneri fought about once every 30 days for 14 years. He fought a total of 18 times against International Boxing Hall of Fame inductees: Lou Ambers, Baby Arizmendi, Benny Bass, Jack "Kid" Berg, Eligio "Kid Chocolate" Sardinas Montalvo, Johnny Dundee, Sammy Mandell, Jimmy McLarnin, Barney Ross, and Bud Taylor.

Canzoneri won 11 of those bouts, beating Ambers, Arizmendi, Bass, Berg, Kid Chocolate, Dundee, McLarnin and Taylor at least once.

Sure, he was shut out by Ross in two tries; lost to Ambers, Taylor, Berg and Mandell once; and drew Taylor another time. But it is impossible to overstate the quality that those opponents brought into the ring and how difficult it would have been to run the table against them.

With the exception of Bass and Taylor, all of those fighters had the rare but prestigious honor of getting inducted separately into the World Boxing Hall of Fame. Fleischer had Dundee and Kid Chocolate as the fourth- and sixth-best featherweights of all time. Taylor at one point was Fleischer's fifth-best at bantamweight.

Ross and McLarnin were considered by Flesicher to be the ninth-best and tenth-best ever at the heavier division of welterweight.

Furthermore, there were titles on the line for at least 12 of Tony's bouts with those legends. He won half of those match-ups.

But here's the thing: to many, winning or losing in those kinds of contests isn't as important as simply either challenging for or defending those titles against decent opposition. Tony bet on himself to take or expose those titles against actual all-time greats a full dozen times.

Some boxers who are presented as champions to fans now don't face an all-time great a single time in their entire careers.

As action-packed as it can be, at least some of the time, when Haney, Davis, Lomachenko and Lopez climb into the ring, it took years for the first two to simply fight the number of bouts Canzoneri lost throughout his career (24). The latter pair hadn't gotten there as of the spring of 2023, when they each had fewer than 20 professional fights to their names and Lopez was preparing to fight at junior welterweight.

All would certainly need years more to fight the number of bouts Canzoneri[3] won by knockout (44) – if they ever get there at all.

And this is not at all to diminish guys like Haney, Lomachenko, Lopez or Davis. They have believed – justifiably, many would say – that they could beat anybody in the world from any era, anytime and anywhere.

But the fighters' promoters – and ultimately the boxers themselves – have taken loads of criticism for not making bouts among them happen. Of the four mentioned here, only Lomachenko and Lopez had faced each other in October 2020, with Lopez beating Lomachenko for a load of belts before later losing them unexpectedly to George Kambosos.

Haney, considered to be the lineal champion, was scheduled to fight Lomachenko in the spring of 2023. But Lopez and Haney hadn't faced each other, and Davis had not mixed it up with any of the other three at all. Meanwhile, modern welterweight titleists Errol Spence Jr. and Terence Crawford – with combined records of 67-0 and with knockout victory rates of 79 and 78 percent, respectively – had not faced each other for the division's undisputed championship as the spring of 2023 began despite facing years of fan as well as media pressure to do so.

All of that has helped make accusations of "ducking" away from facing the best one of the most common insults hurled at modern boxers. And the coronavirus pandemic only further delayed the possibility of any compelling matchups that hadn't happened yet from ever taking place. These boxers mentioned here are far from the only ones. They're just named because they're in weight classes where Tony Canzoneri or his rivals competed.

There are relatively obvious reasons why some fights never take place these days if the situation is viewed strictly through a marketing standpoint. Fights involving an undefeated boxer can be easier to sell. Fights are an easier sell even for a boxer with a single loss because anyone could

---

3   This biography could not claim to have been written by a New Orleanian if the author didn't list Canzoneri among the five other boxers – at least – who hailed from the Crescent City and won world championships. Four of the others were from last century: Pete Herman, Joe Brown, Ralph Dupas and Willie Pastrano. One, Regis Prograis, was from the 21st century. There's no way that Tony Canzoneri is not at least in consideration of being New Orleans's greatest ever boxer, though the city's other world champions have cases made for them by the passionate supporters that they still have locally.

have a bad night or a questionable decision against them on a given night.

And delaying a showdown between undefeated titleists in the same weight class, chasing recognition as the undisputed champ in the division, can create so much anticipation that it translates into multi-million dollar purses, sellout crowds and a pay-per-view audience in the millions.

"Today, you lose to three fighters, and people start asking, 'What's wrong with them?'" former Ring magazine editor Steve Farhood said. "It's a totally different era today than back then."

Our knowledge of the physical toll that boxing takes on its practitioners is also bounds and leaps ahead of where it was when Canzoneri was making a name for himself. It is, to be absolutely sure, a good thing that boxers and their handlers know now that 30 days in between fights for 14 years will with virtual certainty take a vicious, life-shortening toll on the health of boxers, who are always one brain-rattling blow away from having their lives drastically changed for the worse.

And of course, if one single punch doesn't do it, the accumulation of blows over the span of a career can do the same during what are supposed to be their golden years. The year before this biography of Tony Canzoneri started taking shape, four boxers died as a direct result of injuries they sustained in the ring. That was a devastating reminder about boxing's brutality that no one needed but got anyway.

Yet it is that astonishing level of activity to which Canzoneri and some of his contemporaries subjected themselves which makes it all but impossible to meaningfully debate how they would fare against modern stars.

Canzoneri quite literally took on all comers, multiple times, even if they were more skilled than him, bigger than him, punched more powerfully than him, or were likely to beat him. He was undeniably elite himself, wielding a crowd-pleasing, high-pressure, forward-charging style relying on a volume of punches to, as he hoped, overwhelm his opponent.

And when the best fight the best, more often than not, they will struggle to knock each other out, as Farhood pointed out repeatedly when discussing Canzoneri's legacy.

That is why Tony won only a minority of his fights by knockout. It is why only the last opponent he ever faced during his hellaciously paced career managed to knock him out. It is why most of his biggest fights went the allotted distance, where often a point here or a point there on the scorecards marked the slimmest margin between riveting triumph or heartbreaking, career-altering defeat.

In Canzoneri's case, his slate of opponents "did not have very many easy fights, easy giveaways," Farhood said when asked to reflect on the New Orleans native's career. "They're not just Hall of Famers. They're legends."

Tony and his peers, Farhood added, "were fearless in how often they fought, and in who they fought."

Canzoneri's resume would be one for the ages if the only top opponents with whom he clashed were the boxing hall of famers. It would be worthy of being included in the conversation of all-time best resumes if his only other distinction was being the first to reclaim the lightweight world championship after having lost it.

The same would be true of his being the first to ever win back the junior welterweight title after losing it. Same goes for his half-dozen title bout wins against the very best fighters of his era and some of the greatest ever. And the same goes for his 28 fights as a pro at Madison Square Garden – a veritable cathedral of boxing.

All fighters would be proud to have any of those things individually as some of their dossier's brightest highlights. Yet Tony Canzoneri had all of them.

And those accomplishments were far from all that Canzoneri had. He also faced a handful of other fighters who may or may not be universally considered all-time greats but, in their day, undoubtedly ranked among the best which the world had to offer.

For instance, Johnny Jadick, Frankie Klick, Andre Routis, Jose "Battling Shaw" Flores, and Al Singer were all at least champions at some point in their careers. Billy Petrolle was a top contender when Tony Canzoneri accepted a challenge from him and exposed the lineal lightweight crown.

Canzoneri was at different junctures in his trajectory when he met every single one of those six. In other words, Tony faced them without caring if he was still on the rise, was at his peak or was considered to be over the hill.

He won 10, lost five, and drew one against that group of fighters, beating each of them at least once. And often there was plenty on the line in those fights, too. He successfully defended his lightweight world championship against Petrolle. Battling Shaw was the lineal junior welterweight title holder when he challenged him. He took Singer's world lightweight championship.

The sheer number of times Canzoneri clashed with Hall of Famers, contemporary champions and the worthiest of contenders – at least 33, by this count – would in many cases surpass the total number of bouts several modern boxers fought during their entire careers.

To be fair, that doesn't necessarily take away from prizefighters past or present. All of them had to channel courage and self-confidence many of us just do not possess simply to take the ring – shirtless at that! – and battle one-on-one, hand-to-hand, sometimes with much of the world watching.

But few if any fighters today ever risked more than Tony Canzoneri did, as often as he did, against elite competition like he did. And that is the simplest explanation for why boxing pundits overlook his low knockout victory rate to include him in discussions about the fight game's all-time greats.

"Tony ... ducked no one," as Ring magazine once put. "The names of the men he fought look like a register of great bantams, featherweights, lights and welters."

That's a full four divisions of opponents between 118 and 147 pounds, packed with fighters who often were naturally heavier and therefore should have theoretically had a great chance at hitting harder than Tony Canzoneri could.

In a conversation with Mike Silver, the author of *The Arc of Boxing: The Rise and Decline of the Sweet Science*, well-regarded Marine Corps boxing coach Mike Capriano Jr. summed it up as well as anyone has. "What today's huge knockout percentages tell me is that these fighters are being matched with improper opponents – someone that shouldn't be in the ring with them," Capriano Jr. said.

New York boxing trainer and commentator Teddy Atlas echoed Capriano in his own conversation with Silver, who also sought to contextualize the downside of using the metric of knockout percentages to compare pugilists from different eras.

"You did not see so many knockouts years ago because the old timers were fighting good fighters," Atlas said. "It's that simple."

Maybe one day it will again be the norm for the best to fight the best. But, at least for now, and most unfortunately for the sport of professional boxing, those days are as gone as the great and unforgettable Tony Canzoneri is.

CHAPTER THIRTEEN

GOOD FIGHTERS

—

I f those who have been fascinated by Tony Canzoneri's life believed his exploits in and out of the ring were colorful, his friends, associates and rivals' stories more than held their own against his.

Here is how life turned out for some of those who helped Tony turn into what he became either by standing in his corner, leaving everything they had in the ring in battles they had against him, or otherwise populating the very world that he once was at the top of.

JOHN GALWAY

Tony's first boxing coach at New Orleans's Gayoso Athletic Club did well for himself financially after his skilled pupil shot to international superstardom. John Galway rose within New Orleans's municipal government to a position which put him in charge of the city's public buildings. He also owned four racehorses, earning enough to be able to accessorize his wardrobe with diamonds for his stickpin, collar, belt buckle and on his ring finger.

Galway would say the stones were tokens of his hard work, and they inspired at least one of the local newspapers to give him the nickname "Diamond John." Nonetheless, Tony – who once asked Galway to adopt him, unsuccessfully – surely did not appear to leave things on the greatest of terms with the trainer who introduced him to boxing.

It angered Galway that Canzoneri failed to mention him and his Gayoso athletic club during the radio interview that Tony gave moments after he knocked Al Singer out to win his first lightweight championship of the world. The New Orleanian whom Canzoneri thanked for teaching him everything he knew about boxing instead was champion fighter Pete Herman.

Galway also hated that, after his retirement, Canzoneri continued insisting that his boxing mentor during his days in New Orleans was Pete Herman and only Pete Herman.

In a news interview that Galway gave during his final years, he also complained that Tony never gave him any gifts expressing his appreciation for the role that Galway played in fostering Tony's early development.

"He never so much as sent me back a necktie," Galway said of Canzoneri in that July 13, 1946, interview with The New Orleans Item. "Fighters are an ungrateful lot."

Carrying on with a very similar tone, Galway once suggested that Pete Herman denied him his due recognition for helping that world champion's career out immensely as well. Galway claimed he watched as Herman, then an amateur, spoke of quitting after a loss by decision to Johnny Fisse, an opponent who turned out to be a bit of an also-ran. Herman was so dispirited after the defeat he endured that day at the intersection of 7th and Magazine streets – in New Orleans's Irish Channel neighborhood – that he wanted to "throw his boxing gloves and everything out of the street car window," Galway recalled once.

According to Galway, during that street car ride, "Pete said he'd never fight again." But Galway encouraged the budding superstar to stick with it. Herman listened, and of course, the rest is history: he went on to win the world's bantamweight championship in 1917 and 1921.

Galway said he turned down the chance to become a full-time manager of prizefighters because he preferred the steadier, more predictable work that his longtime job at the public New Orleans agency which handled the city's sewers and water service. That profession let him support his family much better than managing spurious boxers ever would, he liked to say.

Galway later moved from where the Gayoso club proudly stood to a bungalow closer to New Orleans's City Park. He was 67 years old when he died on June 11, 1948. His survivors at the time included his wife, Hortense; two daughters; and a son, who became familiar to many New Orleanians in his own right through his work as a Fire Department captain.

PETE HERMAN

After his retirement from boxing, Pete Herman became both a saloon keeper and one of many well-known characters in New Orleans's French Quarter neighborhood. He regaled loved ones, patrons and tourists with stories from his boxing days and from his two reigns as the world champion of the bantamweight division.

Reportedly, he eventually went blind after an opponent's thumb injured one of his eyes in a charity boxing match. But at a time when many famed boxers died penniless, Herman's business investments left him financially comfortable through his death on April 13, 1973.

"Pete ... seemed to excel at everything," Dick Anderson, who has studied Herman's life for years, told New Orleans television station WWL.

SAMMY GOLDMAN

Following a long illness, Goldman died in New York on August 27, 1964, at age 74. Besides his son, Al, his survivors included his wife, Hannah, and a daughter, Anita Coppel. The funeral was at the Forest Park Chapel in New York.

Boxing aficionados forever remember Goldman for guiding Herman in his efforts to recapture the world bantamweight championship he had lost. Of course, after helping Canzoneri win his featherweight, lightweight and junior welterweight titles, he also helped Tony regain the latter two of them after he lost them.

Alfred Goldman once used the word "love" when writing up a description of his father's relationship with Herman and Tony.

"His relationship with Pete and Tony was never just business," Alfred Goldman wrote. "All three were from New Orleans. All three were gentlemen. All three of them were champions."

BASIL GALIANO

Basil Galiano, the New Orleans-born fighter who also had a role in connecting Goldman and Canzoneri, finished his boxing career in 1930 with a record of 47 wins (14 by knockout), 29 defeats and seven draws. He later found work as an officer in the police force that patrolled New Orleans's public boating docks. He was 36 when he died on August 21, 1938, after a two-month battle with influenza.

BUD TAYLOR

Indiana's Bud Taylor, the Blonde Terror of Terre Haute, who was arguably Tony Canzoneri's first major rival, relinquished the world bantamweight championship he won in 1927 to campaign at featherweight. His defeat when facing a heavier Tony Canzoneri presaged what awaited him at featherweight – he never again challenged for a world title.

After retiring from the ring in 1931 with a record of 70 wins (35 by knockout), 23 defeats, six draws and 58 no decisions, he both managed and promoted boxers. He died at age 58 in Los Angeles on March 8, 1962, and was inducted into the International Boxing Hall of Fame in Canastota, New York, in 2005.

THE BONANNOS

Joseph Bonanno – the high-profile mobster who often vacationed at the resort which the Canzoneris built on the upstate New York farm that Tony bought for his parents after fighting Bud Taylor – died in 2002 at age 97. His son Bill Bonanno, who spent a lot of time vacationing at the Canzoneri resort as well, died in 2008 when he was 75 after a career that also saw him produce television films about his family.

JOHNNY DUNDEE

If the activity level of Tony or any of his other contemporaries was impressive, it is astonishing to take a closer look at the career of Johnny Dundee, who lost a New York State Athletic Commission featherweight title fight by decision to a relatively young Tony Canzoneri in 1927. Dundee began fighting in 1910 and didn't retire until 1932, fighting more than 320 times in the meantime. He won 90 and lost 31, with all but one of the remaining bouts resulting in no decision, according to one count.

The resume, for sure, is far from typical, even in a sport where one comes to expect the unexpected. Yet it bears repeating that the longtime editor of the Ring magazine, Nat Fleischer, at one point considered Dundee the fourth-best featherweight ever – two spots ahead of another renowned Canzoneri opponent, Sergio "Kid Chocolate" Eligio Sardinas Montalvo.

Dundee's defeat to Canzoneri was the last significant fight of his career, according to the International Boxing Hall of Fame, which inducted him in 1991. A World Boxing Hall of Fame inductee as well, he died at age 71 in East Orange, New Jersey.

BENNY BASS

Benny Bass, who lost twice to Canzoneri and was the man whom Tony defeated when he won his first undisputed world championship as a boxer, knocked out Seattle's Tod Morgan at the end of 1929 to win a world title at junior lightweight. Cuba's Kid Chocolate then knocked Bass out in the summer of 1931 to take that title for himself, which was the first time Bass ever lost a fight due to a stoppage.

Bass fought until 1940, when he retired with a record of 158-29-6, with 72 of his wins coming by knockout. He died on June 25, 1975, at age 70 and was inducted into the International Boxing Hall of Fame in 2002.

KID CHOCOLATE

The so-called Kid Chocolate, who lost both contests in his two-fight series with Canzoneri, had mixed fortunes in trying to fulfill predictions that he would be one of the best lightweights ever. After losing the junior lightweight championship that he had won from Bass, he was never able to gain it back. And he never managed to successfully campaign for a championship at the lightweight division, at the step immediately above, which of course Canzoneri lorded over for a time.

Nonetheless, Kid Chocolate was remembered fondly for a 12th-round knockout over Lew Feldman that secured him the vacant New York State Athletic Commission featherweight championship, which of course at the time was still considered a major laurel. And Ring magazine in its January 2002 issue listed him as the fifth-best featherweight ever, having gained a spot from an earlier ranking that the publication's former editor Nat Fleischer compiled.

And it is Sardinas who fight fans, boxing historians, and most others associate with the "Kid Chocolate" moniker that a handful of other pugilists[1] have sought to use for themselves over the decades.

---

1   These included American boxer Peter Quillin, whose father is Cuban and who held a World Boxing Organization middleweight title from 2012 to 2014. Meanwhile, the original Kid Chocolate had another nickname derived from a confection: the Cuban Bon Bon.

The resource website BoxRec.com nowadays cautions that Kid Chocolate possibly owed some of his reputation as an unusually dangerous opponent for his contemporaries to incorrect listings of his record – as well as some intentional misinformation – before his debut in the United States in 1928. Ring record books printed before the 1980s erroneously showed he went 21-0, with each victory by knockout, to kick off his career. At least one Ring Record Book – from 1970 – showed he won all 100 of his amateur fights, with all but 14 of those victories coming by way of knockout.

BoxRec.com, however, said experts later concluded that Kid Chocolate's record prior to his American debut had apparently been fabricated by his manager, Luis "Pincho" Gutierrez. The website reported that boxing historian Enrique Encinosa went through Cuban newspapers of Kid Chocolate's era – which meticulously reported on amateur cards for their fight-crazed readerships – and found 22 bouts against a total of 19 opponents between 1922 and 1927. He won all of those contests, but there were no details about whether they came by decision or stoppage, and some bouts didn't even have dates associated with them, Encinosa's research showed. "It is likely that this," the BoxRec site added, "is the entirety of Chocolate's full amateur record."

Despite all that, there were plenty of other reasons for Kid Chocolate to command the respect of boxing scholars in perpetuity. He was the first world titleist from a Caribbean island country that has turned out some of boxing's finest ever fighters. Canzoneri himself at one point called him the toughest man he ever faced in the ring. And all-time great US boxer Sugar Ray Robinson at one point even confirmed reports that he looked up to Kid Chocolate as well as implemented some aspects of his style into his own fight game, including his slick foot and head movement.

There is no indication that boxing insiders were aware that some of Kid Chocolate's credentials had been exaggerated to enhance his reputation as potentially hazardous for risk-averse fighters to take on. And even if it later turned out that Kid Chocolate's credentials were overstated to an extent, Canzoneri had no qualms about facing him when that hadn't been revealed, beating him twice in two of the most recounted episodes of his career.

BoxRec lists Kid Chocolate's record as 136 victories (51 by knockout), 10 defeats (two by KO) and six draws before his retirement in

1938. Cuban state radio reported that Kid Chocolate died in his home country's capital of Havana in 1988 at age 78, according to the New York Times. He is an inductee of both the International Boxing and World Boxing Halls of Fame.

Reports said Kid Chocolate had moved back to Cuba to run a gym after spending his earnings basking in the glow of his celebrity as well as New York's nightlife. The communist regime in charge of Cuba at one point awarded Kid Chocolate a government pension because his athletic successes brought glory to his country in the Caribbean, but otherwise he lived largely out of public view, The New York Times reported.

Cuban state radio did not give any details about a cause of death for Kid Chocolate or who his survivors included. As the Times at one point put it: "The former boxing champion died ... under ..., if not mysterious circumstances, then certainly unrevealed circumstances."

HARRY BLITMAN

Blitman's decision win over Tony Canzoneri in 1928 went down in the record books as an exhibition, but it had a significance that such bouts usually do not. Firstly, for a fleeting but brilliant moment for him, Blitman was – in his words – "the golden boy," celebrating his victory by spending the rest of that night and much of the next day at a Philadelphia gambling joint known as the Turf Club.

Furthermore, Canonzeri personally counted it as one of the two worst defeats in his career – the other in that group was the knockout loss to Bummy Davis that sent him into retirement.

And maybe best of all for Blitman, the triumph also helped him set up a Philly on Philly showdown with Benny Bass, the winner of which would then fight Canzoneri for the full title.

But Blitman was not equal to the moment. Bass dropped Blitman in the second round and then stopped him in the sixth. Though Blitman – whose father was in attendance – left the bout with a $25,000 purse, he was denied a shot against Canzoneri with the championship belt on the line.

"Benny was punching me at will," Blitman would say many years later. "I cried my heart out in the dressing room."

Blitman said it later became clear to him that his win over Canzoneri was as good as it was going to get for him in the fight game.

"I didn't know it, but (that) was the real peak of my career," Blitman said to the Saturday Evening Post at one point. "I clearly outboxed the champ."

He retired following a loss to a fighter named Mike Marshall in 1934. He left boxing having accumulated 54 wins (26 by knockout), 11 defeats (including six by KO), and four draws. He spent his career under the guidance of Max Hoff, who reputedly used his stable of fighters as a front for his bootlegging and gambling enterprise.

Like Canzoneri and other contemporaries, Blitman was regularly around gun-carrying men involved in organized crime. However, after his retirement, Blitman reportedly favored the idea of work that was more honest than his manager purportedly pursued.

He wrote a series of newspaper articles about past fighters and contributed to other daily periodicals. He also worked at a Ford Motor Company plant outside Philadelphia, helped conduct physical training for US navy sailors when the second world war started, and advocated for medical examinations of prizefighters to be more thorough, according to information compiled and published online by the Philadelphia Jewish Sports Hall of Fame.

Blitman was 62 years old when he died in 1972.

ANDRE ROUTIS

The Frenchmen who dethroned Tony Canzoneri as the world's featherweight champion at the end of September 1928 lost his title nearly a year later, having successfully defended it once. Andre Routis lost his championship during what was his fifth consecutive defeat in a losing streak that reached six matches, prompting at least some who have the benefit of hindsight to question exactly how it was that he beat Tony.

Routis retired with a record of 55-25-7 (12 victories by knockout) following a loss to Davey Abad[2] on November 5, 1929, fewer than 14 months after winning his lone world title. He died in France on July 16, 1969, at age 69.

---

2   Abad, you may remember, handed Tony Canzoneri the first loss of his pro boxing career.

AL SINGER

After Tony Canzoneri dealt him a first-round defeat in 1930 to win the world's lightweight championship, Al Singer cemented himself in one of the strangest places in boxing history. His first-round win over Sammy Mandell to collect the world championship and then his opening-frame loss to Canzoneri which cost him the crown left him as the only prizefighter ever to win and lose that particular title in the combined time of two minutes and 52 seconds.

"A product of his time, Al Singer did everything fast," the November 1965 issue of Boxing International said in jest.

Singer, following his defeat to Canzoneri, collected one more big payday by facing Bat Battalino in 1931, Boxing International added. He lost by a second-round technical knockout to an opponent chosen as a last-minute replacement for Kid Chocolate, who had been arrested, says an entry on BoxRec.com, without elaborating.

Al retired in 1935 with a record of 62 wins (26 KOs), nine defeats and two draws. He later served in the US military during World War II, participating in exhibition boxing matches to entertain his fellow service members. He also became a New York State Boxing Commission judge.

In details that mirrored some in Tony's life, he married a showgirl – Billy Boze[3] – and tried his hand at several businesses, including restaurants and theater. He died from a heart attack in his New York City apartment on April 20, 1961, calling to mind Tony's death at the same age – from the same cause and in the same city – not even two years earlier.

The International Jewish Sports Hall of Fame posthumously enshrined Singer as a member in 2006.

JACK BERG

Jack "Kid" Berg, who lost his junior welterweight championship to Canzoneri while challenging for Tony's lightweight crown in 1931, retired in 1945 with a record of 157 wins (61 by knockout), 26 losses and nine draws. Berg – who was born in London as Judah Bergman – lived until he was 81. He died in 1991 after a long illness.

---

3   His obituary doesn't mention Boze, whose name was Wilhelmma Connely Boze.

In a 1986 interview with author John Harding, Berg made clear that he never got over losing the closing chapter of his trilogy with Tony Canzoneri, who created controversy over the bout's outcome by hitting Berg with an unpunished low blow that was hard enough to make the Londoner go down to the canvas in pain.

Losing the finale of his trilogy with Canzoneri under those circumstances "hurt me a lot" not just physically but emotionally as well, the World Boxing Hall of Fame and International Boxing Hall of Fame inductee said to Harding. "After this fight, I disappeared. Nobody knew where I went for three weeks. I was disillusioned about fighting, I packed a bag and I went somewhere. ... And when I came home, I was dirty, uncombed."

He remembered people asking him where he'd been and recalled how that defeat was a turning point for the worse before he chose to walk away from prizefighting for good.

BARNEY ROSS

After dethroning Tony Canzoneri as the lightweight champion of the world, Barney Ross waged a trilogy against Jimmy McLarnin for the world welterweight title three times in 1934 and 1935.

Everyone cautioned Ross against fighting McLarnin largely because of Jimmy's devastating right hand. Ross's co-managers, Art Winch and Sam Pian, purportedly refused to even try to set him up to face McLarnin. So Ross had to get the series for himself, flying out with his brother to New York – where McLarnin trained – to negotiate with him.

"I lived with McLarnin for a month," Ross would later say, explaining how he moved into the gymnasium where they both trained. "Every time I punched the bag, I saw McLarnin. When I ran up the road, he ran with me. All my sparring partners looked like him. I fell asleep thinking of McLarnin ... and woke up thinking of him."

It all paid off when Ross, working by himself and for him, returned with an agreement to fight McLarnin, including once in front of 60,000 fans in an outdoor arena in Long Island City known as the Madison Square Garden Bowl, according to BoxRec.com.

Ross won twice by decision and lost once in the same manner, answering every potent punch he took during those affairs with his own powerful shots and getting up from the only knockdown of a career that ultimately spanned 81 bouts.

His winning record from his series against McLarnin, in addition to his pair of victories over Tony Canzoneri, helped immortalize Ross as one of the era's greats. He retired after he lost a lopsided, 15-round decision as well as his welterweight belt to Henry Armstrong in 1938. He walked away from the fight game with a mark of 72 wins (22 by knockout), four losses, three draws and a pair of no contests.

Ross did not take it easy in retirement. After Japan's military attacked Hawaii's Pearl Harbor in 1941, he enlisted in the US Marines despite being in his 30s and beyond the age at which he could get drafted into the service. The Marines wanted to make him a boxing instructor, but he asked to be sent into combat. They granted Ross his wish and deployed him to Guadalcanal for one of the United States' most brutal battles during the second world war.

One night while he was out on the front lines, Japanese troops shot three of Ross's fellow servicemen while he conducted a patrol with them, as Knockout Magazine and the reference website J-Grit: The Internet Index of Tough Jews both recounted. Ross brought his wounded colleagues into a crater hole and laid down cover fire for them, shooting more than 200 rounds of ammunition and tossing more than 20 grenades at enemies as he defended his compatriots and himself throughout the night.

"I was scared half to death," Ross would later say. "I never expected to get out alive. I was crying and praying and shooting and throwing grenades. Half the time, I guess, I was out of my head."

Military officials said Ross killed more than 20 Japanese combatants. Two of his colleagues died from their wounds, but he was able to save himself while also carrying his other compatriot to safety after reinforcements arrived.

"Then it was morning, and some other Marines moved up and got us out of there," Ross said about the end of his ordeal. For the valor he showed that day, he earned three prestigious military decorations: the Silver Star, the Purple Heart and the Presidential Citation.

Ross did not escape that harrowing night unscathed despite the citations he earned. He not only emerged with combat wounds that sent him to the hospital, as J-Grit noted. He also contracted malaria during his hospital stay, and he became addicted to morphine after he was given the drug as part of his treatment.

The addiction, at its height, drove Ross to spend more than $500 daily to support the habit. But he ultimately beat the addiction by undergoing drug rehabilitation treatment. And he became an anti-drug spokesperson and lectured in high schools across the US about the dangers of substance abuse.

"I am doing this in the hope that the publicity which my case is receiving will encourage others, suffering as I have suffered, to take the step that I [took]," Ross later said. "I [was] a victim of kindness, just as others in my condition [were] – doctors with the best motives gave me drugs when I was in pain.

"Guys in the hospitals with me smuggled drugs to me when the effects of the drugs that the doctors gave me wore off. They didn't want to see me suffer. I am grateful to the doctors and to the guys because they thought they were doing something for me – as, at the time, I thought they were."

One of his other roles in his post-boxing life saw him testify as a character witness in the 1964 trial of his close friend Jack Ruby, who was convicted of shooting and murdering Lee Harvey Oswald. Two days before Ruby killed him in November 1963, Oswald[4] had shot and assassinated President John F. Kennedy, according to investigators.

Ross died of throat cancer in Chicago in early 1967, two weeks after Ruby had died himself of lung cancer. The former champion was later inducted into such institutions as the International Boxing, World Boxing, and National Jewish Sports Halls of Fame.

"Guts? He had plenty," Pian said in the United Press International news wire reporting the ex-world titleist's death. "They couldn't kill him in the Marines with malaria and [Japanese] shrapnel. Dope couldn't kill him. He was a dope addict and he beat it. He beat everybody."

JIMMY McLARNIN

Born in Ireland and growing up in Canada, McLarnin retired in 1936 after scoring back-to-back wins over Canzoneri and Lou Ambers. He ultimately won 55 of his 69 fights (21 by knockout). Of the

---

4   If Canzoneri was one of the most famous people to spend part of their childhoods in New Orleans, Oswald was among its most infamous.

remaining 14, he lost 11 – just one by knockout – and drew three, according to BoxRec.

He appeared in a few movies – mostly about boxing – after walking away from prizefighting. He lived until the age of 96, dying at an assisted living home in Washington state in 2004, according to his obituary in the New York Times. The widower's survivors included a son, three daughters, and six grandchildren.

BoxRec.com considers McLarnin to be Ireland's greatest ever boxer and the sport's number two pound-for-pound fighter of all time, which is recognition that speaks for itself. He is also a World Boxing and International Boxing Hall of Fame inductee.

LOU AMBERS

In 1938, a little more than a year after he defeated him for a second time, Lou Ambers took the world lightweight crown that he swiped from Tony Canzoneri and exposed the title against Henry Armstrong. Armstrong dropped Ambers in both the fifth and sixth rounds, leaving audience members with doubts about whether the affair would end much earlier than many predicted.

Ambers won some respect back by getting up each time and then inflicting gashes near one of Armstrong's eyes and his mouth. But, swallowing the blood near his mouth so that the referee wouldn't halt the bout, Armstrong finished out strongly enough to take a split decision against Ambers and seize the world championship belt for himself.

Ambers enjoyed a second reign as the division's monarch after facing off with Armstrong in a rematch in New York's Yankee Stadium the following year. The clash was particularly brutal, with Armstrong giving away a full five rounds to his challenger because he illegally hit him below the belt line, according to reporting from James Roberts and Alexander Skutt in The Boxing Register. Ambers ultimately tied up his record against Armstrong by consistently landing strong punches on the champion's face – leaving one of his eyes swollen shut – and securing a split decision in his favor.

That's how things ended between the two as a third fight that the entire boxing world wanted never came to fruition. Ambers in 1940 lost the lightweight title to Lew Jenkins, who needed just three rounds to stop and dethrone the two-time champion he had challenged. Ambers got a rematch with Jenkins but lost by technical knockout in seven rounds and retired.

He later became a boxing instructor at the Manhattan Beach Coast Guard training station during the second world war. Like so many prize-fighting stars did in those days, Ambers eventually opened a restaurant that sought to capitalize on his championship pedigree. He also worked in public relations before his induction to the International Boxing Hall of Fame in 1992. He died in 1995 at age 81, according to that hall of fame's citation for him. The World Boxing Hall of Fame also inducted Ambers.

AL "BUMMY" DAVIS

Tony Canzoneri was not the only New York-based fighter of his era who had figures of the criminal underworld swirling around him seemingly all the time but managed to find a way to keep them at arm's length throughout his career.

The only man who knocked Tony out of a fight, the highly-ranked contender Al "Bummy" Davis, was another prime example.

Bummy Davis grew up in a Brooklyn neighborhood that was largely Jewish before World War II. The Ron Ross-written biography "Bummy Davis and Murder Inc." points out that Davis's profile as a boxer rose as loan sharks, extortionists, bookmaker and even killers surrounded him.

However, historians agree that Davis lived life straight and on the right side of the law. And that may have been a harder feat for him than it ever was for Tony Canzoneri.

One of Davis's brothers, nicknamed "Big Gangy," was reputed to be an associate of the Brooklyn mob organization which earned the chilling nickname of Murder Inc. Davis's other brother? He was a Murder Inc. affiliate, too.

At one point, Murder Inc. gunman Frankie Carbo, who later became a powerful promoter in pro boxing, campaigned to acquire Davis's contract in order to manage – well, control – his career. But Davis always rebuffed Carbo's overtures. And his reward for that was a clean reputation among boxing historians and fans.

Ross posits that Davis fought as much to clear his family name because of how he believed his brothers stained it than he did for the money at stake in any of his prizefights.

Born Albert Abraham Davidoff, Davis's signature victory did come at the expense of Canzoneri's career. Yet his time on earth was even more fleeting than that of the man whom he knocked into retirement and to whom his legacy is inextricably linked.

That's because the misfortune and short fuses that can be staples of the kind of environments that both Davis and Canzoneri had to learn to navigate cut Bummy's life short before he had even turned 26.

Already retired, Bummy was in a Brooklyn restaurant bar that he was selling when four robbers on a spree of tavern hold-ups barged in that early morning in November 1945. Davis punched one robber for roughing up the man who had gone there to buy the restaurant.

At least one of the intruders then shot Davis, immediately, three times. The other robbers tried to flee. Whether he just didn't want them to get away without consequences or truly feared that they might hurt someone else, Davis chased after the stick-up men. He got shot again, died outside the bar and left behind his widow and their toddler.

Some of those who adored Canzoneri had once reportedly vilified Davis for the harsh fashion in which he sent Tony into retirement. But ironically, in his death, Davis was lionized – almost universally – as a hero trying to do the right thing in the face of lawlessness.

"His redemption was complete," as John J. Raspanti wrote for the website MaxBoxing.com in 2020. "But what a price he had to pay."

TONY CANZONERI

Tony Canzoneri is an inductee of the World Boxing and International Boxing Halls of Fame, as well as the National Italian American Sports Hall of Fame, among other such institutions.

Whoever wants to discredit the notion that knockout percentages are deceptive measuring sticks that do not tell the full story of a prizefighter should study a boxer other than Tony in their search for grounds to stand on.

There's no evidence in Canzoneri's career to support their arguments – not when he took every one of his chances to face the best and very nearly logged a total of 260 rounds of action in championship fights alone, according to a count from the National Italian American Sports Hall of Fame.

Boxing historian and commentator Steve Farhood summarized Tony Canzoneri's prizefighting career and legacy as well as anyone could hope to do it.

"Tony Canzoneri fought everybody," Farhood said. "He lost sometimes. But look at who he lost to."

Just as importantly, look at who Tony Canzoneri beat. And, while you're at it, look at everything else that he beat, too.

APPENDIX

———

Tony Canzoneri fought more than 170 times during his professional boxing career between the ages of 16 and 30. He won 137 of those bouts (44 by knockout), lost 24 (just one by KO), and drew 10 times.

Below is a list of all of his known results, listed in reverse chronological order from the most recent. He won his lone world featherweight championship in February 1928 against Benny Bass, his first world lightweight championship in November 1930 against Al Singer and his first world junior welterweight championship against Jack Berg in September 1931.

He won a second junior welterweight title against Battling Shaw in May 1933 and his historic second world lightweight championship in May 1935 against Lou Ambers.

TABLE KEY

Win or loss, TKO = The outcome was determined when the referee determined one of the fighters could not safely continue fighting. Sometimes this happens after a knockdown but without counting to 10. The number indicates the round the stoppage occurred in.

Win or loss, KO = The outcome was determined when one of the fighters was knocked down and couldn't get back up before the count of 10. The number indicates the round the stoppage occurred in.

Win, loss, or draw, PTS = The outcome was a decision determined on points from a single official's scorecard.

Win or loss, SD = Split decision. Two officials scored for one side, and the third scored it for the other side.

Win or loss, UD = Unanimous decision.

Win or loss, MD = Majority decision. Two officials scored for one side, and the third scored it a draw.

Draw, MD = Majority draw. One official picked one side, and the other two picked a draw.

Draw, SD = Split draw. One official picked one side, a second official picked the other side, and the third picked a draw.

NWS = Newspaper decision.

Win or loss, DQ = The match ended in a win or loss because one of the fighters was disqualified.

Bout #	Date	His Age	Opponent	Outcome	Result
175	11/1/1939	30	Al Bummy Davis	Loss	TKO3
174	9/19/1939	30	Eddie Brink	Win	PTS
173	8/26/1939	30	Gerald D'Elia	Win	PTS
172	8/18/1939	30	Frankie Wallace	Win	PTS
171	8/3/1939	30	Joe De Jesus	Win	PTS
170	7/17/1939	30	Ambrose Logan	Win	PTS
169	7/6/1939	30	Joe De Jesus	Win	PTS
168	6/5/1939	30	Harris Blake	Loss	PTS
167	5/15/1939	30	Nick Camarata	Draw	SD
166	5/1/1939	30	Jimmy Tygh	Loss	SD
165	4/11/1939	30	Jimmy Vaughn	Draw	PTS
164	3/28/1939	30	Eddie Brink	Loss	SD
163	3/7/1939	30	Eddie Brink	Win	PTS
162	2/7/1939	30	Bobby Pacho	Win	PTS
161	1/31/1939	30	Everett Simington	Win	TKO3

Bout #	Date	His Age	Opponent	Outcome	Result
160	1/27/1939	30	Joe Govras	Win	TKO2
159	1/19/1939	30	Wally Hally	Win	UD
158	12/30/1938	30	Eddie Zivic	Win	PTS
157	12/1/1938	30	Jimmy Murray	Win	PTS
156	11/22/1938	30	Howard Scott	Win	MD
155	11/1/1938	29	Al Dunbard	Win	KO3
154	10/26/1938	29	Howard Scott	Win	PTS
153	10/17/1938	29	Eddie Zivic	Loss	MD
152	5/7/1937	28	Lou Ambers	Loss	UD
151	4/24/1937	28	Joey Zodda	Win	KO7
150	4/13/1937	28	Frankie Wallace	Win	PTS
149	4/5/1937	28	George Levy	Win	TKO7
148	10/5/1936	27	Jimmy McLarnin	Loss	UD
147	9/3/1936	27	Lou Ambers	Loss	UD
146	5/8/1936	27	Jimmy McLarnin	Win	UD
145	4/9/1936	27	Jimmy McLarnin	Win	PTS
144	3/2/1936	27	Steve Halaiko	Win	KO2
143	2/15/1936	27	Billy Hogan	Win	KO4
142	1/30/1936	27	Tootsie Bashara	Win	TKO3
141	1/22/1936	27	Midget Mexico	Win	TKO9
140	10/4/1935	26	Al Roth	Win	UD
139	9/13/1935	26	Joe Ghnouly	Win	UD
138	8/19/1935	26	Frankie Klick	Win	PTS
137	7/25/1935	26	Bobby Pacho	Win	PTS
136	6/10/1935	26	Frankie Klick	Win	SD
135	5/10/1935	26	Lou Ambers	Win	UD
134	4/25/1935	26	Eddie Zivic	Win	TKO7
133	3/15/1935	26	Chuck Woods	Win	UD
132	2/26/1935	26	Chuck Woods	Loss	PTS
131	1/31/1935	26	Leo Rodak	Win	UD
130	1/21/1935	26	Honeyboy Hughes	Win	PTS
129	1/7/1935	26	Eddie Ran	Win	KO2
128	9/26/1934	25	Harry Dublinsky	Win	PTS

Bout #	Date	His Age	Opponent	Outcome	Result
127	8/29/1934	25	Harry Dublinsky	Loss	PTS
126	6/28/1934	25	Frankie Klick	Win	TKO9
125	3/13/1934	25	Baby Arizmendi	Win	PTS
124	3/1/1934	25	Pete Nebo	Win	PTS
123	2/2/1934	25	Cleto Locatelli	Win	MD
122	12/15/1933	25	Cleto Locatelli	Win	UD
121	12/4/1933	25	Cecil Payne	Win	KO5
120	11/24/1933	25	Kid Chocolate	Win	KO2
119	10/28/1933	24	Frankie Klick	Win	UD
118	9/12/1933	24	Barney Ross	Loss	SD
117	6/23/1933	24	Barney Ross	Loss	MD
116	5/21/1933	24	Battling Shaw	Win	UD
115	4/20/1933	24	Wesley Ramey	Loss	PTS
114	2/23/1933	24	Pete Nebo	Win	PTS
113	2/3/1933	24	Billy Townsend	Win	KO1
112	11/4/1932	23	Billy Petrolle	Win	UD
111	10/12/1932	23	Frankie Petrolle	Win	KO3
110	9/29/1932	23	Lew Kirsch	Win	TKO3
109	7/18/1932	23	Johnny Jadick	Loss	SD
108	6/16/1932	23	Harry Dublinsky	Win	SD
107	5/23/1932	23	Battling Gizzy	Win	PTS
106	4/4/1932	23	Ray Kiser	Win	UD
105	2/15/1932	23	Lew Massey	Win	UD
104	1/18/1932	23	Johnny Jadick	Loss	UD
103	11/20/1931	23	Kid Chocolate	Win	SD
102	10/29/1931	22	Philly Griffin	Win	UD
101	9/10/1931	22	Jack Kid Berg	Win	UD
100	7/13/1931	22	Cecil Payne	Win	PTS
99	6/25/1931	22	Herman Perlick	Win	PTS
98	4/24/1931	22	Jack Kid Berg	Win	KO3
97	3/23/1931	22	Tommy Grogan	Win	PTS
96	3/6/1931	22	Sammy Fuller	Loss	UD
95	2/25/1931	22	Joey Kaufman	Win	TKO1

Bout #	Date	His Age	Opponent	Outcome	Result
94	1/26/1931	22	Johnny Farr	Win	NWS
93	11/14/1930	22	Al Singer	Win	KO1
92	9/11/1930	21	Billy Petrolle	Loss	PTS
91	8/28/1930	21	Goldie Hess	Win	PTS
90	7/21/1930	21	Benny Bass	Win	UD
89	6/24/1930	21	Tommy Grogan	Win	PTS
88	6/4/1930	21	Joe Glick	Win	PTS
87	5/14/1930	21	Johnny Farr	Win	PTS
86	5/5/1930	21	Harry Carlton	Win	UD
85	4/8/1930	21	Frankie LaFay	Win	TKO1
84	4/1/1930	21	Steve Smith	Win	TKO7
83	3/14/1930	21	Stanislaus Loayza	Win	UD
82	3/4/1930	21	Solly Ritz	Win	TKO1
81	1/17/1930	21	Jack Kid Berg	Loss	SD
80	10/30/1929	20	Stanislaus Loayza	Win	UD
79	10/18/1929	20	Johnny Farr	Win	PTS
78	9/27/1929	20	Eddie Mack	Win	TKO8
77	9/20/1929	20	Eddie Wolfe	Win	PTS
76	8/2/1929	20	Sammy Mandell	Loss	SD
75	7/9/1929	20	Phil McGraw	Win	PTS
74	6/4/1929	20	Ignacio Fernandez	Win	PTS
73	5/10/1929	20	André Routis	Win	UD
72	4/26/1929	20	Sammy Dorfman	Win	PTS
71	4/9/1929	20	Cowboy Eddie Anderson	Win	NWS
70	3/8/1929	20	Cecil Payne	Win	PTS
69	2/26/1929	20	Ignacio Fernandez	Win	UD
68	2/6/1929	20	Joey Sangor	Win	TKO7
67	1/18/1929	20	Armando Santiago	Win	KO5
66	12/14/1929	21	Al Singer	Draw	MD
65	12/8/1928	20	Chick Suggs	Win	KO6
64	10/29/1928	19	Gaston Charles	Win	PTS
63	9/28/1928	19	André Routis	Loss	SD
62	8/28/1928	19	Bobby Garcia	Win	KO1

Bout #	Date	His Age	Opponent	Outcome	Result
61	6/27/1928	19	Harry Blitman	Loss	PTS
60	6/13/1928	19	Vic Foley	Win	PTS
59	5/28/1928	19	Claude Wilson	Win	TKO1
58	2/23/1928	19	Pete Passifiume	Win	PTS
57	2/10/1928	19	Benny Bass	Win	SD
56	1/30/1928	19	Pete Nebo	Draw	SD
55	12/30/1927	19	Bud Taylor	Win	UD
54	12/1/1927	19	Ignacio Fernandez	Win	UD
53	11/22/1927	19	Vincent DiLeo	Win	TKO1
52	11/7/1927	19	Billy Henry	Win	KO2
51	10/24/1927	18	Johnny Dundee	Win	UD
50	10/3/1927	18	Tommy Ryan	Win	PTS
49	9/2/1927	18	Cowboy Eddie Anderson	Loss	DQ
48	8/25/1927	18	Joe Rivers	Win	NWS
47	8/17/1927	18	Pete Sarmiento	Win	KO1
46	8/9/1927	18	Cowboy Eddie Anderson	Win	PTS
45	7/27/1927	18	California Joe Lynch	Win	PTS
44	6/24/1927	18	Bud Taylor	Loss	UD
43	5/3/1927	18	Ray Rychell	Win	TKO7
42	4/24/1927	18	Harold Smith	Win	TKO3
41	4/18/1927	18	Vic Burrone	Draw	PTS
40	3/26/1927	18	Bud Taylor	Draw	PTS
39	3/7/1927	18	California Joe Lynch	Win	PTS
38	2/4/1927	18	Johnny Green	Win	PTS
37	1/22/1927	18	Vic Burrone	Win	PTS
36	1/12/1927	18	Joe Ryder	Draw	PTS
35	12/17/1926	18	Bushy Graham	Win	PTS
34	11/22/1926	18	André Routis	Win	PTS
33	11/13/1926	18	Enrique Savaardo	Win	TKO5
32	11/6/1926	18	Davey Abad	Loss	PTS
31	10/5/1926	17	Benny Hall	Win	PTS
30	9/20/1926	17	George Marks	Win	PTS
29	8/28/1926	17	Georgie Mack	Draw	PTS

Bout #	Date	His Age	Opponent	Outcome	Result
28	8/14/1926	17	Buck Josephs	Win	PTS
27	8/9/1926	17	Young Montreal	Win	PTS
26	7/26/1926	17	Manny Wexler	Win	KO5
25	6/25/1926	17	Archie Bell	Win	TKO5
24	6/21/1926	17	Willie Suess	Win	PTS
23	6/16/1926	17	Sonny Smith	Win	PTS
22	5/28/1926	17	Sammy Nable	Win	TKO5
21	5/8/1926	17	Benny Hall	Draw	PTS
20	3/25/1926	17	Mike Esposito	Draw	PTS
19	3/20/1926	17	Tommy Milton	Win	PTS
18	3/11/1926	17	Jacinto Valdez	Win	PTS
17	3/6/1926	17	Bobby Wolgast	Win	PTS
16	2/18/1926	17	Al Scorda	Win	PTS
15	2/13/1926	17	Romeo Vaughn	Win	PTS
14	1/26/1926	17	Mickey Lewis	Win	PTS
13	1/21/1926	17	Kid Rash	Win	PTS
12	1/13/1926	17	George Nickfor	Win	TKO4
11	12/23/1925	17	Danny Terris	Win	KO4
10	12/7/1925	17	Danny Terris	Win	PTS
9	11/26/1925	17	Ralph Nischo	Win	PTS
8	11/12/1925	17	Harry Brandon	Win	PTS
7	11/7/1925	17	Henry Molinari	Win	KO1
6	10/10/1925	16	Johnny Huber	Win	PTS
5	9/12/1925	16	Paulie Porter	Win	KO5
4	8/22/1925	16	Henry Usse	Win	PTS
3	8/8/1925	16	Henry Usse	Win	PTS
2	8/5/1925	16	Ray Cummings	Win	NWS
1	7/24/1925	16	Jack Grodner	Win	KO1

SELECTED SOURCES

———

CHAPTER 1

Boneno, Roselyn Bologna. "From Migrant to Millionaire: The Story of the Italian-American in New Orleans, 1880-1910." Louisiana State University Historical Dissertations and Theses. 1986. https://digitalcommons.lsu.edu/gradschool_disstheses.

Branley, Edward. "NOLA History: New Orleans Neighborhood 'P-Town.'" January 13, 2014. https://gonola.com/things-to-do-in-new-orleans/history/nola-history-new-orleans-neighborhood-p-town. Accessed May 5, 2020.

Brasted, Chelsea. "How New Orleans neighborhoods got their names." Nola.com. June 19, 2017. https://www.nola.com/archive/article_e6adefd3-0020-5cde-b8f0-277f7b11319b.html

"Canzoneri, George." Ancestry.com. U.S. City Directories, 1822-1995 [database on-line]. Provo, Utah, USA: Ancestry.com Operations, Inc., 2011.

Canzoneri, Robert. *A Highly Ramified Tree: An American Writer Returns to His Father's Roots in Sicily.* The Viking Press. New York. 1976.

Canzoneri, Tony and Stanley Weston. "This Is My Life by Tony Canzoneri." Boxing & Wrestling magazine. June 1955.

"George Canzoneri." Ancestry.com. New York, State and Federal Naturalization Records, 1794-1943 [database on-line]. Provo, Utah, USA: Ancestry.com Operations, Inc., 2013.

Haas, Edward. "Guns, Goats and Italians: The Tallulah Lynching of 1899." North Louisiana Historical Association, volume XIII, numbers 2 & 3, 1982.

"Josephine Canzoneri." Ancestry.com. 1930 United States Federal Census [database on-line]. Provo, Utah, USA: Ancestry.com Operations Inc, 2002.

Maragavio, Anthony V. and Jerome Salomone. *Bread and Respect: The Italians of America.* Pelican Publishing Company. Gretna, Louisiana. 2002.

"New Orleans." History.com. https://www.history.com/topics/us-states/new-orleans.

Rose, Murray. "Tony Canzoneri Found Dead in Hotel Room." The Associated Press, via The Times-Picayune. New Orleans, Louisiana. December 11, 1958. Pages 34 and 37.

"Tony Canzoneri Is Dead at 51; Held 3 Boxing Championships." The New York Times. New York, New York. December 11, 1959. Sports, Page 33.

CHAPTER 2

Benedict, Chris. "The Twilight Rounds, Rod Serling explores the dark side of boxing – Round three." April 17, 2020. https://thegruelingtruth.com/boxing/the-twilight-rounds-rod-serling-explores-the-dark-side-of-boxing-round-three/. Accessed May 7, 2020.

Casey, Mike. "From New Orleans To New York: Unforgettable Tony Canzoneri." www.cyberboxingzone.com/boxing/casey/MC_Canzoneri.htl. Accessed May 17, 2020.

Canzoneri, Tony and Stanley Weston. "This Is My Life by Tony Canzoneri." Boxing & Wrestling magazine. June 1955.

"Harry Traub wins in AAU title bout ... Canzoneri also triumphs." The New York Times. New York, New York. March 13, 1925. Sports, Page 17.

"Jack Coleman wins State Boxing title." The New York Times. New York, New York. January 9, 1925. Sports, Page 10.

Keefe, Wm. McG. "Viewing the News: Canzoneri's Start." The Times-Picayune. New Orleans, Louisiana. November 20, 1930. Page 14.

Martinez, Harry. "Canzoneri's Parents Tried Hard to Keep Him Out of the Ring". New Orleans States. New Orleans, Louisiana. May 24, 1928. Page 20.

Martinez, Harry. "Goldman Was Boxing Figure Here." New Orleans
    States-Item. New Orleans, Louisiana. Page 11.
"One of the Greatest Little Men in Ring Annals: Canzoneri Had
    Tough Time Winning First Title." The National Police Gazette.
    August 1955.
Smith, Red. "Down Yonder in New Orleans." The New York Times.
    New York, New York. April 9, 1979. Section C, Page 3.
Smith, Red. "Pete and Tony." The New York Times. New York, New
    York. June 17, 1979, Sports, Page 3.
"Tony Canzoneri is dead at 51." The New York Times. New York, New
    York. December 11, 1959. Sports, Page 33.
"Tony Canzoneri – The Man and the Legend". Boxing Illustrated. May
    1983.
Tauzier, Al. "Tony Canzoneri started ring career at 13." The Item-
    Tribune. New Orleans, Louisiana. April 24, 1927. Page 17.

CHAPTER 3

Casey, Mike. "From New Orleans To New York: Unforgettable Tony
    Canzoneri." www.cyberboxingzone.com/boxing/casey/MC_
    Canzoneri.htm. Accessed May 19, 2020.
Canzoneri, Tony and Stanley Weston. "This Is My Life by Tony
    Canzoneri." Boxing & Wrestling magazine. June 1955.
"Canzoneri defeats Routis on points." The New York Times. New
    York, New York. November 23, 1926. Sports, Page 32.
"Canzoneri is defeated." The New York Times. New York, New York.
    November 7, 1926. Sports, Page 8.
"Canzoneri stops Wexler in fifth." The New York Times. New York,
    New York. July 27, 1926. Sports, Page 13.
Martinez, Harry. "Bass Toughest Opponent He Has Met, Says
    Canzoneri." The New Orleans States. New Orleans, Louisiana. May
    25, 1928. Page 16.
"Taylor-Canzoneri Draw Leaves Promoter With the Title Belt." The
    New York Times. March 28, 1927. Sports, Page 16.
"Taylor wins bout from Canzoneri." The New York Times. New York,
    New York. June 25, 1927. Sports, Page 11.
Wright, John. *The Terror of Terre Haute: Bud Taylor and the 1920s*.
    Dog Ear Publishing LLC. November 12, 2008.

"Tony Canzoneri." BoxRec.com website. boxrec.com/en/proboxer/9003.

CHAPTER 4

Canzoneri, Tony and Stanley Weston. "This Is My Life by Tony Canzoneri." Boxing & Wrestling magazine. June 1955.

Dawson, James. "Dundee outpointed by Tony Canzoneri." The New York Times. New York, New York. October 25, 1927. Sports, Page 34.

Dawson, James. "Dundee Will Essay Comeback Tonight." The New York Times. New York, New York. October 24, 1927. Sports, Page 17.

Dawson, James. "Bass in hospital; Canzoneri hailed." The New York Times. New York, New York. February 12, 1928. Sports, Page 154.

"Canzoneri to try for speed in work." New York Times. New York, New York. February 6, 1928. Sports, Page 14.

Dawson, James. "Canzoneri and Bass to settle dispute." The New York Times. New York, New York. Sports, Page 152.

Dawson, James. "Canzoneri Battles for title tonight." The New York Times. New York, New York. February 10, 1928. Sports, Page 20.

Dawson, James. "Canzoneri Defeats Bass In Title Bout." The New York Times. New York, New York. February 11, 1928. Sports, Page 12.

Martinez, Harry. "Bass Toughest Opponent He Has Met, Says Canzoneri." The New Orleans States. New Orleans, Louisiana. May 25, 1928. Page 16.

"Tony Canzoneri." BoxRec.com website. boxrec.com/en/proboxer/9003.

CHAPTER 5

Bonanno, Bill and Gary B. Abromovitz. *The Last Testament of Bill Bonanno: The Final Secrets of a Life in the Mafia.* Harper. New York. 2011.

Burns, Deborah. *Saturday's Child, A Daughter's Memoir.* She Writes Press. 2019.

Canzoneri, Tony and Stanley Weston. "This Is My Life by Tony Canzoneri." Boxing & Wrestling magazine. June 1955.

Critchley, David. *The Origin of Organized Crime in America: The New York City Mafia, 1891-1931.* Routledge. New York. 2009.

Digby, Fred. "They Don't Keep It Long." The New Orleans Item. New Orleans, Louisiana. September 30, 1928. Page 13.

Digby, Fred. "Tony's Appetite Costly." The New Orleans Item. New Orleans, Louisiana. October 30, 1928. Page 2.

Dufour, Charles. "Knockout first in Wilson's career." The Times-Picayune. New Orleans, Louisiana. May 29, 1928. Page 12.

"Fight: 16768." BoxRec.com website. https://boxrec.com/media/index.php?title=Fight:16768

Gould, Alan. "Canzoneri beaten by Andre Routis in title bout." The Montreal Gazette. Montreal, Canada. September 29, 1928. Page 21.

Hall, Quin. "The New Featherweight King." The New Orleans States. New Orleans, Louisiana. December 11, 1928. Page 21.

"Josephine Canzoneri." Ancestry.com. 1930 United States Federal Census [database online]. Provo, Utah, USA. Ancestry.com Operations Inc., 2002.

Keefe, Wm. McG. "Tony Canzoneri 'Back Home' to Start Hard Training Today." The Times-Picayune. New Orleans, Louisiana. May 23, 1928. Page 20.

Smith, Red. "Pete and Tony." The New York Times. New York, New York. June 17, 1979, Sports, Page 3.

"Tony Canzoneri and His Manager Banquet Guests." The Times-Picayune. New Orleans, Louisiana. May 26, 1928. Page 15.

"Tony Canzoneri." BoxRec.com website. boxrec.com/en/proboxer/9003.

CHAPTER 6

Baker, Mark Allen. *Between the Ropes at Madison Square Garden: The History of an Iconic Boxing Ring, 1925-2007.* McFarland. North Carolina. 2019.

"Canzoneri, Berg will fight tonight." The New York Times, via the Associated Press. New York, New York. April 24, 1931. Page 31.

"Canzoneri gives all credit to Pete Herman." New Orleans States. New Orleans, Louisiana. November 18, 1930. Page 18.

"Canzoneri stops Berg in 3rd round." The New York Times, via The Associated Press. New York, New York. April 25, 1931. Page 23.

"Canzoneri to take rest under crown." The New York Times. New York, New York, November 16, 1930. Page 115.

Digby, Fred. "Looking 'Em Over: So It Was Fixed, Eh?" The New
   Orleans Item. New Orleans, Louisiana. May 3, 1931. Page 57.

"Eddie Wolfe." BoxRec.com website. boxrec.com/en/proboxer/52940.

Gustkey, Earl. "An Old Warrior: McLarnin, 81, recalls hard days
   of boxing." The Los Angeles Times. Los Angeles, California.
   September 26, 1989. Sports Page 1.

"Hoovervilles." History.com Editors. https://www.history.com/topics/
   great-depression/hoovervilles. Accessed May 30, 2020.

"Jack Kid Berg talks about his fights with Tony Canzoneri and
   Billy Petrolle." YouTube. Londonboxers. Published on June
   7, 2020. 1986 video interview with Berg conducted by John
   Harding, author of "The Jack 'Kid' Berg Story: The Whitechapel
   Whirlwind."

"Jimmy McLarnin." BoxRec.com website. https://boxrec.com/en/
   proboxer/9024

Keefe, Wm. McG. "Viewing the News: Canzoneri's Start." The Times-
   Picayune. New Orleans, Louisiana. November 20, 1930. Page 14.

Martinez, Harry. "Berlier-Wolfe Box Monday." The New Orleans
   States. New Orleans, Louisiana. May 31, 1931. Page 29.

Martinez, Harry. "Canzoneri crowned world's lightweight champion."
   The New Orleans States. New Orleans, Louisiana. November 15,
   1930. Page 12.

"New champion began ringing career in 1925." The New York Times.
   New York, New York. November 15, 1930. Page 25.

Rose, Murray. "Tony Canzoneri Found Dead in Hotel Room." The
   Associated Press, via The Times-Picayune. New Orleans, Louisiana.
   December 11, 1958. Pages 34 and 37.

"Sammy Mandell." BoxRec.com website. https://boxrec.com/en/
   proboxer/10116

"Singer 9-5 choice to retain title." New York Times. New York, New
   York. November 14, 1930. Page 32.

"Stock Market Crash of 1929." History.com Editors. https://www.
   history.com/topics/great-depression/1929-stock-market-crash.
   Accessed May 30, 2020.

"Tony Canzoneri." BoxRec.com website. boxrec.com/en/proboxer/9003.

"Tony Canzoneri Finally Wins Crown." The Times-Picayune. New
   Orleans, Louisiana. November 16, 1930, Page 3.

"Tony Puts Hopes in Good Right" and "'Papa' Canzoneri Will Lead
    Cheer Corps for Tony." The New Orleans Item, via the Associated
    Press. New Orleans, Louisiana. July 30, 1929, Page 13.
Weekes, William. "Canzoneri Double Ring Champ After Kayoing
    Kid Berg." The Times-Picayune, via the Associated Press. April 25.
    1931. Page 6.
"Wolfe, Canzoneri Spasm Is Recalled." Jacobs, Howard. The Times-
    Picayune. New Orleans, Louisiana. December 29, 1972.

CHAPTER 7

Barker, Herbert. "Canzoneri Risking His Titles Against Kid
    Chocolate." The New Orleans States, via the Associated Press. New
    Orleans, Louisiana. November 20, 1931. Page 19.
Barker, Herbert; and Henry McLemore. "Canzoneri Keeps Title In
    Bitter Scrap With 'Keed'; Pronounced Boos Greet Tony." The
    New Orleans Item, via the Associated Press and United Press. New
    Orleans, Louisiana. November 21, 1931.
BoxRec.com. "Tony Canzoneri vs. Billy Petrolle, 2nd meeting."
    https://boxrec.com/media/index.php/Tony_Canzoneri_vs._Billy_
    Petrolle_(2nd_meeting). July 27, 2020.
Canzoneri, Robert. *A Highly Ramified Tree: An American Writer Returns
    to His Father's Roots in Sicily.* The Viking Press. New York. 1976.
"Canzoneri wins verdict." The New York Times. New York, New York.
    June 26, 1931, Page 32.
"Forgotten Noir Fridays: Ringside (1949)." Thrilling Days of
    Yesteryear blog. http://thrillingdaysofyesteryear.blogspot.
    com/2016/11/forgotten-noir-fridays-ringside-1949.html.
Isaacs, Stan. "Boxing Fans Taste Chocolate." Florida Sun-Sentinel, via
    Newsday. August 17, 1991.
"Jadick wins title from Canzoneri." The New Orleans States. New
    Orleans, Louisiana. January 19, 1932. Page 14.
"Johnny Jadick Is Again Winner Over Tony Canzoneri." The New
    Orleans States, via the Associated Press. New Orleans, Louisiana.
    July 19, 1932. Page 12.
Neil, Edward. "Ross Defeats Canzoneri in Close, Hard-Fought
    15-Round Title Bout." The Times-Picayune, via the Associated
    Press. New Orleans, Louisiana. September 13, 1933. Page 14.

Neil, Edward J. "Tony Canzoneri Hammers Title Aspirations." The Times-Picayune, via the Associated Press. New Orleans, Louisiana. September 11, 1931. Page 15.

Shocket, Dan. "Ross! A Man Who Couldn't Quit." Knockout Magazine, summer 1993.

"Tony Canzoneri (I) (1908-1959): Actor." IMDB.com. https://www. imdb.com/name/nm0134856/?ref_=ttfc_fc_cl_t18

"Tony Canzoneri, Billy Petrolle to Box Oct. 16." The Times-Picayune. New Orleans, Louisiana. September 12, 1931. Page 10.

"Tony Canzoneri Title Go Looms." International News Service, via The Times-Picayune. New Orleans, Louisiana. September 15, 1933. Page 14.

"Tony Floors Payne In First, Then Coasts To Point Victory." The New Orleans Item, via the Associated Press. July 13, 1941. Page 17.

Wallace, Francis. "Barney Ross, Canzoneri in Title Match." The Times-Picayune. New Orleans, Louisiana. June 23, 1933. Page 13.

Wallace, Francis. "Tony Canzoneri Loses Lightweight Championship to Barney Ross." The Times-Picayune. New Orleans, Louisiana. June 24, 1933. Page 9.

CHAPTERS 8 AND 9

Baird. Pete. "Hooks and jabs." The Times-Picayune New Orleans States. New Orleans, Louisiana. September 17, 1933. Page 38.

"Reports Insist Tony Canzoneri Will Retire After Lou Ambers." Il Messaggero. Paterson, New Jersey. August 20, 1936. Page 6.

Canzoneri, Robert. *A Highly Ramified Tree: An American Writer Returns to His Father's Roots in Sicily.* The Viking Press. New York. 1976.

Isaacs, Stan. "Boxing Fans Taste Chocolate." Florida Sun-Sentinel, via Newsday. Fort Lauderdale, Florida. August 17, 1991.

Kieran, John. "Sports of the Times: Tony and Lou." The New York Times. New York, New York. May 10, 1935.

"Martin Burke Offers $30,000 for Title Bout Here With Canzoneri." The Times-Picayune. New Orleans, Louisiana. September 14, 1933. Page 11.

Martinez, Harry. "Another Break for Tony Canzoneri." New Orleans States. New Orleans, Louisiana. April 16, 1935. Page 10.

Neil, Edward. "Ambers Once Hitch-Hiked to See Canzoneri, His Idol, in Ring Bout." The Associated Press, via The New Orleans States. New Orleans, Louisiana. May 8, 1935. Page 10.

Nichols, Joseph. "McLarnin 7-5 Favorite to Defeat Canzoneri in Garden Ring Tomorrow." The New York Times. New York, New York. October 5, 1936. Sports Page 29.

Nichols, Joseph. "19,000 Watch Ambers Outpoint Canzoneri for World's Lightweight Crown." The New York Times. New York, New York. September 4, 1936. Sports, Page 13.

Smith, Red. "Pete and Tony." The New York Times. New York, New York. June 17, 1979. Sports, Page 3.

CHAPTER 10

Boxrec.com. "Tony Canzoneri vs. Jimmy McLarnin (2nd meeting)." https://boxrec.com/media/index.php/Tony_Canzoneri_vs._Jimmy_McLarnin_(2nd_meeting).

Burns, Deborah. Saturday's Child, A Daughter's Memoir. She Writes Press. 2019.

"Canzoneri in bow as actor tonight." The New York Times. New York, New York. February 13, 1942.

Digby, Fred. "Fans Argue Over Fight As Officials Vote Draw." The New Orleans Item. New Orleans, Louisiana. May 16, 1939. Page 14.

Interview with Jay Honold on May 6, 2020.

Martinez, Harry. "Tony Canzoneri Just Won't Stay Put." The New Orleans States. New Orleans, Louisiana. October 18, 1938. Page 14.

Nichols, Joseph. "Canzoneri Halted in Comeback Try." The New York Times. New York, New York. November 2, 1939.

Rose, Aaron. "A Boxer Named Tony." The American Citizen. New York, New York. Summer 1993.

Smith, Red. "Down Yonder in New Orleans." The New York Times. New York, New York. April 9, 1979.

"Tony Canzoneri is dead at 51." The New York Times. December 11, 1959. New York, New York. Page 33.

"Tony Canzoneri – The Man and the Legend". Boxing Illustrated. May 1983.

White, Bill. "Journey's End For Canzoneri." The Associated Press, via

The Times-Picayune. New Orleans, Louisiana. November 2, 1939. Page 22.

CHAPTER 11

Benedict, Chris. "The Twilight Rounds: Rod Serling explores the dark side of boxing – Round three." https://thegruelingtruth.com/boxing/the-twilight-rounds-rod-serling-explores-the-dark-side-of-boxing-round-three/ Accessed May 8, 2020.

Canzoneri, Robert. *A Highly Ramified Tree: An American Writer Returns to His Father's Roots in Sicily.* The Viking Press. New York. 1976.

Canzoneri, Tony. http://www.cyberboxingzone.com/boxing/canzon-t.htm. Accessed May 8, 2020.

"Ex-boxer's brother safe, couple seized as his kidnappers." The New York Times. New York, New York. September 30, 1971. Page 34.

Getlen, Larry. "The Kennedy meth." April 21, 2013. The New York Post. New York, New York. https://nypost.com/2013/04/21/the-kennedy-meth/. Accessed May 8, 2020.

"Jack Kid Berg talks about his fights with Tony Canzoneri and Billy Petrolle." YouTube. Londonboxers. Published on June 7, 2020. 1986 video interview with Berg conducted by John Harding, author of "The Jack 'Kid' Berg Story: The Whitechapel Whirlwind."

Keefe, Bill. "State Hall of Fame." The Times-Picayune. New Orleans, Louisiana. January 22, 1959. Page 69.

Lockley, Mike. "Reflection of Perfection." Sunday Mercury. Birmingham, England. June 14, 2015.

Rose, Aaron. "A Boxer Named Tony." The American Citizen. New York, New York. Summer 1993.

Tosches, Nick. "Dino: Living High in the Dirty Business of Dreams."

Variety Staff. "Rita Chandler." June 12, 2000. https://variety.com/2000/scene/people-news/rita-chandler-1117796861/

CHAPTER 12

Author's analysis of BoxRec.com and Ring magazine information.

Original interview with boxing commentator and former Ring magazine editor Steve Farhood.

Other sources cited in-line.

CHAPTER 13

"Al Singer." Boxrec.com website. https://boxrec.com/en/proboxer/10110.

"Al Singer Dies; 30, Champ," The New York Daily News. New York, New York. April 21, 1961. Page 33.

"Al Singer." Jewishsports.net. https://web.archive.org/web/20101226200032/http://jewishsports.net/BioPages/AlSinger.html. Accessed May 31, 2020.

"Andre Routis." BoxRec.com website. https://boxrec.com/en/proboxer/9866

"Benny Bass." International Boxing Hall of Fame website. http://www.ibhof.com/pages/about/inductees/oldtimer/bass.html

"Benny Bass, boxer, ex-champion, 70." The New York Times, via the Associated Press. New York, New York. June 28, 1975. Page 30.

"Benny Bass." BoxRec.com website. boxrec.com/en/proboxer/9585?offset=0

Berkow, Ira. "Sports of the Times: The Riddle of Kid Chocolate." The New York Times. New York, New York. August 21, 1988. Section 8, Page 5.

"Book Review – Bummy Davis and Murder Inc.: The Rise and Fall of the Jewish Mafia and an Ill-fated Prizefighter." https://www.boxinginsider.com/book-reviews/bummy-davis-and-murder-inc/

BoxRec.com. "Kid Chocolate." https://boxrec.com/wiki/index.php/Kid_Chocolate

Blady, Ken. The Jewish Boxer's Hall of Fame. Shapolsky Publishing: New York, New York. 1988. Pages 194-199.

Bruning, Bill. "Basil Galiano, Boxing Idol of New Orleans in '20s, Dies After Illness of Two Months." The Times-Picayune. August 22, 1939. Page 11.

"Bud Taylor." International Boxing Hall of Fame website. http://www.ibhof.com/pages/about/inductees/oldtimer/taylorcharles.html

"Bud Taylor." BoxRec.com website. boxrec.com/en/proboxer/10094

Griffin, Thomas. "'Diamond John Galway' Has Woes." New Orleans Item. New Orleans, Louisiana. July 13, 1945. Page 5.

"Jack 'Kid' Berg." BoxRec.com website. https://boxrec.com/en/proboxer/010121.

"Jack (Kid) Berg; Boxer, 81." The New York Times. New York, New York. April 24, 1991. Page 25.

Keefe, Wm. McG. "Viewing the News: Canzoneri's Start." The Times-Picayune. New Orleans, Louisiana. November 20, 1930. Page 14.

Martinez, Harry. "Goldman Was Boxing Figure Here." New Orleans States-Item. New Orleans, Louisiana. August 29, 1964. Page 11.

Meyer, Daniel. "Barney Ross - Jewish Boxer and War Hero." J-Grit: The Internet Index of Tough Jews. J-Grit.com. March 2023. <http://www.j-grit.com>.

"New York City Killings Mount." The Wilkes-Barre Record, Wilkes-Barre, Pennsylvania. November 22, 1945. Page 10.

Obituary of John Henry Galway Sr. The Times-Picayune. New Orleans, Louisiana. June 12, 1948. Page 2.

Shocket, Dan. "Ross! A Man Who Couldn't Quit." Knockout Magazine, summer 1993.

Silver, Mike. *Stars of the Ring*. Roman and Littlefield. Los Angeles. 2016. Pages 252-254.

Smith, Red. "Down Yonder in New Orleans." The New York Times. New York, New York. April 9, 1979.

APPENDIX

"Tony Canzoneri Record & Stats." MartialBot.com. https://www.martialbot.com/boxing/t/tony-canzoneri.html

"Tony Canzoneri." BoxRec.com website. boxrec.com/en/proboxer/9003.

INDEX

ABOUT THE AUTHOR

—

RAMON ANTONIO VARGAS has lived most of his life in Metairie, Louisiana, just outside of New Orleans. He is a graduate of Stuart Hall School, Jesuit High School and Loyola University New Orleans. He won multiple journalism awards working as a reporter for New Orleans's daily newspapers the Times-Picayune and the Advocate. He now works as an editor for the US office of the international news organization the Guardian, whose global headquarters are in London.

 Family, Gangsters & Champions: Boxer Tony Canzoneri's Life & World is his third book. He previously authored *Fight, Grin and Squarely Play the Game: The 1945 Loyola New Orleans Basketball Championship & Legacy* and co-authored *Contraflow: From New Orleans to Houston - A story of leadership witnessed after Hurricane Katrina.*

Printed in Great Britain
by Amazon